ANGUS CALDER is a poet and historiaɪ
has taught in universities off and on, with spells in severaɪ Aɪrican
universities and 14 years as Staff Tutor in Arts for the Open
University in Scotland. His verse has been widely published. His
collections include *Waking in Waikato* (1997), *Colours of Grief*
(2002) and *Sun Behind the Castle* (2004). His historical study of
The People's War: Britain 1939–1945 has been in print as a
standard work of reference since 1969. *Revolutionary Empire: The
Rise of the English Speaking Empires* (1981) attracted a Scottish
Arts Council Award and has recently been republished in
paperback. *The Myth of the Blitz* (1991) returned to examine the
place of the Second World War in British culture with
'interdisciplinary' techniques. *Revolving Culture: Notes from the
Scottish Republic* (1994), collected essays about Scottish history,
literature, art, theatre and 'popular culture' and won Calder a
second SAC Book Award. *Scotlands of the Mind* similarly displays
Calder's wide interests, in pieces which range from brief reviews to
major articles. Various perspectives are provided on Scotland's
achievement of 'Home Rule'. The first section presents
unashamedly personal insights, the second ranges over Scottish
history, from the mythical Scota to the present, with large essays
on Protestantism and Disruption, strong emphasis on Scotland's
participation in the British empire and an original and overdue
evaluation of the 'Scottishness' of David Livingstone.

By the same author

History:
The People's War: Britain 1939–45
Revolutionary Empire: The Rise of the English-Speaking Empires from the Fifteenth Century to the 1780s
The Myth of the Blitz
Gods, Mongrels and Demons: 101 Brief but Essential Lives
Disasters and Heroes: War, Memory and Representation

Edited by:
Speak for Yourself: A Mass Observation Anthology
(with Dorothy Sheridan)
Time to Kill: The Soldier's Experience of World War II in the West
(with Paul Addison)
The Souls of the Dead are Taking the Best Seats: 50 World Poets on War
(with Beth Junor)

Literary Criticism:
Russia Discovered: Nineteenth-Century Fiction from Pushkin to Chekhov
T.S. Eliot
Byron

Essays:
Revolting Culture: Notes from the Scottish Republic

Verse:
Waking in Waikato
Horace in Tollcross
Colours of Grief
Dipa's Bowl
Sun Behind the Castle

Scotlands of the Mind

ANGUS CALDER

Luath Press Limited

EDINBURGH

www.luath.co.uk

First published 2002
Reprinted 2004

The paper used in this book is recyclable.
It is made from low-chlorine pulps produced in a low-energy,
low-emission manner from renewable forests.

The publisher acknowledges subsidy from

 Scottish
Arts Council

towards publication of this volume.

Printed and bound by DigiSource GB Ltd., Livingston

Edited and typeset in 10.5 point Sabon
by Jennie Renton

Acknowledgements

PARTS ONE AND THREE of 'Three Days of Scotland' were first published in *SNaPshot*, and part two in *Six Seasons Review* (Dhaka); 'On First Looking into *In Memoriam James Joyce*' in *Chapman*; 'Describing Scottish Culture' in Scotlands; 'The Disruption in Fiction' in *Scotland in the Age of the Disruption*, edited by Stewart J. Brown and Michael Fry (Edinburgh University Press, 1993); 'Livingstone, Self-Help and Scotland' in *David Livingstone and the Victorian Encounter with Africa* (National Galleries, 1996); 'Imperialism and Scottish Culture' in *Scotland, Class and Nation*, edited by Chris Bambery (Bookmarks, 1999); 'By the Water of Leith I Sat Down and Wept' in *New Scottish Writing: Soho Square Seven*, edited by Harry Ritchie (Bloomsbury, 1996). 'Poetry, Language and Empire' was published as a booklet by the University of Waikato Scottish Studies Association (Avizandum Editions No.4) and in *Span*, journal of the South Pacific Association for Commonwealth Literature and Language Studies, 'Iain Crichton Smith' in *Scotia Review*. and 'Once and Future Knox' in *Edinburgh Review*. Items not listed above appeared in *The Herald, The Independent, Scotland on Sunday* and *The Scotsman*, to whose editorial staff, much thanks. 'When Was Scotland?' appears here for the first time. Titles of some pieces have been changed since first publication, and essays have been adapted for book publication.

Contents

Introduction

DOES SCOTLAND AS A 'NATION' have any real existence? There is manifestly no Scottish 'nation state'. If we have no Scottish nationality now, in what sense did we ever have it?

Some patriot remarked, in the days of his native land's partition between three empires, that 'Poland is a state of mind'. We have latterly been instructed by most sound scholars that similar observations are true of all 'imagined communities' of people who define themselves as belonging to this or that 'nation'.

Just what would independence mean for Scotland? More scones for tea? Finer mince with the tatties? Extra golf on Sundays? Better results for Scottish football teams in Europe? More than one broadsheet daily newspaper worth reading? And in a Europe of the regions with European currency and European law, is independence no more than a new name for local government?

I would like to live in an independent Scotland. Even independence within Europe would mean that Scotland might, for instance, subsidise conversion of its entire arable area to organic farming or seriously explore the potential of windpower. (New-style windmills, gracefully dwarfing old pylons and telegraph poles are, in my opinion, an unsung aesthetic delight.)

Even within its limited powers, the Scottish Parliament has reinstalled the idea of free university education, at least during the learning period, in advance of such a move in England.

In terms of identity, Scotland's complex history is marked by whopping fissures. If it is true that everyone senses, crossing the border from England, that a different country has been entered, how does one weigh the effect of alighting, after a train journey from Edinburgh, at Aberdeen Station, asking directions, and finding the reply wholly incomprehensible?

From the centre of Edinburgh, in George Street, on any reasonably clear day, one can look across the Firth of Forth to the hills of the proudly self-styled 'Kingdom' of Fife. From there, one spies the Grampians, clearly, and from the Grampians the mountains of the west coast and the waters of the Moray Firth will be visible. 'Scotland small? Our multiform, our infinite Scotland *small*?' exclaimed Hugh MacDiarmid in one of his great, rambling, long poems. He touched on a paradox that all thoughtful Scots sense frequently: Scotland, so often discussed carelessly as if it were a province of England, has a population of five million people – aligning it with Denmark and Finland – yet within this population's shared sense of Scottishness is expressed a plethora of cultural identities.

The Glasgow region and 'West of Scotland' dominate outsiders' perceptions of what the typical urban Scot is like, not surprisingly since about half of us originate in that area. But the legendary *hauteur* of the Edinburgh middle classes towards the savages of the Wild West is matched by the fighting contempt for 'Weegies' displayed by the Capital's dissolute dispossessed featuring in Irvine Welsh's best-selling fiction, and Ian Rankin has shown in his Inspector Rebus novels that the criminal culture of Auld Reekie may be as rich in its own way as that of the Dear Green Place. Dundee, Aberdeen and Inverness are so distinctive that Scotland might dissolve in some forthcoming 'Europe of the Regions' into five city semi-states. But then what becomes of the Borders, with their string of fiercely competitive small towns, and the islands: where mountainous Skye is utterly different in atmosphere from flat Lewis, Orkney is a considerable centre of High Culture, and Shetland, closer to Norway than Edinburgh, is a post-Norse world of its own?

It may seem a mystery, as one contemplates the social and even linguistic distance between a Buchan farmer and a Govan ship-yard worker, an Edinburgh lawyer and a Stornoway fisherman, that they can all identify with a singular country called 'Scotland'. Yet this happens very palpably when we are engaged in interna-tional sporting activities. In the 1980s a further apparent miracle turned the Scots, who might well on their home form have gained a reputation as the most vicious football followers in Europe, into the model of 'travelling support'. Somehow Rangers and Celtic devotees, fanatical Hibees and dedicated Jamboes transcended tra-ditions of internecine hatred and contempt to join (with a prepon-derance of fans of lesser clubs) a 'Tartan Army' which turned up in European towns and cities determined to fraternise with all com-ers, local residents and opposition supporters alike. The kilts and bagpipes characteristic of the toughest and most ruthless elements in Britain's Imperial battalions were transformed into endearing symbols of innocent goodwill towards all peoples. It is perfectly clear why this occurred. It was a way of scoring against England, some of whose support, most notoriously, turned up abroad full of hate and received it in return.

The key to Scotland's story in the last third of the twentieth century was a swelling sense of difference from England. This was what the Tartan Army spontaneously expressed. If the English were the worst football hooligans in Europe, Scots were going to prove by their behaviour, that Scotland was somewhere quite distinct. This addiction to difference, ruinously for the Scottish Conserva-tive and Unionist Party, achieved critical mass *vis à vis* Margaret Thatcher. Resentment of her imposition on Scotland of policies applauded in the English Home Counties was the chief single fac-tor which ensured that as soon as the Tories lost control of the UK Parliament, Scotland would regain its own Parliament. The pres-sure on the Labour Party to make good its founder Keir Hardie's commitment to Home Rule had become wholly irresistible. The unfortunate side effect of this process was that Scotland and Scots were defined by what they were 'not'. And so Scotland enters the twenty-first century with its not-Englishness embodied in a Parliament which is self-consciously not-Westminster.

This book was compiled on a watershed. Quite what difference the arrival of the Scottish Parliament in May 1999 has made and will make is not yet wholly clear. But that hill has been climbed, and we peer through the mists on the other side at what must be at least a fresh, if not necessarily a beautiful, prospect.

Not long after the Parliament opened, an old comrade in what might be called the Culture Wars wrote to me that he felt somewhat disorientated. Our minds, after the humiliating failure of Scots to vote in sufficient numbers in the referendum of 1979 to secure the more limited Parliament which was then on offer, were concentrated, with something akin to paranoia, on fearful inspection of every possible barrier to future success. Speaking for myself, I am now ashamed that I badmouthed George Orwell because his vision of England seemed to me to be dangerously influential. My attitudes to sport became painfully cramped. After rejoicing in England's *Boys Own Paper* victory over Australia in the Ashes series of 1981 (thanks to the heroic efforts of 'Beefy' Botham), audited avidly by me over the radio in Ross-shire, I lurched into supporting every other Test-playing nation against England. Especially after cricket-loving John Major succeeded Thatcher, any sporting triumph which boosted English morale seemed good for the Tories and bad for the Scottish cause. Signs that Scottish prosperity might be increasing – and many Scots certainly were enjoying new late-capitalist affluence – raised the horrid spectre that the broad alliance of three quarters of us against the Tories and in favour of home rule might melt away like snow on the hills in spring. Which brings us to another interesting mystery. Why, by 1997, had even the prosperous bourgeoisies of the Pentlands constituency of Edinburgh and the Eastwood suburb of Glasgow ceased to vote in Tory MPs? I think the habit of being not-English had soaked so deeply into younger voters, that as older ones died off, the Unionist party was doomed to wipeout. This happened in local government elections in 1995, and in 1999, the Tories failed to

return a single elected member in first the Westminster, then the
Scottish polls.

So, 'we' won. By 'we' I suppose I mean all the people who tried
to keep the political cutting edge of non-Englishness as sharp as
possible. These included folksingers and Fringe playwrights, certain rock stars and a high proportion of the tribe of scribblers. I
guess that future historians may notice how many ideas now taken
for granted first arose in the Eighties, either in small circulation,
high-octane magazines – *Radical Scotland, Chapman, Cencrastus*
– or in prophetic pieces by literati published in Scotland's broadsheet newspapers. I think, for instance, that we owe the notion
that Scotland is a 'mongrel' nation to William McIlvanney writing
in some public print. This is now an indispensable political tool. It
provides a short cut to distinguishing the national feeling of Scotland from the ethnic nationalism of Serbs, Hutus and Fijians, though
many decent English people can't grasp this distinction, and write
and talk as if Scottish independence would necessarily prelude racial cleansing of Englishpersons and the installation of louts with
kalashnikovs at the border. The concept of mongrelism also makes
it easier to affirm diversity as, paradoxically, a basis for our unity.
Nothing was so delightful in the *annus mirabilis*, 1999, as the creation, by Scottish Sikhs, of a new Sikh tartan.

The publication of Alasdair Gray's novel *Lanark* in 1981 seemed
even at the time to mark an epoch. On the face of it, the book was
pessimistic, ending in the apocalyptic destruction of Glasgow. But
the scale of its conception and the wit of its execution were both
inspirational. I think it was on the lusciously embossed cover of
the hardback edition of *Unlikely Stories Mostly*, published by
Canongate in 1983, that Gray first enunciated what has become
his characteristic slogan – 'Work as if you were living in the early
days of a better nation'.

The tradition of violence, the legacy of Knoxian Calvinism, the
inheritance of Empire, the yearnings of Socialism, are interrogated
in the best of contemporary Scottish writing without pretentious-
ness or portentousness. We are starting to live with our own past

and may stop introducing the English, or their language, at every point to excuse what has gone wrong with us.

Books are helping to recreate Scotland. Every significant act of writing is 'political' in the broad, original sense of that word – it bears on the *polis*, the polity. The English intelligentsia, right and left alike, now that Scotland is adrift and Wales partly so, can't decide what the remainder of their island means and have no sense, such as now amply exists in Scotland, that creative writing is an essential part of the political process.

Let me mention a few of the icons assailed in the essays collected here. They range from that easy target, the ridiculous Stone of Scone, through the very grave matter that so many Scots have pretended for so long that the English 'colonised' and 'exploited' us, whereas the stark truth is that Scots were proud and eager collaborators in the colonisation and exploitation of lands overseas by the British empire. I also have a go at certain contemporary 'shibboleths' – the absurdities of 'Scots language' purists, the inanity of most talk about 'tourism'.

As for Scottish national identity, I think the matter of mongrelism is of cardinal importance. (Most, if not all, nationalities are genetically mongrel.) When I was helping Polly Rewt research her *Roots* exhibition about the history of black people in Scotland, it was astonishing how quickly one turned up evidence of African and Afro-Caribbean participants in Scottish life down the ages who definitely added to our gene pool, but have been all but written out of our history. (How many of the historians who have extolled the presumed epic of the Red Clyde have noted a large and nasty race riot against black people beside that river in 1919?) It is crucial that we establish in everyone's thick head the fact that there is no such thing as a 'pure' Scot, genetically or linguistically.

There have however, been very strong, distinctively Scottish, cultural formations. The tendency has been to derive Scottish dourness from the 'evil' influence of John Knox. (There is, for instance, the fatuous idea that Knox, by disapproving of theatre, prevented us from rivalling the achievements of Shakespeare. The

simple facts are that Knox did not disapprove of theatre and that
Edinburgh was too small to support the explosion of popular culture which threw up Shakespeare and his fine rivals in London.) It
is probably the case that the doctrines of Knox and his Presbyterian successor Melville matched tendencies to censoriousness and
thriftiness already present in Scottish culture. In the nineteenth
century, these cultural attributes marched in perverse-seeming step
alongside the world-wide success of Scottish Romantic literature
and the musical and lusty cult of Burns. The frosty-faced but up-
right and devoted Scottish doctor might be caught with tears in his
eyes as his wife sang 'A Red, Red Rose' at the Burns Supper. The
god-fearing engineer erecting and tending machinery in Africa or
Eastern Europe prided himself on having 'Tam o' Shanter' by heart.
Kipling got this right in 'McAndrew's Hymn' (1893) – 'Lord, send
a man like Robbie Burns to sing the Song o' Steam' – incidentally
proving, to the confoundment of language purists, or 'tongue troopers' as they are known in Quebec, that an English nationalist born
in India could write excellent 'Scots'.

Ignorant leftists have dismissed the cult of self-help associated
with that eminent Scot, Samuel Smiles, as a Victorian mechanism
for blaming the poor for their own poverty. On the contrary – it
was the engine of working class advancement, the foundation of
trade unionism and the Labour Movement, and the basis of the
Co-operative Wholesale Societies. Equally culpable ignorance assimilates the Free Church, which broke away from the established
Church of Scotland in 1843, with the 'Wee Frees' who separated
from the Free Church itself and acquired a puritanical and bigoted
grip on parts of the Highlands and Islands. The unification of the
not-Wee Free Church with the United Presbyterian dissenters in
1900 was followed in 1929 by merger of the 'United Free Church'
with the Church of Scotland, at a time when systematic theology
on former lines was falling out of fashion. A dozy liberalism increasingly prevailed. Hence we have lost touch with one of the
bases of Scottish culture as it has come down to us. Robert Louis
Stevenson, for instance, saw the Calvinist tradition not as a cold-

handed, wholly restrictive thing, but in terms of the problematic living faith of his loved, loving and indulgent father. Hence the importance of certain novels I discuss here which can bring that living faith – with its problems, yes – back to life for us.

Through the mists beyond our watershed, I hope that what I think I can glimpse might actually emerge – a nation without the disastrous paraphernalia of the nation-state. A nation empowered by acceptance of the realities of its past and ready to generate new Scotlands of the mind, and recreate itself as a land without prejudice.

Edinburgh, March 2002

PART ONE

Living Somewhere

Three Days of Scotland

One

MY FRIENDLY-NEIGHBOURHOOD-BOOKSELLER (and publisher) Sally Evans reckoned we should go up Castle Rock to see to the new Scottish Parliament begin. The day before I asked Directory Enquiries for 'Scottish Parliament'. The British Telecom Lady (when does the New Scotland get a replacement with a Kelvinside accent?) told me that the number I required was not available. But Sally remembered that one of Saturday's papers had given a ticketline number. This worked, but the 144 seats allocated to the general public had all been snapped up; MSPs, we were informed, would be entering the Church of Scotland Assembly Hall, interim Parliament, from the Mound rather than the Lawnmarket. With Sally's husband Ian King, the other half of Old Grindles Bookshop and diehard publishing, we duly arrived on the Mound at 8.45 AM on The Day.

Overcast, and damn few folk there. A representative Worker in regulation cloth cap was in charge of two large banners demanding 'Prosecute Occidental'. Tourists with cameras, some from the Far East, had heard about it, but very few local Scots had turned up. The show was stolen by two fine-looking lads who seemed at first sight to have been sent by Central Casting, but said they were just concerned citizens from the New Town. One wore antique leather jerkin and kilt and sported a huge broadsword, which the police decided, rather against the odds, that he was entitled to carry. The other, in belted plaid, held a large Saltire. At one point, there must have been twenty press and TV cameras on them.

There wasn't much else for the cameras. The Lib Dems, one

learnt later, slunk in *en masse* through the back, Lawnmarket, entrance. Margo Macdonald MSP (SNP, Lothian list), arrived *en masse* in black cab. A lorry from Denny came past with placards protesting Gordon Brown's increase of petrol tax. Next time it showed, Dorothy Grace Elder MSP (SNP, Glasgow list), a Noted Press Columnist jumped daintily from the driver's cab into the arms of the media. Nice one, Dorothy... A man who looked like Dennis Canavan MP, defiantly elected for Falkirk with a huge majority as an Independent after New Labour had refused to select him, arrived and Sally and Ian and I clapped. He showed us a sour face and we realised it wasn't Dennis. Tommy Sheridan, now Britain's lone Socialist Parliamentarian, appeared, chatting of course at length to the Anti-Occidental Worker. Then came the real Canavan, who also talked to the Worker. We clapped again and he gave us a shy smile. Gallant, unlucky losers arrived – Canon Kenyon Wright, Convener of the Constitutional Convention, who had a moral claim to get in as an independent, but didn't, and Keith Geddes, long-serving Labour stalwart in Local Government, who missed out on the list in South of Scotland, and who has surely forgotten that I once caught him behind the wicket when I was keeping for Carlton Seconds against Holy Cross Accies. Both managed sort-of smiles.

John McAllion, New Labour's major Token Leftist, hovered a while, looking reserved. Alex Salmond appeared, to be mobbed with mikes. Sally slipped into the media scrum like a groupie and Alex shook her hand. Wonderful what they can do with Virtual Reality these days. The Alexander Clones, brother and sister, created by Millbank as infallible spokespersons for New Blairism, appeared severally, both moving for all the world like actual human beings, with muscles and bones and things. In a cloud of minders, mikes and soundmen, Donald Dewar at last walked rather grimly past.

Normally, the Church of Scotland Assembly Hall is physically part of Edinburgh University's New College. A man fell off a bicycle at the foot of the road up from the Mound proper. It transpired that he was a New College theology student keen to get in

3

and proceed with his work. For the rest of Edinburgh, too, it was clearly Business as Usual. As everything became even calmer, I asked a couple of policemen what was happening. 'The MSPs are in there swearing. Then this afternoon they'll elect a Presiding Officer.' I reflected that part of his job will be to stop them swearing any more... The Queen? 'Not till the first of July'.

Around ten, as I slipped down to Princes Street to shop, I realised, with the start of a tear in my eye, that many of the perfectly ordinary looking people who had arrived in cars and cabs with old folk and children – families, entitled to seats inside – or walked quietly past us towards the hall, must have been new MSPs whom we didn't recognise. Just as it should be, our own new Parliament, people like us setting about their business in grey Edinburgh five years to the day after John Smith MP, who had willed it so strongly to happen, had died. In just such grey May weather I stood in a very large crowd outside the church in Morningside where his funeral was held, much more of a State Occasion than this one. But today's lowkey opening was what he would have wanted, matter of fact, part of the ordinary life of a normal nation, with no higher drama than Tommy Sheridan's clenched fist, seen on TV later as, after protesting, he took the oath of loyalty to his sovereign – just 'Elizabeth' here, not 'The Second', since we had no prior Elizabeth.

Two

THE 1999 WORLD CRICKET CUP will be remembered by many millions in several continents for myriad reasons. Not so much for the Final, where the young Pakistanis froze and failed to give Australia much of a fight, as for the majestic play of the first five Indian batsmen; the elegance of Kenya's Steve Tikolo; the spinning guile of Saqlain Mushtaq and Shane Warne; Shoaib Akhtar, 'the Rawalpindi Express', as fast a bowler as has ever been seen; the glorious quick scoring down the order of Moin Khan and of Lance Klusener – 'Zulu' to his South African comrades, the huge hitter from the rustic outback, at the wicket in the last possible over of that astonishing semi-final against Australia, when he called Alan Donald 'White Lightning', for what would have been the winning run, and the great speed bowler made the schoolboy error of turning to see where the ball had gone rather than putting his head down to sprint those few yards down the wicket for certain victory.

It was widely recorded that this 'Carnival of Cricket', as the inept English organisers styled it, derived its richest atmosphere from the tumultuous support for four teams from the Indian Sub-Continent. But the Tartan Army was in attendance. We Were There, not of course, for the winning, but for the taking part. It was easily predictable that Scotland would perform worst of the twelve teams in contention. We had scraped in by the width of varnish on a bail, by beating Ireland for third place in the eliminating tournament for minnows in Kuala Lumpur, behind accomplished Kenya and fervent Bangladesh. This was an achievement not to be underestimated, for a national side almost wholly amateur, from a land distinguished by its overwhelming passion for football, with rugby as a sometimes-successful sideline.

Not that cricket is rare in Scotland. In the north and west Highlands it has barely existed. But Perthshire has notable grounds, large and small. In the far north prong of Lowland country, where Gaelic was spoken well into the twentieth century, Tain in Easter Ross had three cricket clubs in the 1920s. Along the Moray Firth, the game has thrived in relatively dry summers with long northern evenings. A few years ago, it was reported that Aberdeenshire had more active cricketers per head of population than any other part of Britain. After bagpipers marched into Lords, Freuchie from Fife, back in the Eighties, won the national 'English' Village Cricket Championship. East and West Central Belt have distinguished old clubs, and Mike Denness from Ayr once captained England. The idea that cricket is a boring English game for poofters and jessies, now sadly commonplace in Scottish bars, seems to be of recent origin. Early in the twentieth century, as in England, working men played football in winter, cricket in summer. As a young man, Willie

Gallacher, leader of the Shop Stewards Movement on the Red Clyde and later Communist MP for West Fife, put on the pads with his mates.

So we've played a lot of cricket in Scotland. But despite the employment as club pros here at various times of such greats as Rohan Kanhai and Gordon Greenidge (West Indies) and Intikhab Alam (Pakistan), few of us have managed to play it well at the highest level. Since, before the 1914–18 war, the legendary Gregor McGregor (rugby for Scotland, cricket for Middlesex and England) stood up, as wicket keeper, to the fastest pacemen of his day, few Scots have sustained first class careers.

So, in May 1999, it was mind-bendingly wonderful just To Be There.

We were in the tough half of the draw, as it happened, pitted against Australia and Pakistan, the eventual finalists, New Zealand, always a good bet to reach the later stages, Bangladesh, desperate to assert their claim to full Test status, and, well, the formerly near-invincible West Indies.

When I arrived by taxi at the Leicestershire County ground at Grace Road, on the brilliantly hot day we took on the West Indies, the first startling thing which happened was that not one, but two, ingratiating gentlemen separately approached me to ask if I had any spare tickets. Jings-crivvens! Touts outside a cricket match involving Scotland. Unbelievable!

My elder son, who teaches philosophy at Cardiff University, eventually joined me at the gate, brimming with statistics and shrewd prognoses. I am so delighted that I passed on to Gideon my love of this great multicultural game, which he never saw me perform very competently. (On a good day, I was a satisfactory second eleven wicketkeeper and swish-and-hoick pinch-hitter.) We enter to the ripple of Trinidadian steel drums, laid on by the Cup organisers to create Carnival atmosphere. The ground fills up around us with a diverse assembly.

There are 57 varieties of cheerful Caribbeans. There is the Tartan Army with kilts, silly hats and the blue and white Scotland cricket shirt with the St Andrew's Cross, rated by connoisseurs of design the best of the competing twelve. And there are little old ladies and clean old men, now the backbone of cricket-watching in England. These appear to be somewhat bewildered.

The sun being pitiless, I seek a hat and fancy the browny-maroony West Indian one. Since I am wearing the Scotland shirt, my semiotic self-contradiction draws loud comment from West Indian fans – 'You supparting the right team, maan?' I explain that while my heart is with Scotland, my head backs Brian Lara's men to win.

Back in the Fifties, when cricket drew large working-class crowds in the London of my exiled youth, the atmosphere was never like this. 'Flower of Scotland' vied with Caribbean drumming. Shouts and counter-shouts were incessant. Good-natured obscenities were rarely absent.

George Salmond the Scottish captain had outraged the Leicestershire committee, as one learnt later, by electing to bat when he won the toss. They wanted their local supporters to see the great Lara score maybe 150 runs. Salmond, I surmise, understood that it was his duty to think like a man whose side could win, and feared a West Indian total of 300 or even 400 from the statutory 50 overs, which Scotland could not possibly chase. Whereas, if we got as many as 150, the West Indies might lose daft wickets and fall short pursuing such a modest target. This was not a vintage West Indian side. Beside Lara, it had just one other master bats-man, Chanderpaul, and both batting and bowling were largely sustained by mediocre all-rounders. However, Curtly Ambrose and Courtney Walsh, great pace bowlers still, though now in their late thirties, had decided to take this game very seriously.

These men are 'awesome' – very tall and very accurate. Only Gavin Hamilton, a successful professional with Yorkshire, could do much against them. Ironic cheers went up as Scotland passed 45, the lowest score ever recorded in the Cricket World Cup (by Canada) – just one less as it happens, than England's score in a five day Test in Trinidad in 1994, when the same Ambrose and Walsh cropped the flower of that green and pleasant land. In Leicester, we made 68 in the end. There was the brief treat of Chanderpaul's timing – the little man is so exquisitely poised that even his defensive strokes are a joy to watch – and some whiplash hitting by Lara. All over back of 2 PM. English newspapers the next day would speak scornfully of Scotland's humiliation.

So far as Gid and I were concerned they missed the point. It had been a privilege to see our boys on the same park as fabled giants. Also, the sequel alone was well worth the train fares and entry charge.

As 'colourful' characters converged on the ground in front of the pavilion for presentation of cheques to the captains and Man of the Match, Gid said, 'What's that flag?' A vast national flag was being waved by a mob of Caribbean enthusiasts. Enquiries established that it belonged to Dominica, a 'small island' (pop. 71,000), famous only for the great novelist Jean Rhys. Further questions later in a bar by Leicester station elicited from a scholarly West Indian that Dominica produced, long ago, two cricketing internationals, cousins called Shillingford.

Also present in front of the pavilion was the Whale Called Warne, whom I had met before at World Cup matches in Chester-le-Street and Edinburgh, and would see again when Scotland lost their last match, at home, to New Zealand, surrounded by Kiwis chanting 'All Aussies Are Wankers!' This plump, black and white, inflated creature was by that stage signed by every player in all six teams in the section, except for the corpulent Australian leg-spin genius, Shane Warne, who had declined. In Leicester, one also noticed 'Ronaldo', a man in the golden Brazil football strip, no doubt a trophy from the Tartan Army's occupation of France during the 1998 Football World Cup, when, as ever, the samba drums and the skirling pipes had mingled in social, if not musical, harmony.

As small boys from local primary schools played little 'demonstration' matches with plastic bats and rubber balls – such was a feature of all World Cup games – and the West Indies side (Jimmy Adams wearing a Scotland shirt) limbered up for serious practice with an impromptu game of soccer, the steel band drummed on and the Tartan Army stripped the willow to its beat. Gid and I retreated past this through the torrid air to the cool of the Leicestershire members' bar, where we paid attention through the window to further happenings. We knew that Courtney Walsh was signing copies of his just-published memoirs. (Gid eventually got his autograph for me.) We thought we detected Brian Lara in a black shirt amongst the crowd lingering below us. I further conjectured that the elderly West Indian in a suit chatting intently to a comely woman might be the legendary Barbadian batsman, Clyde Walcott. (One of the all-conquering 'three Ws'. While Everton Weekes had been named after the Liverpool soccer club, Clyde's dad had gone for the less illustrious Scottish side – all to do with Football Pools, I suppose.)

We went down to investigate. Walcott, my man wasn't, but a retired engineer, 73 years old, called Johnson. Lara, as one should have realised, had hot-footed it to Manchester to join his footballer friend Dwight Yorke, from Tobago, in the city-wide celebrations over United's astonishing last-minute win in the European Cup Final against Bayern Munich in Barcelona the night before. So what? Alan and Lesley from K. Jackson's bar, my local in Edinburgh, hailed me. Gid and I settled down on the boundary near them as the true Match of the Day unfolded.

Someone had hijacked a plastic bat and a rubber ball from the juniors. A trash can served as wicket, 'kept' by agile worthies in the front row of the seating. Directed, to some extent, by the black shirted Lara-lookalike, an impromptu game unfolded. Fielders appeared wherever, whenever. A man in kilt and tammie, fine white shirt, fag in mouth, set his pint of lager down by the fence and bowled quite neatly. When a Caribbean bloke wearing dark glasses took over the ball, Tartan rowdies sang out, 'Come on, Stevie Wonder'. Mr Johnson from Barbados deserted his lovely lady for long enough to show some batting class. An equally aged Caribbean of Asian mien likewise played some deft shots, unperturbed by Tartan 'sledging'.

This exuberant *mêlée* was like a delicious dream. Under clear blue sky, in the green centre of Deep England, love of the game, spiced with genial irony, briefly brought into community the braes of Angus and the beaches of Barbados. An *English* game? Awa wi ye – dinna dare say that in Calcutta or Antigua. A game for jessies? Not if you face Ambrose and Walsh.

Three

ON I JULY, FROM THE Ceilidh Place in Ullapool, I phone George Gunn in Thurso about this playwriting competition he's asked me to help adjudicate for his Grey Coast Theatre Company. George is surprised that I'm not at home in Edinburgh. I am surprised by George's reason for being surprised. The very considerable bulk of republican, socialist, anti-establishmentarian George is parked, it seems, in front of his TV so that he can watch the Queen's ceremonial opening of the first Scottish Parliament since 1707. 'Historic day, man,' he grits out, 'this is History.'

I go downstairs to meet Donny O'Rourke in the cafe. What has happened is that C. and I arrived in Ullapool three days ago to find that Donny is carpentered into the Ceilidh Place programme as a kind of Writer in Residence, with a notion that he would gather some talented friends together for little shows in the Clubhouse over several days. Alas, Donny has found that the people he wanted can't make it. He is stuck, by sheer accident, with me. We've never properly met before but find that our minds overlap usefully. We are planning an event where he and I will present, read from, and gossip personally about, four great Scottish poets: Sorley Maclean, Norman MacCaig, Edwin Morgan and Iain Crichton Smith. (The loss of Iain last October still grieves both of us, and we have the same reaction – he was so unassuming and self-deprecating that it wasn't until he died quite suddenly that one realised that he was a great poet.)

So Donny and I are parked in the café volleying Douglas Dunn's *Faber Book of Twentieth Century Scottish Verse* between us when in comes Jean Urquhart, who founded the Ceilidh Place with her husband, the late, great actor Robert, back in 1970 – this unique combination of comfortable hotel, good food, friendly bars, bookshop, art gallery and venue for concerts and touring plays. Jean was in Edinburgh last night, at the deftly timed premiere of Sean Connery's new movie – Big Tam, who will be at the opening of Parliament as an invited guest is combining business with what one must suppose is great pleasure. So I am surprised to see her, back up so early, and she is surprised to see me. Again, *why* am I not in Edinburgh? Well, apart from being republican, socialist etc, I live so damn near the Castle and the ceremonial route that the Historic event could upset me deeply. Apart from the barriers up blocking nearby streets to traffic and the crowds and litter on my home paving stones, there will be troops all over the place, the brutish arm of the Brit state.

One peculiarity of the Ceilidh Place is that Jean has excluded radios, let alone TV, from its bars and bedrooms. I only just discovered yesterday that a couple of TVs are secretly kept for guests who adamantly insist on one. I have duly hijacked a TV to watch not the opening, but the Test cricket. Now here is Jean herself, Lord save us, getting the other set manhandled into the café and set up where we can see it. Weird. Donny and I resume our anecdotes and discriminations.

Unnoticed by us, the TV disappears. Jean has taken it to Reception or somewhere. And here she is upon us.

'It's over,' she says. 'It was most moving. I cried.'

I cut up to my room soon after and flick on the set. Aftermath happenings. Parliamentarians and Celebs are moving through the crowds. Big Tam waves to his people like the monarch he truly is. MSPs and MPs not ranked or sorted out in any order stroll peaceably, party mingled with party, suddenly greeting friends among the bystanders. That honest man Donald Dewar shambles through the *mêlée* looking shy. Now I'm in tears. Cut to studio. Liz Lochhead is there, flanked by Andrew Neill of *The Scotsman* and Ian Hamilton QC, who long ago Stole the Stone. (The first time I came to the Ceilidh Place was when I did a Scottish Book Week gig with him here five years ago.) Kirsty Wark asks Liz what she found most memorable. Liz replies, 'The poetry.'

Gradually over the next few days, from TV highlights, returned eyewitnesses, and press reports, I piece together a version of what happened vivid enough to serve as direct memory when my senile mind drifts loose and wanders. Yes, there is foosty pomp and circumstance, with the Royal Carriage etcetera, Chookie Embro being stiff and, no doubt, nippy, security goons and sodjers rampant. But all this has been ambushed, so to speak, by well-planned informality.

Amid great controversy a few weeks back, Sheena Wellington was appointed to sing 'A Man's a Man for A' That' at the Opening. She herself insisted that it was not a male-chauvinist anthem. Her singing is what so moves Jean on the day. Towards the end, Sheena's voice changes gear – come all ye – and out go her arms, hands, beckoning. So the MSPs join in, associating themselves with Burns's contempt for yon birkies ca'd lords and asserting the siblinghood of all humankind. Another touch (this must be what pleases Liz Lochhead): a very young actress recites a prize poem, from Thurso of all places, which will chuff George Gunn, by an 11-year-old, celebrating the Scottishness of, amongst other things, mince 'n tatties and Oor Wullie. So the spiky-haired sage on his bucket achieves spectral emanation before Her Majesty.

The crowds, I am told, were tense before the Opening. Lots of nervous parents of jittery schoolkids bussed in for the occasion. But afterwards everyone relaxes in fine sunshine. God has abated his war against Scotland and let there be no rain. Musical events, from classical to rock, break out all over Princes Street Gardens.

Meanwhile the Ceilidh Place has been set up as one of four contestants in a BBC Radio cross-Scotland Pub Quiz, with Lesley Riddoch calling the questions. Five questions only. Sudden death. We are against some howff in Arbroath and whoever wins goes through to the instant final. A radio is perched on the bar, around which gather a score of locals, including one lady who has brought several fat reference books, which are of no use in this quiz. All the questions are about Scotland. Jean, on a telephone hook-up, relays our answers. We are undone thus: the grazing of ten, not twenty sheep is sufficient to classify a lump of land as an 'island'. Moans of 'fix' ring out. But at least we have dotted Ullapool onto the media map of the Great Day.

It's sunny here, too. In the evening, C and I buy excellent fish and chips and eat them in the carpark near the harbour where the local junior pipe band is performing, with breaks filled by Highland Dancing by even smaller young people. Furtively, I greet again. Though some of them are barely as big as their instruments, these kids are not bad at all. Even that horrid item 'Scotland the Brave' somehow comes out honest and moving. I say to Jean later that I guess that round here, half their parents are probably English incomers. She says that she thinks not, but reflects that it would be good if it were so. For both of us, all people who live in Scotland by choice are *de facto* Scots.

Grampian TV news, this night, is very huffy about how Inverness and Aberdeen were left out on the Great Day – no open air concerts, no ceremonials. But I think folk in Ullapool feel easy enough, in their trim, quiet port where at this time of year there is virtually no darkness at all, and men fish through the small hours in burns up in the mountains, while wide-awake birds sing.

1999

Like a Stranger in a Strange Land

IN THE WONDROUS GARDENS OF Inverewe, a Frenchman of peasant-like appearance walking amid the many exotic plants, stabs out his stick towards a white rose. 'Rose blanche', he tells his wife emphatically. Slipping down a side alley to give vent to my convulsive laughter, I wonder what purport that moment had. There can be no part of France where white roses are unusual. Was he merely demonstrating the truism that familiar things seen far from home become significant, like the temperate-zone spring and summer flowers I once witnessed blooming in December in Dhaka – wallflowers in Bangladesh?

Some days later, on 2 July 1997, the chief executive of Historic Scotland had himself photographed by the press in front of Edinburgh Castle. Triumphs were to be chronicled. The Castle is Scotland's top paid tourist attraction, with more than a million visitors last year, 120 per cent up on 1995. While New Lanark was down, Urquhart Castle, a favourite spot for Nessie-seekers, was up 20 per cent, etc. From such statistics the chairman of the Scottish Tourist Board elicited 'a healthy picture'. He averred that 'the 1996 results prove that continuing investment in new facilities, marketing, training, service, and hospitality can bring results'. He added that tourism is now one of Scotland's 'largest industries', employing some 177,000 people.

Reading this, instructed as I am by Jean Urquhart, who runs the Ceilidh Place in Ullapool where I am staying, my mind enters with increasing disgust an arena of Orwellian Newspeak. As in Gogol's great novel, there is traffic in 'dead souls' – like Chichikov's dead serfs, 'tourists' exist only on paper. And the 'industry' mentioned is no such thing.

First, the great statistical fantasy of 'tourism'. The MacLellan

Galleries in Glasgow, we are told, had a 'staggering' increase of visitor numbers of 258 per cent in 1996, thanks to the big Charles Rennie Mackintosh exhibition. Well, I 'visited' that and I know at least one fellow-resident of Edinburgh who went twice. Do we become 'tourists' when we flip coins across a counter to see work by one of our own country's great artists? Is it not likely that Scots preponderated among the galleries' 'visitors'? Whisky production is undoubtedly an industry. So is fishing. But tourism isn't an 'industry'. In so far as hotels employ people all the year round in steady jobs, they are working in a specific 'service industry'. Museums, meanwhile, have complex educational and recreative functions for nearby Scots. Sometimes tourists are there, sometimes not.

A few writers produce books specifically for tourists. I don't. To get into and out of the gardens at Inverewe it is necessary to pass through a shop that sells, among other things that tourists are supposed to like, books. Imagine one of mine got on those shelves and was sold, to become part of a statistical agglomerate of sales to 'tourists' in 'tourist' shops. Does that make me part of the 'tourist' industry?

I fancy that the 177,000 'jobs' reported by the STB chairman are largely filled by Gogolian 'dead souls'. The figure must be arrived at by taking those employed in hotels, museums, and other places which would exist irrespective of tourism and adding the people, mostly young, mostly underpaid, recruited in summer to staff places where tourists may arrive in spate. The day I read the newspaper in which the STB was reported to be congratulating itself, I witnessed one of its initiatives in progress. I asked why some ten young persons in the lounge at the Ceilidh Place were dressed up in smart black and white (one had a bow tie). The charming lady in charge of them told me that they were pupils of Ullapool High School undergoing 'Welcome Host' training – hygiene yesterday, serving-at-table today – on the presumption that they would staff the 'tourist industry'. Oh dear. If most of these bright-faced kids can find nothing better than seasonal or precarious low-paid work related to 'tourism', Scotland will be in ruins.

People who should properly be called 'visitors' are recycled as dead-soul 'tourists'. Unlike Jean Urquhart, I believe that 'tourism' actually exists. The French couple mentioned above were, to my mind, 'tourists'. They had come in a bus with other French people. Very probably, they were taken from place to place as part of a set 'tour'. And I've often been a 'package holiday tourist' myself. You pay for sunshine, clean rooms, a swimming pool, a beach. You swim. You read. It is healthy and cheap. But most people who come to Scotland have more in mind than a peaceful flop-out.

When a businessman visiting Edinburgh drops into the National Gallery, he is not a 'tourist'. There are birdwatchers, hillwalkers, people interested in archaeology. There are cousin Katie from Saskatchewan and great uncle Bert from Brisbane, Japs with their cameras, Germans who like sailing, and Yanks with a passion for fiddle music. For people in all these categories, and more, satisfactory facilities were in place before the STB was ever thought of. How many visitors Scotland gets is determined less by marketing than by the position of sterling *vis-à-vis* other currencies and the economic situations prevailing in other countries.

When the STB attributes 177,000 jobs to its own shifts and devices, I am reminded of La Fontaine's great fable of 'The Fly and the Coach'. On a hot day, powerful horses pull a coach up a steep hill. A fly alights on the nose of the foremost and urges them on. When the summit is attained, it applauds itself for directing the operation ... In fact, 'tourism', according to the STB's own figures, is actually down in Scotland over the past few years. What has definitely increased is the 'Tourocracy' of people who are salaried to encourage the fantasy that their activities are boosting a non-existent industry providing more and more naff jobs. If the Tourocracy does by any chance achieve anything, that will probably be bad news. I shudder to read, in a recent STB brochure, of a 'Food Quality Grading Scheme backed by extensive consumer research in the UK and Europe'. So people will come here to eat, not what we enjoy ourselves, but what, outside Scotland, they think they want to eat? As for the 'Tourism and Environment Task Force' which is seeking to develop 'a code of conduct for cetacean watching in the Moray Firth', my guess is that it would probably impede the relaxed observation of dolphins by decent people, but won't stop any nasty person doing rotten things.

The museum of local history housed in Ullapool's oldest church building has excellent features. Anyone can read there, carefully sorted and mounted, documents and letters such as elsewhere would be prised only by dedicated scholars out of dusty library basements. Just one thing jars – a video about the area and its history which runs through cliché after cliché about the land, the fauna, the fishing, the Clearances, and concludes triumphantly that after all their centuries of hardship and struggle the 'people of Ullapool' have at last won through – the area is a tourist attraction! This nauseating junk, wait for it, won last year an award for best video from the Tourocracy.

My own most remarkable moments abroad have been as what the STB calls a 'non-holiday tourist' – in other words, I was there for a purpose. I once went with a Scottish cultural delegation to the Baltic States. In Talinn, Estonia, we attended one of those ghastly functions where local bureaucrats talked Soviet tosh about international friendship. I did, however, actually achieve a brief friendship at this event, with a teacher who spoke excellent English. As we paced the streets together, he talked gloomily about how boring Talinn was. (I thought it very interesting.) Where, I asked him, had he perfected his English? 'In Leicester', he responded, with a sigh which I can still hear – 'Aaah, Leicester'. Few British cities can be less attractive to 'tourists'. But he had met a different kind of people from his own. Maybe he had loved brick suburban buildings such as we take for granted. Perhaps warm English beer seemed to him delicious.

Meanwhile, I had enjoyed something routine for him but fascinating to me – a production of *Traviata* where the chorus sang in Estonian, but the three principals used Italian – a fine tenor from Finland, a truly glorious baritone from Moscow, and the local *diva*, not too bad.

Work – a British Council lecture tour – deposited me more recently in Rajshahi, a town in Bangladesh on the banks of the Ganges. Near sunset I was taken out on the river by three students who were in charge of me. That night we visited one of their lecturers, a man who himself had been a student in Stirling. After more-or-less convincing me that Buddhist thinkers of the first millennium had anticipated all the characteristic ideas of present-day European post-structuralism, he decided a drink would be a good idea. Alcohol? In this dry Muslim country? In a scene reminiscent of comic opera, the lads dashed in and out of alleys leading from a little square, and within minutes we had beer and Indian whisky, smuggled across the great open Ganges. One of the students was later very sick over the floor of my supposedly arid hotel bedroom, but neither the management nor the British Council got back to me about this regrettable eventuality. The whisky, by the way, wasn't bad – more like Bourbon than Scotch – sweet.

My Ganges experience would have been utterly different if instead of going out in a tiny fishing boat hired on the spur of the moment for a few *takas*, I had encountered the river on a posh tourist vessel with superior Scotch in the bar, surrounded by Europeans and Japanese. That evening I was taken a few steps inside a different culture. Engineers abroad to look at factories, churchmen visiting missions, must have similar epiphanies – unexpected friendships, memorable 'scenes' where no 'scenery' was expected. 'Aaah, Leicester'.

Not long before I came to Ullapool, I visited Stonehaven for the first time. I had never stopped there, though I had seen it often from the train. I wanted to check out the Grassic Gibbon Country.

Nor had I ever lingered in Arbroath. I broke my journey there and found a place wondrously innocent of tourism. There was no one at the ticket counter in the famous ruined abbey, nor any board I could see with the text of the great Declaration on it. Seeking in the town centre the kind of hotel where you can sit on a sofa with coffee and biscuits, I found none, but in a pleasant pub the bartender sold me a pint of orange squash so cheaply that she can never have heard of the First Law of Tourism – Always Overcharge Strangers.

In Stonehaven, my steps from the station led me to a small, cheapish, central hotel which shall be nameless. It was so Fawlty, I enjoyed it. There was no radio in my room, no bedlight, and no bedside table. And since there was no lounge I could find, I sat instead on the near-empty beach eating truly excellent catfish and chips, or outside pubs (where I did detect a few English visitors) prospecting the attractive harbour. A slightly precarious walk along the clifftops brought me to Dunnottar Castle, a genuinely awesome spectacle, with its grandiose site on a crag, the scale of its ruins, the lion's den near the entrance where, the custodian assured me, the Earl of Mar had once kept a real lion. Then he sold me his very learned historical guide to the castle, first published some seven decades ago and penny-plain. Ignorance here of the Second Law of Tourism – put glossy covers on such things and retail them at three times the price.

At what seemed to be the poshest hotel in town, I had another fine experience. I discovered (from small print in the newspaper) that Brian McNeill was singing to the local folk club. This was a bargain. McNeill's virtuosity on several instruments and huge personality might have squashed everything else, but didn't. Locals did floor spots after half time, with sincerity and some flair. The event was full of mutual respect and warmth. Though I overheard one or two of the inevitable Antipodean transients, this event was nothing to do with 'tourism'.

It wasn't so good that the open-air swimming-pool in the much-signposted Leisure Complex was closed, and that one saw dilapidation there and scented extinction, or that, careless, I could find no way of getting to the Grassic Gibbon Centre in Arbuthnott on a Sunday afternoon.

But even that had its upside. A pleasant bus trip through the sunny Mearns took me to Laurencekirk, I paced up that town's long main street, observed the sabbath life of a place new to me, before concluding that I might as well take the next bus back. I am certain that I enjoyed Stonehaven and environs so much precisely because they were so 'untouristy'. Apart from the notice on boards that the inventor of the pneumatic tyre was born in Stonehaven, and bits of other information beside old buildings, there was no sign of any attempt to impress outsiders, except, perhaps, the many certificates in the butcher's shop in token of awards made by Smithfield judges. I wonder if it provided the superb black pudding which was the outstanding feature of the erratically served breakfasts at my hotel.

Yet I love Ullapool, which is very definitely geared up for tourism (and has a really smashing new swimming pool). Beside people passing to and from Lewis on the ferry, and ships calling in, there are coaches depositing French and German persons in scores and freer travellers from Europe, North America, and Japan. There are several salubrious hotels, smart guest-houses, a youth hostel, shops selling most things travellers want, from the makings of a picnic lunch to expensive clothing. Transients mostly look happy. They have driven through very beautiful scenery, or stepped off one of the frequent boats which take you out to the Summer Isles up splendid Loch Broom. In light which is glorious even while it's raining, a light which constantly changes as weather casts mountains, sky and water into new relations, the visitors are smiling. And the young people who serve them smile back.

Jean Urquhart employs lots of young people in the Ceilidh Place, her remarkable combination of hotel, art gallery, bookshop and 'little theatre', where there is musical or dramatic activity most nights. It is a happy place to stay, full of beautiful and interesting things; a genuine centre of Scottish culture where the food doesn't 'Taste of Scotland' but of the imaginative preparation of fresh ingredients. There are no TVs. Furthermore, there are none of those tiny rectangles of wrapped-up soap by your wash-hand basin which you find in hotels everywhere. This does not please the Scottish Tourist Board.

It seems that the STB when considering which hotels should get its Crowns shoots off questionnaires about amenities. One question is about soap. Are bars changed every day? Jean's staff put out large scented discs which look like works of art and could last for weeks. Why change them?

The drive of the STB is to 'package' everything saleable to visitors in Scotland. Thus, the Scottish Arts Council, collaborating with the STB, wants organisations it funds to 'develop' their brand. From 'Scotland the Brand' to 'Scotland The Bland' is a short step. And I would far rather Stonehaven stayed exactly as it is than that Ullapool took any further steps in the direction of packagisation. This, damn it, is my country. If someone buys a Canongate Classic in Jean's shop, 'tourism' is irrelevant to the transaction. Bands play at the Ceilidh Place for whoever likes music. We should get on with our own business in our own way. The more we enjoy our own culture on our own terms, the more foreigners should, and will, relish dropping in on it.

1997

By the Water of Leith
I Sat Down and Wept

IN AN EARLY EPISODE OF Irvine Welsh's novel *Trainspotting* the protagonist Renton is drinking on a balcony bar with his vicious 'friend' Franco Begbie whose violent talk and gestures are annoying him. 'Rents' muses:

> Ah hate cunts like that... Cunts that are intae baseball-batting every fucker that's different, pakis, poofs, n what huv ye. Fuckin failures in a country ay failures. It's nae good blaming it oan the English fir colonising us. Ah don't hate the English. They're just wankers. We are colonised by wankers. We can't even pick a decent, vibrant, healthy culture to be colonised by. No. We're ruled by effete arseholes. What does that make us?... The most wretched, servile, miserable, pathetic trash that was ever shat intae creation.

Danny Boyle's highly successful film of the book turns this into a speech made by Rents when his fitness-minded friend Tommy, clean living so far but quite soon to die of AIDS contracted from bad needles, has led a small crew of Leith druggies up to a moorland Ben. They refuse to climb it. The reason for this transposition seems to be that the film's audiences furth of Scotland will associate the country with Beautiful Highland Scenery. Removed from the complex pattern of interactions in Edinburgh where Welsh's book placed them, the words – originally thoughts prompted by the behaviour of one nasty Scot – stand out starkly (but still wittily) as a rant aimed at Scottish identity in general. Americans and Germans will be challenged to set their romantic conceptions of Scotland against the frustrating reality of modern urban life. For alert Scottish filmgoers the message could be more complex. At

the very moment when enhanced and inflamed pride in Scotland is
sustained for many of us by the successes of writers such as Welsh
and film-makers like Boyle, these same creative people sound a
warning: don't imagine that all the literary prizes, all the acclaim
for James Macmillan's compositions, all the successes of painters
like Bellany and Currie, mitigate the misery which makes drugs
attractive to young people. Along with *Trainspotting*, the most
publicised recent work of Scottish fiction has been James Kelman's
Booker-winning novel *How Late It Was How Late*. Kelman's protagonist is much older than Renton, much less educated and articulate, from a working class Glasgow where drink and gambling,
rather than drugs, are the opiates of the underdog. But the two
books have this in common: to survive at all, their protagonists
have to get clear away from Scotland. I recently by chance came
across a paperback, *Famous Scots*, published in 1988 by an obscure London house. Its author, Ian Fellowes Gordon, concentrates
on Scots who left their homeland to make their mark in England
or overseas. Whimsically, he suggests that it might be best for the
world in general, and Scotland in particular, if the whole population followed their example. 'If Baird and Carnegie and Reith and
Adam and Mary Garden had to get out to perform their wonders,
think what five million might do, sweeping across the globe. The
mind boggles.' Mine does, indeed. I remember a journey across
the old East Germany maybe fifteen years ago. The landscape between Leipzig and Dresden resembled much of Central Belt Scotland – an early centre of Industrial Revolution, now in decay. But
in that queer place, the DDR, unemployment officially didn't exist.
Everyone wore decent if unexciting clothes. At Dresden station a
shabby creature shambled in front of me. Unbelievably, it was a
red-nosed hairy Scot, asking for the price of a cup of – whatever.
Latterly, in Glasgow, I unwisely accepted the hospitality of a pleas-
ant-enough-seeming stranger I met in a bar. He harangued me for
hours, in his houseproud high rise flat, on his sorrows and my
inadequacies. It particularly incensed him that I sat drinking his
water while he slowly consumed lager. He told me about his

broken relationships with women, the court charges he was facing. When I tried to slip away he halted me and threatened to pitch me out of his window – he was, he pointed out, a former prison officer and had been trained to batter people properly. So I submitted to his monologue. However one justifies the literary replication of the usages 'fuck' and 'fuckin' once or twice in almost every sentence, characteristic of certain circles in Edinburgh as well as in Glasgow, on this occasion they seemed to issue from the jaws of Hell. My acquaintance was inviting me to share Hell with him. And I couldn't firmly say I wouldn't join him.

Scotland has very beautiful countryside easily accessible from all major centres of population. (How claustrophobic London seems to a Scot.) It has produced gallant soldiers, great philosophers, devoted missionaries, inspired inventors, scientists and engineers, even a few politicians of integrity. It is also the land of the maudlin drunk and the dangerous drunk, of the wife-batterer in the desolate housing scheme. The words 'keelie' (lower-class person) and 'schemie' (inhabitant of a scheme) have no equivalents south of the border. The diminutive 'ie' projects a kind of acceptance, if not affection. It also, to state the obvious, expresses diminution. The Scot who is better off than the keelie or schemie, if only by fractions, may acknowledge and yet spurn, using these words, her or his own kind. We are bound together by a common fate which is not, much of the time, at all attractive. It is limited and limiting. Talented Scots, and even untalented ones, can earn much more money in other countries. However much we love and want our country, it doesn't seem to want most of us. Even cool, cool A.L. Kennedy, in her brilliant novel *So I Am Glad*, has a far from underprivileged narrator, alienated in today's trendy Glasgow, 'find herself', if anywhere, in Paris.

Scottish 'identity' is, of course, a myth. It is given substance only in the corporealities of persons who imagine that they have it. There is nothing outside consciousness which is 'identity', though Scots may invest their individual identities in Scottish landscape or Scottish football, Scottish poetry and music or Scottish beef cattle.

One can demonstrate that over historic time, the prevalent sense, or contending senses, of Scottish identity have changed. After the Reformation, Lowland Scots who had embraced Calvinism came to see theirs, along with ancient Israel, as one of the 'two sworn nations of the Lord.'. Other Scots, Lowland and Highland, identified, in the long run more and more imprudently, with the fortunes and fate of the Stewart dynasty. The Union of 1707 and the Industrial Revolution reduced such identities to sentiment. From the new commercial and industrial Scotland emerged the cult of the Self-Helping Scot, momentously exemplified by Burns and Carlyle, David Livingstone and Andrew Carnegie. The 'man of independent mind', born in a tiny, crowded shepherd's cottage or weaver's flat, educated in a simple village school, or, after toilsome hours of manual labour, by himself, attained by his own dedicated efforts fame if not fortune. Or the mythical 'lad o' pairts', inspired by a devoted dominie, made his way to the university, where he subsisted on porridge and prizes, ultimately emerging as a great divine or scholar or scientist. For family reasons which will emerge later, I cannot help subscribing emotionally to the Self-Help myth.

As Industrial Scotland emerged, blackened with soot from the land's own coal, the success which made Glasgow the shipbuilding and heavy engineering centre of the Greatest Empire the World Had Ever Seen sustained artisans and even labourers as well as the great Captains of Industry. It is certain that very few Scots in the first decade of the twentieth century would have thought of themselves as 'colonised' by the English. We were, rather, proud coadjutors with them, not always hiding from them our sense that we were their superiors. In a *Punch* cartoon of the period, a businessmen just back from London greets his aged father, who asks him how the English are getting on. 'I don't know,' comes the answer. 'I only spoke to the top men.'

The bitterness which came with industrial collapse after the 1914–18 war coincided with strong interest, for a time, among Scottish Labour MPs in the idea of Home Rule and with the arrival of the Scottish National Party. Certain factors conspired to create the notion that Scots were a colonised people who should liberate themselves. One was the success of Irish Nationalism, sparked by an Easter Rising which was led by working-class, Edinburgh-born James Connolly. Another was the sudden creation, at Versailles, of a small host of new nation states carved from the Austrian and Russian empires. If Latvia could be independent, why not Scotland?

Yet the only colonialism affecting Scotland had been directed against Gaels by Lowlanders, with features comparable to those seen in, say, Africa – dispossession of land, erection of new towns as centres of commercial exploitation, attempts to stamp out the native language. In so far as Lowlanders were English-speakers and Englishmen joined in the Lowland effort, one might just speak without absurdity of English colonisation of the Gaeltacht. However, throughout the empire, where Highlanders of all classes proved to be as murderous and rapacious as soldiers and agents of British imperialism as any other sort of people from the UK, many Scottish Gaels prospered exceedingly. What Welsh's Renton, like a very high proportion of young Scots, chooses to forget, or perhaps never knew, is that Scots, whatever harm they did each other at home, were signally fortunate to be able to sally forth together and plunder vast territories secured by an Imperial Navy which employed ships built on the Clyde. Analogies with Latvia, Finland or Slovenia don't bear examination. The upsurge of Scottish Nationalism to electoral credibility in the 1960s was in part a local variant on a world-wide theme, as colony after colony gained independence and Basques and Bretons and Sards began to be noisy. It also had something to do with the fact that loss of Britain's empire meant declining job prospects in warmer places for able young Scots, now compelled to look about them at home.

The Kailyard cult, which had arisen in the late nineteenth century as a complement to, rather than rival of, the triumphalist myth of Industrial Scotland, proved far too strong for the scorn of such major writers as George Douglas Brown and Lewis Grassic Gibbon. Exalting images of rural and small-town Scotland, it survived in the pages of the D.C. Thomson Press and was sustained by Dr Finlay's Casebook in the brave new world of mass TV. Clydesidism revived too, as Scottish heavy industry came back to life with the Second World War and the post-war boom. But as bases of Scottish identity, both now seem almost as tenuous as, say, nineteenth-century Jacobitism, which was a cult for quaint Tories. The shipyards, the mines, the steelworks, have gone. 'Working men' can hardly find a basis for identity in prideful skilled work when such work is no longer there for them. Scottish agribusiness is hardly distinctive. For local councillors and intellectuals, Culture has now become the surviving option. Fortunately, Scottish art and literature and music have achieved notable feats in the last quarter of a century. While in Glasgow, Culture officially replaces shipbuilding as the city's defining activity, the Scottish intelligentsia can find their Scotland and their own identity in their own activities and in the conceptions of Scotland which they themselves use and create. I rejoice that so many fine things have come out of our latest Renaissance, but feel increasingly uneasy. I am not a postmodernist; I am still enough of an old-time Marxist to look for a base as well as a superstructure. A Parliament Of Our Own Again won't provide a base unless it promotes activities and conditions of life in Scotland which widely differ from those seen south of the Border and elsewhere. Perhaps the most encouraging development at present is the new respect officially given to the ways in which we actually speak, and have spoken.

In February 1996, a truly startling anthology appeared under the aegis of the Scottish Consultative Council on the Curriculum, a body advising the Scottish Office, that mighty arm of the UKanian state. *The Kist / A'Chiste* anthology aggregates material selected and supplied by every education authority in Scotland. Some of it is written by schoolchildren themselves. Most of the individual items could be described as poetry, but there are also short stories and plays. And very little of the book is in standard English.

After that vile Education Act of 1871 which, in the interests of the bourgeois state, made schooling compulsory, children were beaten for using at school dialects of Scots, let alone Gaelic, which regimes since the days of James VI had intermittently toyed with extirpating. Now, in complete reversal, anything goes. From the Dundee authority, one guesses, comes a comic strip of 'The Broons', that pawky family featured since what seems like time immemorial in the pages of *The Sunday Post*. Paw Broon, the diminutive cloth-capped patriarch, says to his daughter's new English boyfriend, 'I don't suppose you've ever seen a haggis? My, it's a rare bird an' awfy hard to catch – it can blaw itsel up an' doon just like a balloon.' He invites young Cyril to join him on a haggis shoot and believes he has pulled his leg successfully as the young Sassenach blasts away at fictitious haggises flying past. But Cyril claims in turn that if you dig up a rabbit's burrow at midnight you'll find a haggis sleeping there, and successfully performs the trick. He's been working as a butcher himself, and produces one of his own making...

It must have been Shetland which supplied a parody of Masefield's 'Cargoes' in Norroena/Scots, the tongue of those islands:

Sixareen fae Feddaland
Back ower fae North Roe
Rowin hom troo Yell
In a six knot tide...

One infers that it was Strathclyde which sent in the much-loved 'Lament for lost dinner ticket' by Margaret Hamilton:

See ma mammy
See ma dinner ticket
A pititnma
Pokit an she pititny
Washnmachine...

There are items which could have been found in more staid anthologies – for instance, 'The Ballad of Sir Patrick Spens',

MacDiarmid's great lyric 'Empty Vessel', Derick Thomson's Gaelic poem about the Norsemen arriving and settling on his own island of Lewis. This last, of course, is given, like all the Gaelic contributions, with translation in standard English facing. But a full inventory of the contents of this extraordinary volume would reveal, as a common distinguishing feature from Standard, the tendency of all tongues spoken demotically in Scotland to drive towards humour – dry, grim, warm or biting. Two wonderful facts impress me about *The Kist / A'Chiste*. (They might not seem so amazing to the teachers of English who have for decades now been waging in schools up and down the land their guerrilla campaigns on behalf of the vernacular.) Firstly, education authorities are now positively encouraging children to use in class the tongues they actually speak at home and in the streets. Yet, secondly, all these tongues are, as it were, talking to each other. Joy Hendry, editor of *Chapman* magazine, who was a prime mover for this anthology, was formerly a teacher herself, and she tells me that she used Hamilton's 'Dinner Ticket' poem with its Glaswegian phonetics in classrooms in East Lothian. Teachers in Ayrshire are now encouraged to explore Sheena Blackhall's Aberdeenshire Doric. And the book invites teachers and pupils alike to be curious about Gaelic. The book thus stands for diversity within unity.

The Scots Language Society will probably hate this. Its members seem to be hunting the snark of a single Scots language, with its own teachable grammar and national uniformity. Neil R. MacCallum, editor of the Society's magazine *Lallans*, wrote in his arts column in the SNP's *Scots Independent*, that 'The remarkably consistent literary Scots as represented by Allan Ramsay and Robert Fergusson in the eighteenth century, through to Soutar and his younger contemporaries is a fairly standard language based on a natural spoken tongue.' It is significant that he didn't mention Burns, whose use of Scots was anything but consistent. MacCallum went on to upbraid the published text of Joy Hendry's play about Soutar for 'inconsistencies', such as using both 'school' and 'skule', 'ken' and 'know'. He missed the simple point that people around

Soutar would have switched tongues, as Scots generally do. A play about modern Scots couldn't have characters sticking to Language Society-approved forms and remain veridical.

I was talking about tongue-switching the other day to an acquaintance from Leith who is an authority when he approves of the 'inconsistent' language of Irvine Welsh's fiction. Leith-speak between Leithers is such that outsiders are barred. My acquaintance has a fine story to illustrate this. Hamish Henderson invites him to meet a certain Italian in an Irish bar in Rome called the Fiddler's Elbow. The Italian's (standard) English is good and he and the Leither speak easily together for some time. Then a woman friend of the latter, also from Leith, joins them, and they begin to exchange news. The Italian is stricken with total bafflement, and tells Hamish, 'I can't understand what they're saying.' To which the great expert on Scottish song and story replies, 'Neither can I.'

The notion of a Standard Scots is exploded neatly, and I think decisively, by a squib of Tom Leonard's in his book *Intimate Voices*:

MAKAR'S SOCIETY
GRAN' MEETIN'
THE NICHT
TAE DECIDE THE SPELLIN
O' THIS POSTER

And MacCallum, who writes with some style himself in English, should recognise that English is also a Scottish tongue. The much loved poet Norman MacCaig, whose death just after the outburst by MacCallum which I've quoted seemed to unite all of literary Scotland as one mourning family, wrote exclusively in English, though one heard behind the voice of his poems, its quirks and its rhythms, those of Gaelic ancestors and Scots-speaking friends. Would any Scot of taste care to cast out of some putative canon the splendid English prose of Hume and Stevenson? That hero of the Nationalists, Fletcher of Saltoun, who opposed the 1707 Union so eloquently, wrote smooth English of 'Addisonian' standard well before most Englishmen could.

On the matter of English in Scotland I am personally sensitive. I was once sitting with Hamish Henderson in his second (perhaps first) home, Sandy Bell's Bar, when some sardonic youth accused me of being English because my voice is consistently RP. Hamish said, in that unmistakeable high drawl of his in which I detect, beside his native Perthshire, traces of education at Dulwich College and Cambridge University, 'Oh, no, Angus has a very *good* Scottish accent.' And of course a lot of Scots, not just Tories, use RP. In Edinburgh, RP can arouse resentment, because some folk object to the city's many English incomers, and because class divides have separated posh New Town lawyers and professors from Leith dockers and Craigmillar 'keelies'. In Glasgow I have no problem this way. People just assume that I come from Edinburgh...

Ironically, my mother, who did her best to make her five children speak pure RP, is from Glasgow, where she trained as an elocution teacher. Now, how can I describe my own Scottish identity?

The historian Christopher Harvie once distinguished between 'Black Scots' and 'Red Scots'. The former stayed at home and, so to speak, cultivated the kail in the kailyard and stirred the porridge. The latter, Scotsmen on the make, roamed to every corner of the world.

My father was a typical Red Scot. So were his two brothers, who rose high in the aviation industry, one in England, the other in Canada. Sister Bella stayed in their native Forfar, where their father worked in a jute mill and their mother took in washing. She married a baker, and so became proprietress of that remarkable comestible, the Forfar Bridie (a robust chieftain of the race of bridies, which are mostly fissenless, cheapskate things). She was a Black Scot, and an exceptionally dour one.

Dad was brilliant, but declined the chance of university and left school at 16 to become a newspaper reporter. The D.C. Thomson Press welcomed him. He wrote crime reports for *The Sunday Post* from Glasgow, where he met my mother, a doctor's daughter. By the time they were 21, they were married and settling in London, where Dad rose rapidly in Fleet Street. His remarkable career later included fearless, outspoken reporting of the London Blitz, hijacking by Churchill's government to head 'white' propaganda in the famous Bletchley ensemble, great distinction as a science writer, and a Labour Life Peerage. In the late Fifties, Edinburgh University made him Professor of International Relations (and found they had to give him an honorary MA to legitimate him, since he had never attended any university). This eventually occasioned a return to Scottish base at last, around the time I was leaving university myself.

Meanwhile I had grown up in Sutton, a leafy but boring outer suburb of London. My mother's 'Kelvinside' accent, my father's well-tamed Forfar, were still very apparent over the phone, and in certain tricks of speech. I did, and did not, pass for white. Angus, after all, is a distinctively Scottish name. As a very small boy I wore a kilt – too expensive to replace when I outgrew it. I knew from a very early age that I was different.

My non-related 'aunties' and 'uncles', my parents' oldest friends, were Scottish. (Scottish journalists, James Cameron and Tom Baistow, were the only non-family people present when they celebrated their Golden Wedding, along with Cameron's Indian wife.) We did not go in for Burns Nights at home, but on at least one Hogmanay, since our English neighbours did not understand the custom of first footing, I was sent out with the traditional shortbread, coal and salt in hand, to be readmitted seconds later. Reels were danced in the living room, where most of the poetry books in the bookcase were Scottish, and in Scots.

We were Socialists living in a solidly Tory area, and Congregationalists domiciled opposite an Anglican Church. (Our own minister, a learned and passionate preacher, was Welsh, and a fellow-Socialist.) I attribute a lot of my many problems at successive schools to a complex sense of difference from others. Torment reached a peak with the Scottish gym teacher at my grammar school. This fierce little man also instructed my mother in country dancing at the local Caledonian Society. He taught other boys this form of exercise, but I rejected it. I would not perform his fake sword dance, either. 'The back the side, the front the back, the back the side, the front the back, Calder, stop scratching your balls!' It wasn't till I was 35 that, dragged into Summer School discos, I discovered I could dance in any way at all.

Naturally, however, my first girlfriend was the daughter of Scottish parents. And my first wife, met at Cambridge and married in England, also. I'll try to distinguish what I felt in childhood and youth, or realise now, was 'Scottish' from the Englishness around me.

A degree of warmth? I think so, though of course one knew warm English people. I imagine I'd have found this even in my ferocious gym teacher if I'd met him as an adult. Scottish combativeness in debate and abrasiveness in conversation are not incompatible with warmth. There is an innate propensity, it seems, to 'flyte', as our medieval poets did, exchanging mock abuse in competition. I have often heard men in Scottish pubs, professional men as well as working men, trading insults with great enjoyment.

Puritanism? Certainly, in Scottish circles I remember, sex was not mentioned except when some item in the news aroused cryptic disapproval. But here in Scotland itself one is aware of wide divergencies. The Burns Supper tradition offers even respectable persons disgustingly wide scope for coarseness. Scottish pantomime comedy is innocently broad. Since the days of Dunbar and Lyndsay, there has been tension in Scottish literature between licentiousness and restraint. The language of Covenanting propagandists positively gloats over the iniquities of those who follow the 'whore of Babylon'. Burns picked up and carried to great heights an acceptance of carnality found in popular song. Yet Burns had a puritan streak, too, seen in 'The Cotter's Saturday Night'.

Respect for intellect and science? My father embodied that, and I can barely see past him to judge others. To say that the general attitude towards education in Scotland is more favourable than elsewhere is not to endorse the dubious boast that our institutions are much superior. Yet the fact that the boast is made, and believed south of the Border, so often, is in itself significant.

A democratical, 'man's a man for a' that' spirit? Well, my father talked of Elizabeth Bowes Lyon, from Glamis near Forfar, as a kind of childhood neighbour. Her common touch as George VI's consort probably saved the British monarchy in the crisis following the pro-Nazi Edward VIII's Abdication. My mother's father, the only grandparent I knew, who came to spend his last days in our house, had been an early and passionate advocate of a National Health Service, had chaired meetings for Jimmy Maxton, and had treated poor patients in Bridgeton free. Though I cannot say that I encountered any Scot in my boyhood who was more radical than the Welsh Congregationalist minister whom I mentioned above, there was a general 'come on in, will ye have a dram?' spirit amongst Scots I knew; see under 'warmth' above... This brings me, somewhat crabwise, to two remarkable films which have recently carried images of Scotland into packed cinemas. *Braveheart* first, then *Trainspotting*.

I'd been very squeamish about going to see Mel Gibson's film about 'the' Wallace. When it arrived in Scotland in the autumn of 1995, attended by its swoon-making star-cum-director, the SNP had taken it up for propaganda purposes. Reports from people I respected suggested that the film was not only at an antipodes from factual history (I could stand that – Michael Caton Jones's *Rob Roy*, which travesties early eighteenth century Scotland, is actually a very good 'Wild-South-West-Highland-Western'), but also crassly anti-English.

As a professed 'cultural historian', I had to endure this film. But who to go with? Embarrassing to view it with an English friend, of whom, in Edinburgh, I have many. But my Scottish friends tend to be more-or-less nationalistic, and I dreaded some sterile wrangle afterwards. As the film neared the end of its Edinburgh run, I was talking one Friday night to Joy Hendry and Joyce Macmillan, the sage and principled theatre critic and political columnist of *Scotland on Sunday*. Joy is pro-SNP but declares fiercely 'I'm not a patriot, Scotland's a rotten country'. Joyce is so anti-people-who-are-anti-English that she must be in line for death threats from the mercifully few nutters on the SNP's quasi-Fascist fringe. Giggling like schoolkids, we decided to brave *Braveheart* together the following Monday. But on the day, we all found alternative engagements.

In the end I appealed to my daughter Gowan; as an actor, her main interest was in watching Scottish performers in the film do their bit-parts. Brought up in Scotland, entirely State-schooled, she retains the Anglicised RP accent of both her parents (and complains that it may cost her jobs, as producers look for folk who were reared, or sound as if reared, in Glasgow or Dundee schemes, to cast for yet another despairing or sentimental touring play about slices of working-class Scottish life.)

So Gowan and I sat gobbling chocolate mints through the three hours (plus compassionate intermission) of *Braveheart* in the Dominion, Morningside. The auditorium was barely a third full. That day the tabloid *Daily Record* had reported that 'the *Braveheart* effect' on the Scottish opinion polls had ebbed away. Because of the film's arrival (so legend will have it, and gullible historians will write it), the SNP had shot up to 30 per cent. Now they were back to a 'normal' 23 per cent.

It wasn't too bad. It was *not too* bad, really. Honestly, I mean, it wasn't *so* bad. As Gowan confessed, it was *inspiring*, actually.

There was this Aussie, Gibson, as Wallace, with a consistent and even convincing West of Scotland accent. (Better than Neeson's, the Irishman who played Rob Roy in Caton-Jones's film.) Naebody kens whit the fuck The Wallace talked like. His name suggests Welsh genes. He might have got his tongue round funny-spelt words like you find in Medieval Scots – 'quhilk' for 'which' and so on. He might have called women 'queans' – in Aberdeen they are still 'quines'. He most likely knew a bit of Gaelic – most Scots seem to have had at least a trading knowledge of the Highland tongue in those days, and the poet William Neill was claiming a few years back that he still heard shepherds using it high in the Galloway hills... Anyway, Mel had settled for modern Strathclyde, and had a nice gallus wee grin to go with it. See you ootside, Jimmy, was his attitude to the fuckin English. He cut the throat of the English nobleman who'd cut his wife's throat, rode into the bedroom of a Scottish noble who'd deserted at the Battle of Falkirk, disposed of him, then jumped his horse oot the windae, descending hundreds of feet into the loch below. The hardest of hard men, but charming with it. Kent French and Latin, tae, a bit like one of James Kelman's fuck-saying proletarian philosophers...

In fact Mel, or his scriptwriter, implausibly named Randall Wallace, had got eerily close to the throbbing heart of our current ethnic consciousness. Oz nationalism must be the key to it. The Aussies who, as Churchill complained bitterly when they started narking at him during the Second World War, are largely descended from 'bad Irish stock', tend to define themselves, basically, as anti-Pom. The Poms are all bastards and poofters. (Cf. Irvine Welsh's wankers.) Sure enough, in *Braveheart*, those Poms who aren't extremely nasty officer types, or mindless automaton infantry, are raging queens. There are only these three types of Pom.

The first and second types, as Gibson intuits, now play Rugby for England. They are big and strong and utterly convinced that they are going to beat Scotland. Usually, it has to be admitted, they do. But every so often, by guile and wit, we beat them. (What, *me* cheating, ref?) Aitken and Sole, cheered on alike by latterday Miss Brodies shopping in Jenners and lager-drinking Hibees (Hibernian FC supporters) in pubs on the soon-to-be-named Irvine Welsh Heritage Trail in Leith, led canny, brave fifteens who fucked the English in two recent Grand Slams. We were smaller, see, but we were clever.

At a pregnant moment in *Braveheart*, Brian Cox, playing the boy Wallace's guardian after the English have hacked his father and brother to death, says he'll teach him to read Latin before he teaches him to fight. Tapping of noddles goes on, here and elsewhere in the movie, to indicate that it's in yer heid ye beat the fuckers, ken? Sure enough, at Stirling, the Scots, jeering warmly at each other and throwing the odd friendly punch, go in for clever tactics which fuck the English ooti sight. This is eftir they've all raised their kilts and waved their goolies in defiance.

You can do that if you're wearing a kilt. It is easy to tell who the Scots are in the movie. They wear kilts. I suppose that back in the thirteenth century, Wallace and other Lowlanders did wear plaids, and they might have belted these, producing a kilt effect. But with weather as bad as the film suggests (probably because it was shot in Ireland) they'd no hae been canny not to wear leggings as well. Gibson, though, with swaddled legs and shaggy bootees, wouldn't have had quite that shinny appeal which persuades the French lassie who'll be the next Queen of England (some quean to be a Queen, eh?) that she must sacrifice her body to him. (Without any attendants, she awaits him in a Highland bothy to warn him of her evil father-in-law's latest treacherous plan. Nae tabloid ratpack in those days.) If the film is to be believed, monarchs enthroned in Westminster Abbey ever since descend from the loins of the Wallace – which, come to think of it, renders appropriate the role of that Abbey's choir who, along with the London (sic) Symphony Orchestra garnish the film's soundtrack.

Scots are cheery. Scots make jokes. Kilted Scots are sexy. But Scottish toffs betray prole Scots. That's what the film says. The Bruce, an aristocrat, is a fraught character, torn between toff self-interest and prole destiny, as his large and agonised eyes display. Gowan said afterwards, with her usual acuteness, that the film was really more about class than nationality. The Scottish nobility are shown as a shifty lot, obsessed with their estates in England, and easily bribed. At one point the Wallace declares to the Bruce, 'You think this country exists to provide you with position. I think your position exists to provide our people with freedom.' In response, the Bruce muses, 'From top to bottom this country has no sense of itself.'

We can relate all this to mindsets characteristic of the present-day Scottish intelligentsia... To be Scots is to be prole. To be prole is to be Socialist (so fuck off, Tony Blair, vampire from that Hammer Horror castle, Fettes College.) To be Socialist is to be internationalist. So, we go so far with our Scottish nationalism, join the clamour for a Scottish Parliament, mingle as Artists for Independence, then think: Hell, we're Socialists, really, internationalists really. An independent Scotland run by New Town lawyers and money men, or dominated by fixit Labour councillors from Strathclyde might even be worse than what we have now: a wee country hundreds of miles from London where people can at least unite in girning against Westminster rule. If we couldn't blame the English for most things, we'd blame each other.

Serendipitously, I'd been warmed up for *Braveheart* by a seminar that afternoon at Edinburgh University's Centre of African Studies. It was on the Oromo.

Who? Despite over thirty years of interest in African matters, despite having lived awhile in Kenya, where there are 200,000 Oromo in three groups towards the northern and north-eastern borders, I'd never heard of these people. Over half the population of Ethiopia are Oromo, yet one can read books on the country and never notice them. With European encouragement, Abyssinian kings, Amhara, overran the Oromo country, Southern Ethiopia, or 'Region 4' as it is now. As discussion proceeded after a learned paper, as a couple of Oromo actually present made their rather shy voices heard, one point seemed clearer and clearer: the 20-million-plus Oromo, silenced and overruled, retain a strong sense of common identity despite sharp differences in religion and politics among themselves. Language binds them, and also a common myth of origin – all Oromo groups, inside and outside Ethiopia, trace themselves back to the same place. Kinship and intermarriage help hold identity together. But above all, if you're Oromo, you're not Abyssinian. You're not Amharic. You're not Tigrean.

Scots share no one distinctive language with fellow Scots. We don't have a common myth of origin, unless it's expressed in the every-schoolboy-knows joke that the eponymous Scots originally came from Ireland. Picts, Strathclyde Britons and, yes, Angles, eventually came under the King, not 'of Scotland' but 'of Scots'. Sane Scots know that we were always mongrels. And we are exogamous with it. A typical present-day Scot will have one Highland granny and one English one, with two Lowland grandads and a lot of Canadian cousins. His Dad will have converted to Catholicism on marrying an Italian- or Polish-Scot. My daughter Gowan's origins go back, through her Scots-Jewish grandfather, to the noted ghetto of Vilnius, in Lithuania, and beyond that to the ancient Mediterranean and Middle East.

So we are not much like the Oromo except in one respect. We define ourselves by what we are not. We are not English. I talked a few months back to a bitter man in a pub who'd been made redundant by our local armament makers, Ferranti. In the package of chips on his shoulder, anti-English sentiments jutted out. You go to London. The barman sneers at you because you're a Jock. Fucking English... I forbore to point out that in my experience barmen in London are commonly Irish or Aussie or, yes, Scottish ... Renton's exodus to London (then further) in *Trainspotting* echoes that of so many dissatisfied Scots.

In the ScotRail free magazine, which in February 1996 caught up with the boom in Scottish fiction (meaning critical and commercial success in London), A.L. Kennedy admitted to having something in common with James Kelman and Irvine Welsh. 'We have a dark sense of humour, are politically left-of-centre and not afraid of nastiness in our writing.' These characteristics link all three with Janice Galloway, Duncan MacLean, Alan Warner, Alasdair Gray and Iain Banks. The Scotland of recent fiction has been a grim and dangerous place. Irvine Welsh might seem extremist read in isolation – alongside the others he appears pretty typical. There is a latent contradiction between the left-wingness and the nastiness. If there is any hope, such writers might say, echoing *1984*, it lies with the proles. But the proles, rather than banding together in search of political solutions, are barely coping with confused suffering, and prone to self-mutilation and self-destruction.

Were it not for the scene which I referred to at the start of this piece, the film of *Trainspotting* might be decoded without reference to Scotland or to politics. Young people, variously charming and sinister, damage themselves with drugs and booze, and get involved in petty, then major, crime in a grubby urban setting... With its assured style and brilliantly judged pace, the movie might be taken to be a local response to Quentin Tarantino. It is a very filmy film and its musical soundtrack, which has no obvious Scottish reference, places it firmly in the hands of people who know about the recent past of rock. (The setting, carefully sustained, is the mid-Eighties.)

The specificity of Welsh's Leith and Edinburgh is lost, despite shots of Princes Street and the Castle. Not only is dense Leith idiom avoided, but the accents suggest west as much as east, in Lowland Scottish terms, and local eyes spot the signs that the outside shooting was mostly done in Glasgow. But Renton's outburst about English wankers and shitty Scots ensures that the film is a statement about Scotland, as well as applicable to all cities. Not only the violence of Begbie, but the mental sickness of Sick Boy and the gormless, compulsive thieving of Spud are seen as examples of enslaved and colonised Scottish mentality. When these three confront a suave English drug baron to sell him the heroin which they have stolen, Renton, psychological bystander rather than participant, reflects that such a big operator is bound to make suckers of them – and he does. As the only significant English character in the film, this creep might be taken to represent all the colonisers, the Southrons who manipulate and control Scotland.

Virtues attributed to the Scots are set in ironic light. The braininess of Sick Boy is misapplied to endless drivel about Sean Connery movies. Social sodality, warmth and bonhomie are travestied in a scene where a baby dies and drug-taking mother howls as our charming heroin users sleep through their trances. *Braveheart* solidarity between Renton and his friends is merely an accident arising from a common background; at the end, Renton rejects Begbie and Sick Boy, purloins their share of the price of the drugs, and hands money back only to the good-natured, helpless Spud. Such discrimination accompanies a moral victory over his environment: his Scottish environment.

But all this negativity has positive implications, thanks to Renton's political rant, which suggests that if only the Scots could free themselves, then they might be absolved from the universal types of folly which he and his friends represent. Remove English rule: cure social disease?

Hypers of Scottish Culture should have problems with the *Trainspotting* phenomenon. The image of Scotland which book and film insist on presenting is very nasty, very unheathery. Both times I saw the film early in its run at the Cameo. Looking around the packed audience, I seemed to see almost no one over 30. Irvine Welsh's sales, huge, especially in Edinburgh, mean that young people feel they must buy his books. The phenomenon is uncontrollable and could be lasting.

I am glad that I enjoy Welsh's books, uneven though they are. I myself am not, I hope, swimming outside the current which is flowing to wherever it will flow, with whatever political, social and ethical consequences, over the year of millennium, into an unimaginable future Scotland where Scottish identities, surviving, as I am sure they will, are constructed in ways which I cannot foresee, through language in its habitual state of flux and new songs transforming old ones...

1996

On First Looking into
In Memoriam James Joyce

IN 1965, WHEN WE WERE both 23-year-old postgraduate students, Jenni I lived at a place called Chailey. It was not like the classic Sussex beloved by Bloomsberries and Georgians alike and inspirational for English Nationalist composers, but it was handy for Haywards Heath station and hence for London; and we did get free use of a cottage on a flat stretch of Weald with pylons marching over the field behind. The cottage belonged to Angus Ross, a specialist in eighteenth-century literature who lectured at the new University of Sussex. Dr Ross, though then absent teaching somewhere in the New World, had left behind his books and records. Thus it was that I first heard Ewan McColl's singing and first opened *In Memoriam James Joyce*.

Both Jenni and I had been reared in England by very Scottish parents. Mine kept Barrie's plays and Soutar's poems in the living room. Jenni's father, famous as a pioneering critic of Scottish literature, was a friend of C.M. Grieve. However, my earliest tutor at Cambridge (Helena Shire) had been scunnered by my first essay for her, on the Ballads. I had missed the point completely – no habitat could be less like Liddesdale than the London suburb where I'd grown up. Without undue fuss, Helena started setting me right. In between Chaucer, whom she always called 'Geoffrey', and the later 'Edmund', we studied Henryson and Dunbar. One day Helena told us that 'Jeannie' was coming to Cambridge to sing for the local branch of the Saltire Society. For her King's students, she arranged a special treat. We sat in Helena's living room one morning and Jeannie Robertson sang just for us. Then in the pub Jeannie kept on singing. Later, when I was chairman of the Labour Club, I invited Jeannie back for a joint meeting with the Folk Society. I was on my way home.

Aware that my Cambridge education had been incomplete, at Chailey I took advantage of the rural quiet and rose early to improve myself. I read Pound and couldn't get past his Fascism. I went right through Yeats' *Collected Poems* and didn't like them – it was to be four more years before I got the point and became, perhaps to my cost, a crazed Yeatsophile. In Cuckfield Hospital, while our elder daughter was being born, I sat reading Joyce's *Ulysses*. I tried to translate Lorca and Neruda. And, thanks to the absent Ross, I discovered MacDiarmid.

In 1965, MacDiarmid's poetry was little represented in anthologies – I'm not sure that I'd previously encountered even one lyric. The first *Collected Poems*, very far from complete, had appeared in New York in 1962, but the book wasn't generally available in the UK. Angus Ross had slim volumes of the early lyrics, of which I made little, and 'The Drunk Man', which I found intriguing but indigestible. What hooked me on MacDiarmid was *In Memoriam James Joyce*. The shock of recognition was intense. In a notebook I transcribed, in high excitement, passage after passage from the poem. I was far from realising that some of the statements which struck me as utterly and most importantly true had probably been copied by Grieve himself from the *TLS* or wherever. What was it, in 1965, that made me so completely susceptible to MacDiarmid? Playing records of McColl so much no doubt helped – I was consciously reclaiming the Scottish heritage to which I was connected by parentage but not environment, and Scott's novels began to mean a lot to me about the same time. But the fact that MacDiarmid was Scots weighed, I think, no more than each of three other factors – his Marxism, his commitment to 'science', and his internationalism.

After Helena Shire, the tutor who'd influenced me most had been George Steiner. It may seem odd that Steiner, no sort of left-winger, should have formed more than anyone else my commitment to Marxism. But he did so because he spoke eloquently and incessantly about and from Central European intellectual traditions in which Marx was centrally implicated. Brecht? Of course – but we must also read his polemical adversary Lukacs – and, by the way, Trotsky's *Literature and Revolution*, a dazzling tract, was indispensable, too. Yes, George...

By 1965, l had digested at least a proportion of Steiner's words, was making something of Brecht myself and had begun to explore the vast Neruda. Now here, in *In Memoriam James Joyce*, I encountered a poet, MacDiarmid, who was into high-intellectual uses of Marxist materialism as no other poet, in English, ever had been. And for someone instructed by Steiner, his invocation of the master composer of that Jewish generation which had included Wittgenstein, Lukacs and Adorno was delicious proof of his authentically un-English intellectualism:

> Other masters may conceivably write
> Even yet in C major
> But we – we take the perhaps 'primrose path'
> To the dodecaphonic bonfire.

My father, a science journalist, had passed much of his time with famous scientists. Haldane, Bernal, Bohr and Waddington were tea-table names in our household. No doubt my own literary ambitions were sparked by filial revolt. But the idea that science was a serious matter didn't leave me. In my early twenties I did not realise that for Thomson, Pope, Goethe, Shelley, there had been no barrier between poetic and scientific ways of knowing. I thought that they were somehow opposed. Here, to my relief, was MacDiarmid, thus far uniquely (though I soon discovered Miroslav Holub) eager to assert otherwise:

> Ivar Aasen, Elizabeth Elstob, Rabelais, Browning,
>   Meredith, Remizov,
> Gergj Fishta and Avetik Isaakyan,
> And William Barnes and his sixty languages,
> Browning with his 'to talk as brothers talk
> In half-words, call things by half-names, no balk
> From discontinuing old aids',

– words like the fortune-telling table
Whereby things not yet discovered are foreknown to Science
– as Meldelyev predicted scandium, germanium and polonium,
As astronomers have foretold where a planet should be
and the telescope later has found it – as blue roses
Can never be found, but peas with yellow blossoms
And haricot beans with red blossoms will yet be found,
Guests not yet arrived – whose places await them.

Finally, I was a committed internationalist. MacDiarmid struck me at once as the least parochial writer from the British archipelago I'd ever read. Here was a geographical sweep to match Neruda's, an encyclopaedic celebration of the diversity of human cultures. I learnt, most crucially, from this poem that 'internationalism' should imply not Airline English and Big Macs everywhere, but interaction between distinctive nations, of which Scotland should properly be one – indeed, is one:

Or even as we know
Schweitzer and Cappelletti on the Cimbric language
Of the last descendants of the old Lombobards;
Tibetan influences on Tocharian;
Glottalized Continuants in Navaho, Nootka and Kwakiutl...
And Pirandello's treatise in German on the Sicilian dialect,
Laute und Lautentwicklung der Mundart von Girgentii.

And rejoicing in all those intranational differences which
Each like a flower's scent by its peculiarity sharpens
Appreciation of others as well as bringing
Appreciation of itself, as experiences of gardenia or zinnia
Refine our experience of rose or sweet pea.

Or even as, in the Shetland Islands where I lived,
I know, in the old Norn language, the various names
Applied to all the restless movements of the sea...

I don't now think of *In Memoriam* as MacDiarmid's greatest achievement. 'The Drunk Man' and 'On a Raised Beach' seem to me the prime poems, among many lyrical and meditative items which concentrate MacDiarmidism more powerfully than most of *In Memoriam* But when I thought I wasn't literate in Scots, I needed verse in English to lead me in. I first saw MacDiarmid a couple of years after our brief Chailey residence, flyting with Hamish Henderson at an Edinburgh Festival event. I knew that his denunciation of folksong was wholly wrong (and contradicted by passages in *In Memoriam*). Yet he lived entirely up to expectations – scaldingly eloquent and as uncompromising as a mountain. Then, in 1975, I attended a conference on Commonwealth Literature at Stirling University. For some reason, the MacRobert Centre dining area was almost empty. Two figures sat by the window. Although very shy, I impudently put my tray down at their table. The Vietnam War was still in progress. The Viet Cong were winning. The younger man was trying to reason his friend Chris out of his dogmatic support for these Communist guerillas. I don't think this loving MacCaig–Grieve wrangle was conducted for my benefit but it was some show. Later, after he'd read, I took a new friend over to meet Grieve, the Somali novelist Nuruddin Farah. What everyone says is true: off a platform, outwith a flyting, whisky in hand, fag in mouth, the great man was sweetness personified, as if to meet this young African was an honour. I felt as in the presence of an elderly relation – someone whom, in a sense, I'd known all my life, part of the genealogy. As with family, one could take contradictions and eccentricities for granted, as elements in a pattern without which one couldn't exist.

When he died three years later, I had just been 'teaching' his work for the Open University. I was asked for a tribute for the Course Newsletter. What else could I do but quote *In Memoriam James Joyce*?

This single-minded zeal, this fanatic devotion to art
Is alien to the English poetic temperament, no doubt,

'This narrowing intensity' as the English say,
But I have it even as you had it, Yeats my friend,
And would have it with me as you at the end,
I who am infinitely more un-English than you
And turn Scotland to poetry like those women who
In their passion secrete and turn to
Musk through and through!

So I think of you, Joyce, and of Yeats and others who are dead
As I walk this Autumn and observe
The birch tremulously pendulous in jewels of cairngorm,
The sauch, the osier and the crack-willow
Of the beaten gold of Australia;
The sycamore in rich straw-gold;
The elm bowered in saffron;
The oak in flecks of salmon gold;
The beeches huge torches of living orange.

This brings tears to the eyes. But, reopening *In Memoriam* it's
the man's Byronic humour which strikes me. To appear so erudite,
to demand, page after page, that everyone else should be erudite,
then to demonstrate, with calculated bathos, that the learning de-
manded is not that of *TLS* specialists but something quickening
everyday life...

One thing sticks out. You must agree
Poetry apart, as life you scan,
The whole thing's due, in human terms,
To woman taking a rise out of man.

Full of quotations, *In Memoriam* exists to be quoted. I might
say that my intellectual life since 1965 has mostly consisted of
quoting MacDiarmid imperfectly. And yet somehow he leaves one
free, doesn't he? At a recent OU summer school I set up several
students to perform an 'Edwin Morgan Miscellany'. I persuaded a

rather stiff and pedantic-seeming Englishman to mime 'Little Blue Blue' while Doug from Bedfordshire read the lines. Just before the event, to our dismay, he disappeared without trace. But eventually, right on cue, he burst on stage wearing, beside a blue tracksuit, that selfsame blue rose which *In Memoriam* tells us 'can never be found'. It wasn't natural but never mind.

1992

Allan MacCartney

ALLAN MACCARTNEY'S SUDDEN DEATH at the age of 57 deprives
Scotland and Europe of a politician who could not be spared. As
Deputy Leader of the Scottish National Party he left his beloved
country poised at the point of selecting candidates for its first parliament since 1707. 'National', not 'Nationalist' Party. The first
thing you learned about Allan was that he cared as passionately
for the peoples of southern Africa, and for the Sami minority of
northern Scandinavia, as he did for his ain folk in North-East Scotland, which he represented in the European Parliament from 1994.
Scots for him were one people in a mosaic of equal peoples. The
MEP job specification might have been written for him. Beside several African tongues, and pidgin Gaelic, he spoke German, French
and Dutch. As a political scientist he was particularly interested in
the constitutional issues facing Europe (and Scotland) which baffle
and bore even most 'politically-minded' people.

He was the son of a West African manse, born in Ghana where
his father was a Church of Scotland minister. Brought home, he
was educated in Elgin, that well-set and distinctive capital of
Strathspey whisky country. At Edinburgh University, he became
the founding president of the student SNP in the days when the
party was deeply unfashionable. He returned to Africa as a volun-
teer teacher in Eastern Nigeria, and subsequently lectured for eight
years in the University of Botswana, Lesotho and Swaziland. Back
in Scotland, in the mid-Seventies he completed a PhD thesis for
Edinburgh University on 'Local Government and the Politics of
Development in Botswana'.

The Open University in Scotland gave him an academic base in
Edinburgh as Staff Tutor in Social Science. I joined him there in
1979 as Staff Tutor in Arts and can testify to the pleasures and

strains of that very peculiar role. Responsible for appointing and supervising scores of part-time staff from Galloway to Shetland, we also had the academic duty of contributing to courses created in Milton Keynes. And if we didn't keep stuck in there, our pleasant English colleagues would forget that Scotland had a different legal system, different educational traditions, an established Church of its own and a richly distinctive cultural history. So – Stornoway Tuesday, Milton Keynes Thursday. The good news was that one travelled all over Scotland and Allan could use that to maintain and extend contacts within the SNP, for which he was a spokesman on external affairs from the early 1980s on. The bad news was the travel could drive you mad. Allan, however, stayed impeccably sane.

There were no academic seminars in the OU Edinburgh office. Instead, we academics on flexitime lingered after lunch in the pub round the corner where Allan, red wine in hand, puffing the short cigars which were his one obvious weakness, tended to function as orchestrator of remarkable symposia which included his neo-Marxist colleague Greg Maclennan (son of the Secretary-General of the CPGB); the maverick Tory home-ruler, Michael Fry – a historian like my own *alter ego*, Ian Donnachie; and any full-time or part-time staff who cared to join in. Remaining good humoured as our Senior Counsellor colleague Henry Cowper enjoyed his politically incorrect flytings against women and social scientists, and indulged his Old Labour anti-nationalism, was one of Allan's peculiar graces, as was his utter straightforwardness.

He was one of few Scots outside pipe bands who could wear a kilt without exciting jeers. His marriage to Anne Forsyth straightforwardly endured while his colleagues' crumbled and he leaves three children and four grandchildren. As a political scientist, he was practical, interested in voting systems and the legalities and mechanics of home rule. Though no philistine, he wasn't into fancy Gramscian cultural nationalism. In politics, he sought not self-aggrandisement but political solutions to problems which he understood politically. As an Honorary Fellow of Edinburgh

University, he set up a notable conference there in 1986 on 'Self-Determination in the Commonwealth' and the democratic right of all peoples to self-determination was the liberal groundrock of his own politics. On other issues, he was an uncomplicated social democrat, fully in tune with the SNP's leftward shift in the 1980s. He didn't go on about religion but one knew that regular worship in the Church of Scotland sustained him. In *Who's Who in Scotland*, he listed his recreations as 'music; languages; walking' and wait for it, 'vexillogy'. This word is in neither Chambers nor *OED*. It either has something to do with standards carried in the Roman army or (as I suspect) is a nonce-word related to 'stirring things up'. If so, Allan always stirred up with an unaffected broad grin and wholly unmalicious humour. His former OU colleagues in the administrative and secretarial departments have been in tears. Allan, liked by all, was the natural MC for Christmas parties or our annual 'Burns Lunches'. My own loving memory has him, paper hat on head, filthy Italian cigar in hand, leading us over empty wine bottles into a patriotic song, Hamish Henderson's great 'Freedom Come All Ye', say, in which 'A black boy frae yont Nyanga / Dings the fell gallows of the burghers doon.'

1998

Norman MacCaig

JOE, THE YOUNG BARMAN in the Auld Clachan (not one of the howffs which Norman frequented) said when I showed him the front page news, 'I guess he'll be more famous now that he's deid.' It was typically modest of Norman not to die on Burns's birthday, but good, if a death can be good, that it came in a week when people need reminding that Scotland has other great poets. Joe went to one of the few schools in Scotland which Norman did not visit, under the Scottish Arts Council Writers In Public scheme. While auld wifies on the Edinburgh busses have been mourning the loss of the city's special poet, there are kids all over the country who studied Norman's poetry for exams but, more importantly, saw this ravaged Caesar stride into their lives and read perfect poetry to perfection. I don't know if Ali Smith, the brilliant short story writer, first encountered him that way, but when Joy Hendry, editor of *Chapman* magazine, gathered together the tributes of scores of Scottish writers to celebrate Norman's 85th birthday last year, Ali, who lives in Cambridge now, came up with one of the best.

> Whenever I travel to the rail track home
> I can't help it, I think of that casual MacCaig poem
> The one where he's sitting smiling to himself on the London/
> Edinburgh train
> soaring North, yes, here we go, here it comes again.

Scotland has three languages for poetry. MacCaig's was the English of Edinburgh, where he was born, and became a primary school teacher, never aspiring to be greater, in a worldly sense, than that, though later both Edinburgh and Stirling Universities were honoured to have him on their staff, talking to students about writing with that aversion to bullshit which was his hallmark. The surprise was that this elegant, modest man was the closest friend of King Bullshit, MacDiarmid. They were diametrical opposites. MacDiarmid wrote huge sprawling poems about everything under the sun, especially politics and Anglophobia. Norman, a pacifist who suffered for his principles in World War II by being detained in Wormwood Scrubs, wrote frequently, with vast affection, before and after MacDiarmid's death, about his tankie friend. But MacCaig's politics, what you see in his verse, were those of the independent individual. They are short poems. Each makes, incisively, its point. The affinity, as many have pointed out, is with Herbert and Holub and other great poets of postwar Eastern Europe.

Hard work as a primary school teacher. Weekend evenings in Milne's Bar, in Rose Street, by Hanover Street, just off Princes Street, by the Mound. There he formed one of a legendary quadrumvirate: MacDiarmid, if he was up from Biggar, Sydney Goodsir Smith, and Robert Garioch. The other three wrote, or had written, in Scots. They were all very much aware of the great Gaelic poet, Sorley Maclean. In Norman's verse, you hear, enunciated or echoed, the three leids. And the substratum is Greek and Latin. He studied Classics at Edinburgh University, after going to that school steeped in Classics, the Royal High. He talked about the Celtic feeling for form which he derived from Gaelic forebears, not, usually, about that Classical grounding. But he wrote, in a poem called 'Aesthetics', 'Words with Greek roots/ and American blossoms/ have taken over the pretty garden.'

Summers in Lochinver. Suilven, his special mountain, fishing, walking:

I look up
at the eagle idling over
from Kylescu.
I look away
at the shattering waterblink
of Loch Cama.

Sorley Maclean wrote that Norman had given the Sutherland landscape new meaning. He honoured his Gaelic grannies in very beautiful English.

The career was extraordinary. I am tempted to write 'by-ordinar' and I will. One of the things which Norman confessedly loved about MacDiarmid was the old man's rescue of Scottish expressions. Norman was into his thirties before he published two books of poems. These belonged to the Neo-Apocalyptic School, rampant on the 'Celtic Fringes' in the 1940s. Later, he disavowed them to the extent that one fancied that only an innate respect for scholarship prevented him destroying the copies lodged in the National Library of Scotland. As that School went, they weren't bad. He came into his own, though, in his forties, with *Riding Lights*, published in 1955. At this point he might be, and was, mistaken for a Scottish relative of the Movement. He wrote, Celtically, in formal measures. Another book in the Fifties, and acclaim. Then the verse relaxed. Five books in the Sixties, increasingly deploying that throwaway-seeming free verse. Five later ones, written at an age when most poets have given it up for golf. The *New Collected Poems*, of 1990, did and did not round off a reputation. Even after that, folk young and old in Edinburgh (and I must add, Glasgow and Inverness) listened avidly for the itch of his scribble.

His place in Scottish Literature is unique, as the best recent writer in English, pure English. The achievement wins praise where you don't expect it. I was out on the tiles a few months ago with a young skinhead Scottish writer domiciled on what I suppose we will come to call the Irvine Welsh Heritage Trail. He surprised me by expressing his utter love of Norman's verse. We deplored together the fact that Norman was in failing health, never quite himself again after the loss of his much-loved consort, Isabel. We plotted to surprise Norman with a bottle of whisky in his home in Leamington Terrace. We never did it. I regret that. I offer, too late, this epitaph. 'Your death is beyond belief/ which you never had, anyway/ It comes upon one as a private grief/ – the ultimate enemy.'

1996

Iain Crichton Smith

THE DAY HE DIED, when BBC Scotland TV lunchtime news, after dire remarks about the national football team's latest performance, came up with a well-compiled tribute to Iain Crichton Smith, one didn't know whether to laugh or cry. There he was, the portentously but deceptively rueful downturn of the mouth, the especially complete and candid baldness, but craggier than one remembered somehow, turning into a monument... Yet someone who had met him only recently, a magazine editor whose request for some poetry in Gaelic he had responded to at once, had just said to me, hearing that I was writing an obituary, 'tell everyone how friendly and nice he was with people'. As the rather strange phrase has it, there was 'no side' to him. Since he lived in Argyll it was surprising how often he turned up in Edinburgh for unprestigious literary events. Meeting him thus, one thought, not 'great poet' (with an OBE and three honorary doctorates), but what a witty companion, completely unassuming, muttering briskly in the drily enigmatic accent of his native isle of Lewis, suspended somewhere between censure and send-up, kirk and comedy.

He used that voice to wondrous effect in his marvellous monologues of Murdo, an archetypal, parochial, universal Gaelic fantasist and sluggard, ironic obverse to the values of the Free Church which overarched the Long Island of Iain's childhood and youth. These had audiences in fits. But he read his verse, one would have to say, badly. His compeers Sorley Maclean and Norman MacCaig were in different ways spectacular public readers, and Edwin Morgan happily still is. Iain, Lewis-wise, threw his lovely things away, with rapid off-hand delivery, no bloom on it, as if he was afraid of seeming to show off. This was despite his conviction, uttered in what must be his last pre-posthumous publication, an article in *Chapman* which came out in the week of his death, that poetry above all should be musical. 'We need', he wrote, 'a new music. Not a new imagery but a new music... True originality lies in the music which more than the image is the sign of a new consciousness'.

His own music came to him from a Gaelic tradition, closed to most of us, in which he practised all his life as one of the language's major writers this century, in fiction as well as in verse. Ten years ago he told an interviewer that if he had 'thought there was as much recognition, that I'd reach the same breadth of audience, and that there was as much going on, that there were as many other writers in Gaelic as in English, I believe I'd have chosen Gaelic'. Typically auto-subversive. His first opus, written in Gaelic when he was eleven, was about Neville Chamberlain's wee trip to Munich. 'I think I'd been narrating the event to my family and out of that came my first poem, which was in the oral, rather than literary tradition.'

Bayble, his childhood home, a drab village near Stornoway, without even a decent beach to it, was an unlikely place for either tradition to bear fruit. Grey sea, flat brown island. His atheism as an adult was a reaction against the repressiveness, shades of the prisonhouse, which he sensed in the Free Church hegemony over Lewis. Iain was born on New Year's Day 1928, in Glasgow. His Mother took him straight back to Lewis and he usually suppressed his birthplace, lest he be confused with authentically Glaswegian writers. His Father, a merchant seaman, died of TB, scourge of the isles, when he was an infant. His Mother struggled in poverty, working as a herring gutter, wrecking her hands, to bring up three boys (Iain was the middle one). But Iain attended the Nicolson Institute, that great school which educated so many children so well that they left the island for university, gained fame and fortune, and never came back. Here, in the fifth year, he received as a prize Sorley Maclean's book of poems which melded love and politics and brought Gaelic into the twentieth century, *Dain do Eimhir*, quite recently published. 'It was very progressive of that teacher to give me such a book'. Meanwhile, they taught him Wordsworth and Tennyson and he discovered, for himself, in the magazine *New Writing*, the latest poets, and in the bookshops and library Eliot and Auden, who between them gave him his new music in English. He loved 'Hollow Men', 'Ash Wednesday', 'Marina' and began an on-off affair with Auden's verse which lasted a lifetime. At Aberdeen University he studied English Literature, but was befriended by fellow-student, Derick Thomson, who became a major Gaelic scholar and poet.

Committed to writing, he had to have a job. He taught school in Clydebank for a couple of years. Appointed to the High School in Oban, in 1955, he bought a flat for himself and his Mother in Combie Street. Devoutly Free Kirk, she lived with him till she died, a presence behind many verses about old women. Writing in his spare time, he began to establish a reputation as a rising poet. The English 'Movement' was ascendant over taste, and the rhymed formality of some early Crichton Smith might have fooled readers into thinking that he went along with its aesthetics. But the fourteen-section sequence 'Deer on the High Hills', which he himself continued to think of as his masterpiece, went in its philosophic meditation where the Movement dared not tread, jousting with complexities on its way to a deceptively simple conclusion:

> The deer step out in isolated air.
> Forgive the distance, let the transient journey
> on delicate ice not tragical appear
> for stars are starry and the rain is rainy,
> the stone is stony and the sun is sunny,
> the deer step out in isolated air.

His first novel, *Consider the Lilies*, published in 1968, about an old lady in the Highland Clearances, is now reprinted as a classic and has been much used in schools. It was work commissioned for cash by Giles Gordon, then a publisher with Gollancz, who as editor had first printed 'Deer on the High Hills' in *New Saltire Review* 2, 1961. (I have that magazine in front of me now. It also includes an aggressively 'modernist' poem by Iain's Oban High School pupil Lorn MacIntyre, and an angry article by Edwin Morgan about the failure of Scottish publishers to 'do something about modern Scottish poetry'. Sad that, like Morgan himself, Iain would consolidate an international reputation through publication in Manchester.) Iain thereafter wrote novels, he said, to fill in the gaps between poems. He was addicted to detective fiction. (In my last conversation with him, on the phone, I asked him if it was true that he had once reviewed 50 detective stories in a single weekend. Pause. Hint of a chuckle. 'I think it was only 26.') His own fiction, however, did not involve fancy plotting. It was simple and directly written, usually out of what he knew first hand – though *An Honourable Death* (1992) is very successful in recreating the life of General Sir Hector MacDonald, the crofter's son who became a great imperial war hero and killed himself on his way to face Army proceedings connected with his alleged interference with young boys. One remembers from Iain's novels not plot, but an atmosphere of friendly attention to fellow-humanity, expressed in the title and substance of one of his best, *A Field Full of Folk* (1982). Perhaps *In the Middle of the Wood* (1987) will come to seem his most remarkable achievement in prose. Like Waugh's *Ordeal of Gilbert Pinfold*, it derives directly from a phrase of paranoia, which in Iain's case actually led to a spell in mental hospital.

Iain, I think, really didn't set very great store by his English prose fiction, though now that Alan Warner's novels have made Oban world famous, it is worth noting that *The Tenement* (1985) used that unpropitious locality very effectively years before *Morvern Callar* was dreamt of. Novels were bread-and-butter after he dropped teaching in 1977. ('I said to myself, "There's no shortage of teachers in Scotland. Writers are, perhaps, not quite so available."') Married, late in life, to Donalda Logan, he moved to green and quiet Taynuilt. Prizes flowed in for the poetry, which was was frequently less formal now, displaying the influence of William Carlos Williams in its centring on direct perceptions of the mundane – as in *The Village* (1989). There were radio plays, and plays for the stage which succeeded very well in the new Scottish touring tradition, like a thumping good short one about St Columba I saw in 1997 in a small venue in Ullapool and *Lazybed* which more recently packed out the Traverse. Knowing that he would die soon, he finished, in his last weeks, a new play for the Traverse.

Stewart Conn recalls bumping into Norman MacCaig in Edinburgh. MacCaig says 'I'm very worried about Iain Crichton Smith.' 'Oh dear, why's that?' 'He hasn't published a new book for a whole week.' It would be easy to conclude that Iain wrote too much for his own good – ten novels in English, two in Gaelic; taking both languages together, some dozen volumes of short stories; more than a dozen books of verse in English alone. He wrote addictively, habitually. He did not like revising, and said that he had barely touched 'Deer on the High Hills', which came to him, as he told Lorn MacIntyre when he showed him the MS, in one burst of inspiration. In fact, it is the frankness and freshness of all his work which guarantees its durability. A vestigial Free-Church-like discipline reined back his surge of language, along with the technical rigours of the Gaelic verse tradition.

He did, just days before Carcanet published *The Leaf and the Marble*, which he had dedicated to Donalda, 'with love and gratitude'. This long sequence (64 pages) is the work of a virtuoso with no need to prove his technical mastery. Free verse is plucked together with irregular but effective stitches of rhyme and half-rhyme. Crichton Smith moves with complete freedom somewhere between, say, the conversational rhymed measures of late Yeats and the 'open field' strategies of the mid-twentieth century American avant garde, while subscribing to neither aesthetic. Very simply, the sequence sets up an opposition between the 'light leaves' of spring in Rome, representing love and Donalda, and the marble of Empire and Death. The nearest thing to this I've seen recently was *Freedom Lament and Song* by the great South African poet Mongane Wally Serote, whose technique relates to jazz improvisation, turning melody, motifs, chords, over and over. Crichton Smith cannot 'progress' beyond the stark opposition introduced at once between life and death, freedom and oppression. His atheism leaves no scope for philosophical (theological, metaphysical) transcendence. The grim classical Hades is much invoked as part of the tyrannous domain of marble, along with the straight roads of Roman imperialism. Roman oppression is explicitly and unforgivingly equated with Hebridean Presbyterianism. What Crichton Smith can do is play variation after variation on his theme, affirming life with wry passion again and again. Brilliantly, his epilogue takes us to ancient Egypt, where death and the cults associated with it might seem to have been all-powerful. Paintings mean a lot to Crichton Smith, deprived in his Stornoway youth of direct encounter with good ones. There is an Egyptian painting of King Tutankhamun sitting on the Golden Throne, which has seat and legs of 'lyric blue'. His wife Akhesenamun, standing, eyes level with his, stoops to touch his shoulder:

> Love is here –
> the perfect unadorned gaze.
> This blueness, it is
> calm and silence
> The hands,
> the limbs, are so delicate,
> airy, transcendent. The throne
> tilts into the air, such a fine
> transaction. She touches
> him with wonderment, lightly
> out of the light, amazed
> at finding him there...
> Egyptian
> heaviness is gone, the custom
> of death.
> This is an idyll
> freed even of gravity, the will
> untrammelled, lifted into the air
> of a lucky finding.

Such an image of contingent happenstance still quivering, thanks to art, over millennia was an apt one for Iain to leave us with. Through verse and art, love and beauty survive, as Horace put it, longer than brass. Paradoxically, such brief rovings of feeling as infinite death allows us assure such minds as we have that intimate frail things endure. Leaflike in freshness, an intimate, special music is heard throughout Iain's great bulk of verse, and now that he's gone so suddenly (just weeks from diagnosis of the cancer to his death) I think we will all hear its distinctiveness more clearly. One last wry thought, though – the Bible got him at last. Exactly threescore years and ten...

1998

John Prebble

'A NORTH-EAST WIND PULLED at the flame of the guard-tent lanthorn, and teased the water of the Moray Firth where Rear-Admiral Byng's warships and transports rode at anchor. To the south, across the River Nairn, mist or rain was smoking on the braes of Urchany. It was a morning that soldiers know, and Major Forrester's advanced pickets of the Royal Scots, damp and cold from a night's watch along the high ground at Kildrummie, can have felt no love for it.'

Thus John Prebble set 'Butcher' Cumberland's men off on their march to battle in his book *Culloden*. The passage is typical in two ways. First, Prebble had been a soldier and his experiences during the Allied invasion of Germany in 1944–45 conditioned all his writing about battle: he knew how a squaddie might feel on a dreich April morning. He had known himself what a private of the Royals wrote about – 'Strong rain on our backs and the enemies face.' Secondly, his impeccably detailed use of primary sources is enriched – or vitiated – by imagination. He had no 'authority' for that wind tugging the lantern. He just knew that it must have been so. For such liberties, very few academic historians could forgive him.

Culloden, Prebble's masterpiece, was published in 1961 near the start of a notable, now notorious, decade in British culture. It was soon followed by a book by Prebble's erstwhile comrade in the Communist Party of Great Britain, E.P. Thompson, *The Making of the English Working Class*, in which a rebellious academic sought 'to rescue the poor stockinger, the Luddite cropper, the 'obsolete' handloom weaver, the 'utopian' artisan, and even the deluded follower of Joanna Southcott, from the immense condescension of posterity.' Prebble's project, extended through *The Highland Clearances* (1963), *Glencoe* (1966) and *Mutiny*

(1975), was likewise to 'rescue' the ordinary Gaels of the Scottish Highlands, whom he saw as overborne by Lowlanders and English before, during and after Prince Charlie's rebellion, ultimately betrayed by their own chiefs and evicted from the lands of their ancestors. To their succession of tragedies, he added accounts of other Scottish catastrophes – he had begun with *The High Girders* (1956), detailing the collapse of the Tay Bridge in 1879, and went on to narrate the tale of Scotland's aborted colony in Central America in *The Darien Disaster* (1966). Always, his effort was to recover the experience of common man and woman.

Peter Watkins made a remarkable film of *Culloden*, pioneering the technique of 'documentary' re-enactment of past events now seen on TV *ad nauseam*. Prebble also scripted the film *Zulu* (1964), based on an article he'd written which the director, Cy Endfield had spotted. Telling how a handful of British soldiers had defended the Rorke's Drift Mission against 4,000 Zulus in 1879, the film remains famous, not least because it gave Michael Caine his first starring role. It is infused with Prebble's values. He 'out-Kiplings' Rudyard in his sympathy for the ordinary soldier of the Queen while expressing admiration for the Zulu *impis*. As with his Highlanders, his feeling for Africans relates to his sense, picked up in childhood on the plains of Saskatchewan, of what the white man had done to native North Americans. Having won an audience by the brilliance of his writing, he chose to din into it the realities of oppression, expropriation and betrayal, saucing these with vivid description, dry wit and grim humour, as a tersely ironic stylist not hopelessly outclassed by Edward Gibbon.

Though Prebble never learnt Gaelic, and depended on friends for access to sources in that language, his love affair with Highland Scotland was lifelong and constant. It began in the Canadian township of Sutherland, recently created by a man of that name descended from one of Lord Selkirk's Red River settlers of 1813. His parents had emigrated there after his father, discharged from the Great War Navy, had found only grinding, ill-paid work as a porter in England. They were High Anglicans and devout Tories.

But an uncle who had emigrated to Canada had become a Socialist and pacifist, and the boy John, born in London in 1915, began to acquire in Saskatchewan the inklings of his contumacious spirit.

The Prebbles lived in territory which had seen the last great rebellion in Canadian history, that of half-caste *métis* led by Louis Riel. Prebble's schoolteacher was a Miss Campbell, fiercely proud of the Scotland she had never seen. He was enthralled by the contrast between the mountainous land she evoked and the flat prairies around him. The neighbours, generations away from Scotland, routinely flaunted tartan, 'flame-red or blue-green against the snow in winter'. His father could still get no better work than labouring, and gladly accepted the chance to return to England as caretaker of a church hall in Earls Court. Prebble resided in England for the rest of his life, pleased to be English. He was very proud of his 'Jutish' descent from countless generations of labouring Men of Kent, from a 'Preble' pardoned in the fifteenth century for his part in Jack Cade's uprising, from Abraham 'Preble' who fled from persecution in the 1630s to become a notable man in Puritan New England.

He won a scholarship to Latimer's, a public school for day boys. Here his historical imagination took off. A teacher introduced him to Langland's Piers Plowman and to the story of John Ball's rebellion. He identified (like E.P. Thompson) with the English tradition of radicalism preserved in records of the 'Putney Debate' raised by the Levellers in Cromwell's army. Throughout World War II he carried in his army paybook a quotation from one of these 'Agitators', a London tradesman – 'If we had not a right to the kingdom, we were mere mercenary soldiers.' Simultaneously, Prebble maintained a love affair with Scotland, a country he had not yet seen, shared with a Jewish friend, Walter Flack, who later became a millionaire through property speculation. They invented Highland names to add to their own, and inscribed them on exercise books and 'with impudence upon school and house notice boards.' They chanted aloud verses stuffed with such names by Scott, Aytoun and others. Prebble was not disappointed when he first saw Scotland on holiday, aged 21. In his unorthodox volume of autobiography, *Landscapes and Memories* (1993), each chapter starts off with a Scottish scene replete with minute historical associations for Prebble, who on repeated returns came to know far more about Scotland and its history than most educated Scots.

Prebble's first job, after eighteen months of unemployment, was collecting rents for an estate agent. The poverty with which this confronted him, and the outbreak of civil war in Spain, thrust him into the Communist Party. The Party wouldn't let him go to fight in Spain – he was told they'd already had enough 'middle class martyrs' and now needed some proletarian heroes. Instead he became a journalist. Called up in 1940, he had a curious war, largely in a camp in North Wales, where he specialised in radar engineering, propagandised for the CP, created a controversial 'wall newspaper' and led a kind of mutiny, organising an illicit petition signed by 250 men calling for a Second Front Now to aid Russia. One can only assume that the dignity and courtesy, and air of high intelligence, which he presented in later life were already there, and saved him from serious trouble. As the Allied armies moved towards the Reich, he ran away from his safe posting to join the fighting troops in Europe. He wrote in his memoirs that 'to have been part of the liberation of Europe is still a matter of deep pride to me, and my life would have been poorer without it.' Yet Germany, defeated, was a terrible place to see. In Hamburg, when they spoke of a 'Holocaust', they were talking of nine days in 1943 when the RAF gutted the town. 'The smell of fire, of damp and charred wood, returned on days of rain, even two years later...' Here, out of current experience, he started his second novel, *The Edge of Darkness*. His first, *Where the Sea Breaks*, about Germans arriving in wartime on an imaginary Scottish island, had come out in 1944 from Secker and Warburg.

Post war, he reverted to journalism, initially for Lord Beaverbrook, who completely failed to seduce him – it is clear that Prebble was rather vain about having resisted a charmer who had overwhelmed Michael Foot and Aneurin Bevan. He also abandoned the CP, convinced that 'in the struggle for liberty and justice the cause is more often at risk from its leaders than it may be from its enemies.' Headway as a writer of fiction was made. *The Buffalo Soldiers* (1959) won an award in the USA as best historical novel about the American West. This uncompromisingly grim tale was rather inappropriately marketed afterwards as suitable reading for 'older children.' Then in 1959, during an hour's visit to Culloden, he decided to write the book about the battle and its aftermath which made him the favourite historian of Scotland's 'general readers' and a bogey man for academics.

Nowadays, an excellent new book about Scottish history seems to come out every other week. This was not the case in the early Sixties. The fine efforts early in the century of Hume Brown and Mathieson had been followed by accounts of Scottish history, presented as 'standard' which were variously boring, insipid, and/or just plain wrong. Romantic novelists ruled the roost with their sanitised fantasies. Prebble's avowed aim was to get past the 'Bonnie Prince' and whisky-label sentimentality to the roots of the 'sickness' which he saw as possessing Scotland since, and because of, Culloden. He had discovered in a library before World War II the authentic documents collected after the '45 Rising as *The Lyon in Mourning.* He had also encountered a pamphlet, published in the 1930s, of the nineteenth century writings of Donald Macleod, a Highlander inveighing against the 'Clearances'. He recognised that Macleod was not always accurate and that many of his charges against the landlord class were unsubstantiated. Nevertheless, he accepted the overview that the Gaels had been persecuted out of their land and forced to emigrate. Here, historians quarrel not just with his 'factional' methods, in *The Highland Clearances,* but with his conclusions.

More than a century of large-scale emigration from the Highlands had presented several very different phases. Departure before the American Revolution had usually been voluntary, however mournful at the quayside. During the Napoleonic Wars, landlords had actually resisted emigration by their clan vassals, whose labour was needed to support the boom in kelp collected on Atlantic shores and burnt for potash. Gaels who did get to the New World often prospered there (for instance, controlling the whole vast Canadian fur trade). Highland soldiers were willing participants in the victories of the British Empire. But Prebble saw Highland history over many generations as a kind of rolling sequel to the brutal (though not, in European context, unusual) suppression of the area by Cumberland's forces after Culloden. The well-documented activities of the 'improving' Duke of Sutherland, who 'cleared' his vast estate for sheep, and the caustic anti-Gaelic prejudice of his agent on the ground, Patrick Sellar, were taken as typical of this presumed racist, colonialist malevolence. Prebble's paranoid view of Highlanders as innocent victims of evil capitalism chimed all too well with the bar-room girnings of such Gaelic idiots as still write to the Scottish broadsheets comparing the clearances to Hitler's Holocaust. In fact, the Sutherland family did not profit from their misplaced paternalism, and the departure of tenants from over-crowded Highland acres spared Scotland famine in the 1840s to match Ireland's.

Nevertheless, it is notable that the best scholars to apply themselves to the Clearances since Prebble – Eric Richards and James Hunter – have been much kinder in their remarks about his work than historians famous in other fields. The late Gordon Donaldson, Royal Historiographer in Scotland, denounced Prebble's books, in the 1980s, as 'utter rubbish'. Michael Fry, expert on eighteenth-century politics and Scottish enterprise overseas, responded to news of his death with the view that he was an 'inferior historian' who lacked 'proper respect for evidence'. It is relevant to note that Donaldson was, and Fry is, a Tory. I put it to Prebble in interview once that after he left the CP he substituted a Gael/Sassenach dichotomy for the Marxist one of working class/bourgeoisie. He found this idea interesting. But he was himself profoundly humane in his attitude to people of all ethnic origins and classes. He could not get inside the skin of that complex and talented man Patrick Sellar. But when he wrote *The King's Jaunt* (1988), his mellow and at times hilarious account of George IV's visit to Edinburgh in 1822, his attitude towards the King himself and his Tory pageant-master, Walter Scott, was surprisingly sympathetic.

The Buffalo Soldiers tells of black cavalrymen, ex-slaves, sent West to deal with the Comanches under an officer who is the son of an Irish Fenian evicted and expelled from his own country. Prebble told me that he could never decide which of these three sorts of people commanded his fullest sympathy. He spoke as a man still appalled by the sufferings of ordinary Germans in 1945, even though Irma Grise, mistress of the commandant of Belsen, spat in his face when he was on guard duty over her and other camp personnel. He wrote of 'the long brawl of Scotland's history', and his pessimistic view of the country's past in terms of feuds, tragedies, folly and treachery is in my view extremely misleading. But he brought to bear on it a vision of human nature, vicious and kind, barbaric yet sometimes noble, formed in the mid-century agonies of Europe. However he misread Scotland, he took its people seriously. They responded by making his books enduring bestsellers, and as James Hunter has wisely said, he 'did more than any other single person in the twentieth century to interest a wide general public in the history of Scotland.' Like many others, I was kickstarted by Prebble (and Walter Scott) and moved on.

He was a Fellow of the Royal Society of Literature, but it must have mattered more to him that he was adjudged Scotland's Writer of the Year in 1993, winning the country's largest literary prize, and that Glasgow University gave him an honorary doctorate in 1997.

2001

PART TWO

When Was Scotland?

Stone of Destiny

I HAVE BEFORE ME AS I write, a chunk of stone. It is like a flattened oval of blackened oatmeal smoothed by seas and time. I picked it up on a beach in Orkney 24 years ago. It serves me well as a paper-weight and seems to me beautiful.

Just up the road, Edinburgh Castle displays to tourists a lump of sandstone in two bits joined together. No one, apparently, thinks it beautiful. David Stewart, who tried to steal the Stone of Scone from Westminster Abbey in 1974 and got fined £150, now describes it as 'a really scabby piece of garbage, a random block'. Ian Hamilton QC, who lead the little band who actually retrieved this chunk, or another one, on Christmas Day 1950, opined, when Michael Forsyth, as Secretary of State for Scotland, arranged that the object came back to Scotland, that it was 'meaningless masonry'. Others who thought that Forsyth's exercise was just a vote-seeking stunt had fun with the notion that the Stone had originally been used as a cesspit-cover...

There are people who think the object 'useful' as part of the mumbo-jumbo involved in the anointing and crowning of British monarchs. Some quasi-radioactive current, presumably, must be thought of as proceeding from the stone under the throne through, or between, the monarch's buttocks, from the distant mythical origins of sacred kingship. For upholding the 'Divine Right' of kings, the duly-enstoned Charles I had his tongue – Scottish in accent, from his Dad – silenced by Cromwell's axeman. The Restoration of monarchical nonsense thereafter was superstitious or cynical mystification by the ruling class. Only GMTV viewers fall for such twaddle now – *Sun* readers have too much sense.

For those who care to explore the topic further, Pat Gerber's lively book *Stone of Destiny* (1997) provides copious leads. To peel off the layers. One: the lump in the Castle may or may not be the Stone stolen by Ian Hamilton in 1950. The 'true' Stone of Scone may have been hidden somewhere by Nationalists. But the object in Westminster Abbey, reived by Edward I in 1296, may have been a hastily substituted fake. The 'true' Stone of Destiny on which Kings of Scots had been crowned may lurk almost anywhere. One notion in circulation since 1818 is that Macbeth prudently stowed the Stone somewhere in or around Dunsinane. The idea that Bruce entrusted it to Angus Og, first Lord of the Isles, suggests a Hebridean hiding place.

Flying-saucer groupies and frequent tourists on the lost continent of Atlantis will choose to believe that the Stone was the pillow of the Old Testament patriarch Jacob, transmitted to Ireland by the Egyptian Princess Scota and the prophet Jeremiah c. 500 BC, and thence by the Scots to Dunadd in Argyll. The 150 members of the Scottish Knights Templar know where the real Stone is but won't tell us...

Gerber believes that any real Stone of Destiny would be richly decorated in the Celtic manner. This could be worth seeing. As for the Lump in the Castle, I suggest the Scottish Tourist Board should arrange a photo-opportunity for the world press. Let it be dropped in Loch Ness and we shall see if it rouses our favourite monster. 'Two birds with one Stone?'

1997

A Pict 'N' Mixt Identity

WILLIAM FERGUSON'S REMARKABLE book *The Identity of the Scottish Nation* (1998) will not tell you what makes the Tartan Army tick. It does not attempt to argue why we should preserve the Four Year Honours Degree in an era when internet technology is set to change the face of education everywhere. It is not topically orientated towards the new Holyrood Parliament. Instead, a very learned elder scholar moves, phase by phase, from the Middle Ages down to our own day, exploring what historians, philologians and polemicists have made of certain questions regarded at one time or another as crucial to Scotland's survival as a kingdom or to our identity as a people.

Did Scota, daughter of the Pharoah drowned in the Red Sea in the Book of Exodus, really sail off after that disaster with her husband Nel, a direct descendant of Noah, to seed the Scots through their son Gaedel Glas? Obviously not, so it seems to us, but the legend corresponded to origin-myths flaunted by other European kingdoms – the English had Brutus, descendant of Aeneas, the Trojan who had founded Rome, the French had Frankus, the Danes, Danus. However, till the end of the eleventh century the Latin word 'Scotia' denoted Ireland. As relations with the English king got rough at the end of the thirteenth century, the legend of Scota was deployed along with the idea that Scottish kingship had a very ancient tradition. Or you could argue, as the Declaration of Arbroath did, that the Scots came from Scythia by way of Spain, after which 'Within their realm have reigned 113 kings of royal stock, never an alien upon the throne'. Such kings, like Robert Bruce himself, might have been held to derive their right to rule from the active consent of their people and this was the germ of Scotland's most remarkable contribution to political thought.

The number of Kings of Scotland was a matter of vivid debate for centuries. Their line was pushed back to pre-Christian times. The great Latin scholar George Buchanan, in 1582, plumped for forty kings between the mythical Fergus I and the semi-historical Fergus II, presumed leader of the S cots from Ireland who settled in Argyll in the early sixth century AD. However, Pictish king-lists survived. Granted that Kenneth McAlpin united Scots and Picts under his kingship in the mid-ninth century, how did one fit the Picts into the nation's identity? Terrible unease developed among Lowland Protestants as the Irish – Catholic, conquered, seen as lazy and treacherous – slipped down the scale of ethnic respectability. Could sturdy Scotland really have been, once-upon-a-time, a kind of Irish colony? Who were the Picts?

Since damn-all was known about these folk, it was brilliant of Buchanan, master of linguistics, to work out that they had been what we call 'P-Celts'. That is, their language was distinct from 'Q-Celt' Gaelic, and allied to Welsh and Breton, but closer than these tongues to ancient Gaulish. For the purposes of thinking about Picts, it was unfortunate that Buchanan also argued – following the Arbroath Declaration – for the right of subjects to depose monarchs. So anything he wrote was politically incorrect in the eyes of even moderate Royalists and Anti-Jacobins. Furthermore, (knowing the lass well) he was convinced that Mary Queen of Scots had connived in the murder of her husband Darnley. Even today, millions of people cannot forgive Buchanan for this.

The wildest alternative to Buchanan was proposed in 1789 (fateful year!) by John Pinkerton, whose views gained wide currency among scholars, including Jamieson, the pioneering lexicographer of the Scottish tongue. Besides being a paranoid fraudster, Pinkerton was in the avant-garde of the 'Teutonising' tendency which turned even the ancient Greeks into blonde, blue-eyed Nordics and had appalling consequences under Nazism. Pinkerton thought the Celts stood in relation to the 'Scythians', whom he placed in Scandinavia, 'as a negro to a European', so that 'as all history shows, to see them was to conquer them'. His Nordic Picts spoke a Germanic tongue which developed into Lowland Scots.

Meanwhile, the vast emotional impact of Macpherson's *Ossian*, which set the Fenian heroes on Scottish soil, reinforced the idea that Scottishness began, very anciently, at home. One could argue that the 'Caledonians' who halted the Roman legions already spoke Gaelic. And so on... And so forth...

Ferguson is too good a scholar himself to imagine that the writers he examines can all be dismissed as axe-grinding clerics and scheming hacks – though some of them were. He wrestles throughout with abiding problems about the writing of history. Sound historians respect the judgement of learned predecessors – especially, until quite recently, the methods and statements of the great Roman historians. From the late-eighteenth century onwards, led by Hailes and Gibbon, historians have believed that direct study of original sources can provide a quasi-scientific 'truth'. And nowadays, 'oral history' is given more weight than it had a hundred years ago.

But what if popular traditions are garbled? What if 'original sources' are scanty, tainted with bias, or simply faked? What if scholarly 'authorities' were actually twisting history to make a political case? If the views of the writers he studies now seem wrong, Ferguson can nevertheless discriminate between those who argue soundly and those whose expression is loose. He sets each in turn in political and biographical context. For X, an ardent episcopalian, it is essential that the old Celtic Church of Columbus had Bishops. His Presbyterian adversary Y must needs argue that it repelled, for a time, such Popish abominations. Ferguson can set in a rather attractive context the most hilarious notion that he mentions – an eighteenth-century Kirk minister named Malcolm contended that the inhabitants of St Kilda retained a very ancient form of the Irish language which had certain affinities with Chinese. (Thus, the unity of all humankind could be asserted, as Enlightened Europeans wished it to be.)

Though *The Joys of Pedantry* might not prove a runaway bestseller, there is vast pleasure to be found in minute scholarship.

At times Ferguson's repetitious revolving of his authors' antiquated preoccupations may somewhat tax his readers' patience. But the book is full of fun. Thus, the erudite 'Bluidy Mackenzie', Sir George of Rosehaugh, a lawyer execrated by the Covenanters, is revealed as a gutsy patriot as firm and fierce as Fletcher of Saltoun. Dr Johnson unjustly jibed at 'Ossian' Macpherson as a forger: Ferguson turns the tables and shows – what Boswell doesn't mention – that he had been duped some years before by a Scottish literary fraudster, one Lauder. Once bitten, twice shy.

Ferguson is thoroughly versed in literature, English and Scottish, and this conditions his judicious concluding chapter. The medieval spread of Gaelic over most of Scotland is a firm fact, but we are a mongrel people and notions of Celtic (or 'Teutonic') purity really have no place here. Whatever our 'identity' might be, it would now be under threat from the universal hegemony of American-English culture and 'global gangs of Mammonites that would cheerfully ruin the planet for profit.' Ferguson goes on: 'Against such and other menaces the poets still offer the best prescription.' One might add – poets in all our three or more languages: Gaelic tempered by Norse and English, varieties of spoken and written Scots, and English uttered, to recall R.L. Stevenson's great phrase, by people who retain 'a strong Scots accent of the mind.'

1998

Once and Future Knox

IN 1811, AS THE WAR AGAINST Napoleon thundered towards its end, the Reverend Thomas M'Crie's great biography of John Knox appeared. It was an exercise in the new historical methods so momentously pioneered, after Hume and Robertson, by Edward Gibbon. M'Crie was scrupulous to cite his sources, of which he took a critical view. His book, furthermore, was elegantly composed, with flashes worthy of Gibbon himself, as when he said of James VI and I that 'cowardice alone prevented him from becoming a tyrant.' Though M'Crie was a wholly committed admirer of Knox, he did strive to understand why his hero was not universally loved in Scotland. Two factors he mentions are still worth considering. Firstly, the English on the whole hadn't liked him (any more than their leaders liked Scottish Presbyterianism in general). So they had said bad things about Knox. After the Union of 1707, 'a passion for conformity to our southern neighbours' predisposed Scots to accept negative English views:

> But the greatest torrent of abuse, poured upon his character, has proceeded from those literary champions who have come forward to avenge the wrongs, and vindicate the innocence of the peerless, and immaculate Mary, Queen of Scots. Having conjured up in their imagination the image of an ideal goddess, they have sacrificed to the object of their adoration, all the characters which, in that age, were most estimable for learning, patriotism, integrity, and religion.

M'Crie is thinking here of Buchanan, for instance, defamed when not merely ignored because he wasn't a Scotomariolater. He blames the great Scottish historians, Hume and Robertson, for letting the young queen off lightly.

M'Crie focused a fascinating problem, to do with the inner logic of taletelling. Even if you believe, as is reasonable, that Mary connived in the murder of her husband, you find yourself drawn into a primary, binary opposition – she must be light because Knox is so dark. The paradox is that it is due to Knox's own extraordinary literary talents that this opposition is indelibly vivid.

One could not write the history of the Scottish Reformation without quite frequent reference to Knox. He was a charismatic preacher who at various junctures inspired or rallied others by his words. He was important on the committees which drew up the Scots Confession and the *Book of Discipline* as bases for a new church order. Some of the lords, great and small, whose actions forced forward what was tantamount to a revolution deferred to him, as their source of sound ideas, as he himself deferred (though far from completely) to his master, Calvin. Protestant Europe saw him as a great, brave spirit. As Minister of the High Kirk of Scotland's capital city, a few minutes walk from the Royal Palace, and a man accordingly influential upon the Town Council responsible for governing the Queen's immediate environment, he did have a certain amount of clout. But a succinct narrative of political and ecclesiastical events from the late 1540s through the 1560s could, with continuous plausibility, mention him only in passing...

Knox himself is our prime source of evidence for his interviews with Mary, Queen of Scots (hereinafter MQS). They feature in his *Historie of the Reformatioun in Scotland* which is in effect a memoir, though written in the third person, and is one of the greatest works of Scottish prose. These interviews are wonderfully vivid. They have made him a bugaboo, a byword for crabbit, censorious, bigotted eld stalking (as it were) with his coarse harangues a creature of sweet sensibility and fragrant young flesh. The most judicious person (and I can think of no one more judicious than myself) is ineluctably drawn, by the logic of the tale, to sympathise with her. Damn it, if she went to the bad, wasn't it partly because the man who was in a position to influence her morals for the better was such a brute that he alienated her? The true tragedy which we find in her tale is owed precisely to our perception that she had good qualities – she was charming and intelligent – but struggled in a nightmarish darkness of which Knox was part.

But, I repeat, without Knox's brilliance as a writer we could not see things quite this way. Consider the great interview when he makes her cry.

Rumours abound regarding the Queen's possible re-marriage. Knox is incensed that some of her Protestant courtiers seem to accept that she may marry a Catholic (for diplomatic and dynastic reasons, of course, not because she loved any particular Catholic). He harangues a large congregation on the topic. MQS is very annoyed, and summons him to Holyrood Palace. Various noble supporters accompany him, but only John Erskine of Dun – a notoriously nice man, Good Cop to Knox's Bad Cop – actually goes up with him to the Queen's private cabinet... MQS is 'in a vehement Fume'. She cries out that 'nevir Prince was handilled as she was'. I shall modernise/anglicise what follows:

'I have', said she, 'borne with you in all your rigorous manner of speaking, both against myelf and against my Uncles [leaders of the Guise faction in France]; yea, I have sought your favour by all possible means; I offered unto you presence and audience whensoever it pleased you to admonish me, and yet I cannot be quit of you. I vow to God I shall be once revenged.'

At this point, she chokes on her tears. Her pageboy seeks out more handkerchiefs to dry her eycs. Knox waits 'patiently' till she has calmed down:

'True it is, Madam, your Grace and I have been at divers Controversies, into the whilk I never perceived your Grace to be offended at me. But when it shall please God to deliver you frae that Bondage of Darkness and Error in the which you have been nourished, for the lack of true Doctrine, your Majesty will find the Liberty of my tongue nothing offensive. Without the preaching Place, Madam, I think few have occasion to be offended at me; and there, Madam, I am not master of myself , but maun obey him who commands me to speak plain, and to flatter no flesh upon the face of the earth.'

'But what have you to do,' said she, 'with my marriage?'

The gist of Knox's reply is that God hasn't sent him to 'wait upon the courts of Princes, or upon the chalmers [chambers] of ladies', but to preach Christ's 'Evangell', which has two parts, Repentance and Faith. Preaching the first entails pointing out to his hearers what sins they are committing. Most of the nobility are so 'addicted' to the 'affections' of MQS – in other words, are so charmed by her – 'that neither God's Word, nor yet their Commonwealth are rightly regarded; and therefore it becomes me so to speak that they may know their duty.' (Their duty at this moment is to oppose any Catholic marriage by their Queen. Knox, a preacher in England, fled to the Continent with many colleagues to escape the murderous, heretic-burning persecution of Mary I after her marriage to Philip II of Spain. He does not want anything like that to happen here. One of the bizarre astigmatisms of anti-Knoxian Scotomariolaters is that they assume that Catholics in her day were all perfectly pleasant people, and only Protestants were 'bigots'.)

What follows may rightly be recognised as one of the great moments, representative and inspiring, in the movement of Europeans towards our present day ideas of democracy. MQS repeats her question:

'What have you to do with my marriage? Or what are ye in the Common-wealth?'

'A subject born within the same, Madam. And albeit I be neither Earl, Lord, nor Baron within it, yet has God made me (how abject that ever I be in your eyes) a profitable

SCOTLANDS OF THE MIND

member within the same: Yea, Madam, to me it appertains no less to forewarn of such things as may hurt it, if I foresee them, than it doth to any of the Nobility; for both my voca- tion and conscience crave plainness of me. And therefore, Madam, to yourself I say that whilk I spake in public Place. Whensoever that the Nobility of this Realm shall consent, that ye be subject to an unfaithful [non-Protestant] husband, they do as much as in them lieth to renounce Christ, to ban- ish his Truth from them, to betray the freedom of this realm, and perchance shall in the end do small comfort to your- self.'

At this point MQS goes into hysterics again. Erskine tries to calm her down, and gives her 'many pleasing words of her beauty, of her excellency, and how that all the Princes of Europe would be glad to seek her favour.' But this just casts 'oil in the flaming fire'. Knox stands still 'without any alteration of countenance for a long session', and finally astounds us with this:

'Madam, in God's presence I speak, I never delighted in the weeping of any of God's creatures; yea, I can scarcely abide the tears of my own boys, whom my own hand corrects, much less can I rejoice in your Majesty weeping. But seeing that I have offered you no just occasion to be offended, but have spoken the Truth, as my vocation craves of me, I maun sustain (albeit unwillingly) your Majesty's tears, rather than I dare hurt my conscience or betray my Common-wealth, through my silence.'

At this the Queen is 'more offended'. She orders Knox out. The 'meek and gentle' Dun remains with her, Lord John of Coldingham goes in, and they stay with her for about an hour. Meanwhile, outside, Knox finds that everyone except Lord Ochiltree is pre- tending not to know him. So he turns to the ladies of the court, sitting there in their 'gorgeous apparel' and says 'merrily':

'O fair ladies, how pleasing was this life of yours, if it should ever abide, and then in the end that we might pass to heaven with all this gay gear? But fie upon that knave Death, that will come whether we will or not, and when he has laid in his arrest, the foul worms will be busy with this flesh, be it never so fair and so tender; and the silly Soul, I fear, shall be so feeble, that it can neither carry with it gold, garnishing, targating [tasselled borders], pearl, nor precious stones.'

So Knox chats away with the women till Erskine of Dun comes out to take him home.

It should have been superfluous to quote this extraordinary passage at such length. But whereas every reader of every biography of MQS (and these have proliferated like midges in summer) encounters the gist of it – Knox made MQS cry – very few people now look at Knox's amazing *Historie*. When they do, they encounter, as I hope I have shown, great drama in all but format.

Suppose, for purposes of argument, that Knox, who was not taking notes at the time, much later elaborated imaginatively around a scene of less consequence than he would have us suppose? In that case, he was a great novelist born out of his time. Assuming, as I do, that a man so addicted to truth honestly set down what he remembered, observe that he did not need to give us so much detail. He displays a passion to expose the complexity of this exchange. Yes, he dramatises himself favourably, as the honest pastor who like Luther before him 'can do no other' than what he does, irrespective of human feelings, and as the loving father who hates chastising his small sons. And yes, he represents MQS as absurdly out of control, tempestuously irrational. But he leaves us scope to feel with her, as the young woman contending (perhaps) with her conscience, rendered unsure of her own position as queen by what is put to her by this grave, forceful man (with his very long beard, not mentioned). Why did Knox feel compelled to report that, thrust out, he resorted to the company of court ladies? Well, it gives him scope for an exemplary admonition such as any divine of the period, Catholic or Protestant, might have delivered. But note the sense of humour displayed by the word 'merrily'. He knows fine that readers may be amused that instead of lavishing compliments, as Erskine might have done, upon these gorgeous creatures, softening them up, he pitches himself at once into his all-flesh-is-but-grass routine. *And yet they converse with him.*

Determined Knox-haters may sneer that he is merely trying to prove to us that MQS is exceptional amongst young women in her obduracy in defiance of God's Truth. And yes, that could explain the inclusion of this otherwise gratuitous detail. It does not follow that the scene is implausible. Robert Louis Stevenson published a justly famous essay on Knox's relations with women, in which he makes one point in particular which is fundamental, and is still seized by shrewd historians: women in Knox's day were brought up to confess to male priests. Knox was a great preacher, but in the first instance a reluctant one, dragged into the role by admirers within the besieged community in the castle of St Andrews gathered around the men who had murdered Cardinal Beaton in 1546. However, once he settled into that role, as a pastor in Berwick and Newcastle, his charisma would attract well-to-do ladies used to pouring out their spiritual, and no doubt other, troubles to whatever acceptable cleric was on hand. Hence Knox's remarkable relationship with the Englishwoman Elizabeth Bowes, who became his mother-in-law and, going with her daughter, deserted her husband to be with him in Geneva. She was one of several – it has been suggested that Anna Locke, wife of a Protestant London mercer, may actually have been the love, so to speak, of his life, though in no carnal sense. Knox, an insecure and timorous man by disposition, seems to have felt more comfortable with women than with men. Stevenson characterises him as 'a man of many woman friends; a man of some expansion toward the other sex; a man ever ready to comfort weeping women, and to weep along with them.' It was mortifying to him, therefore, that MQS did not respond to his sincere goodwill. He was not a quarrelsome man – he got on well with fellow clerics, no mean feat in any age. In private, where in his later days he was surrounded by devoted women and beloved children, he was cheerfully companionable. Scotomariolaters dwell on how much he hurt MQS. Few have wondered how much she may have hurt the private feelings of John Knox.

Dr Rosalind Marshall's biography of Knox is not put off by the monstrous bluster of Knox's pamphlet *The First Blast of the Trumpet against the Monstrous Regiment of Women*, directed against Mary of England. As she says, 'Knox was not conjuring up a picture of a huge army of women on the march against the opposite sex. In his day, "regiment" meant rule, and so he was attacking the monstrous (meaning unnatural) rule of women.' No one – literally no one – in Knox's day would have disagreed with the basis of his argument, that women should always be subordinate to men. But in practice, women might function as queens and regents. What shocked Jean Calvin and many other people when they saw Knox's pamphlet was its wider application. Knox, in a Scottish tradition which we first see blinking in daylight as early as the Declaration of Arbroath, believed that subjects might rise up and depose bad rulers. Stevenson quotes with approval a marvellous statement from the pamphlet: 'we are debtors to more than princes, to wit, to the great multitude of our brethren'. Dr Marshall, succinctly and most readably, makes complete sense of Knox in his times and produces, without hero-worship, a complex and attractive human being.

Liz Lochhead, in her seminal play *Mary Queen of Scots Got Her Head Chopped Off,* likewise notes and responds to complexity. Her Knox appears, for instance, in conversation with Bothwell, who murdered Mary's first husband and became her second. With some evidence to back her, she represents the two men as kinsmen, and her Knox says with vehemence in confidential privacy what the historical Knox said in public:

If the word of God teaches men that all earthly palaces and power systems are robbers' caves then the punishment o' wicked princes is the *duty* of their subjects. I will leave it

unto God to deal with the prince o' this realm. I am shair
the Good Lord will protect her, if she deserve to be protectit.
Neither I, nor the yane true kirk have ony richt tae interfere.
And I'd advise you no' tae either Maister Hepburn O'
Bothwell.

Yet, even as well played as he was in the original Communicado
production by the director himself, Gerry Mulgrew, Lochhead's
Knox cannot escape the logic of the tale. In the final scene where
the characters in the play are transformed into children in the street,
'Wee Knoxxy' is teased and his head is forced up a girl's skirt. He
is terrified. 'Yuck it, youse! Yuck it. Dinnae! Ah doan't like lassies.
Ma faither says I'm no' tae play wi' lasses.' The historical Knox
did like lassies. But 'Wee Knoxxy's faither represents the dark tradition of denial which is, as I have stressed, ineluctably present in
that image, which we owe to Knox's own writing, of the domi-
neering preacher refusing to allow a young woman 'free' choice in
marriage.

However, Lochhead's quite sympathetic presentation of the historical Knox is an exception proving the general rule that since
Stevenson Scotland's best writers have tended to use 'Knox' as short-
hand for 'grim repressive Calvinism', and leave it at that. One could
make a film much more moving and intelligent than *Braveheart*
out of the extraordinary tale of the lad from East Lothian of obscure, plebeian origins who suddenly in his thirties found his vocation as a great preacher, suffered as a slave in the French galleys,
emerged to charm the ladies of Northern England, to befriend in
exile the greatest theologian of his day, to return to spearhead (with
tongue, not sword) a revolution in his native land, and to die with
the Reformed Church he had craved rearing itself tentatively up-
right. But while one may amuse oneself casting the movie (Harrison
Ford as Knox? Catherine Zeta Jones as MQS?), it will quite certainly not be produced in our lifetimes. All we can do for the moment is rescue Knox from the idiotic imputation that more or less
single handed he destroyed Scottish culture, while noticing the

strengths as well as weaknesses of the Calvinist tradition which undoubtedly looked back to his life and writings while it assumed fitful and partial (not continuous and complete) control of Scottish social and emotional life.

In a very late essay (1976), Hugh MacDiarmid quoted, with contempt, a Lanarkshire newspaper: 'During the Reformation, John Knox, who had a hatred of art in any form, smashed many church windows'. In fact, Knox distanced himself from the actions of the 'rascal multitude' (his term) who vandalised ecclesiastical property after he preached that famous, inspiring sermon at Perth on 11 May 1559, at the outset of revolution. Much artwork had gone already, due to English invasions and Scotttish neglect. Stevenson refers wrily to the prevalent notion of Knox 'breaking beautifully carved work in abbeys and cathedrals, that had long smoked themselves out and were no more than sorry ruins, while he was still quietly teaching children in a country gentleman's family'. Nevertheless, it is plausible to suggest that he approved of austere churches, such as Dutch Calvinism later favoured, and such as might have appealed to many others simply on grounds of cost. The widespread, at times obsessional, conviction that he single-handed stamped out Scottish drama, and prevented it matching the achievements of Shakespeare et al by the Thames, deserves rather more space here.

In his *Literary History of Scotland* (1903), J.H. Miller produced what is now a familiar scenario. With the Reformation:

> The old sports and pastimes of the poor were suppressed with a heavy hand... For well-nigh a hundred and fifty years [down, we observe, to the ever-blessed Union of 1707] the desolating influence of a gloomy and intolerant fanaticism brooded over the country... If we may judge by Lyndsay's *Satyre*, no nation could have showed a fairer promise of playing a worthy part in the dramatic revival which is the glory of English literature at the end of the sixteenth and the beginning of the seventeenth century. But... that promise was irretrievably blasted.

Edwin Muir quoted this in his wee tract *Scott and Scotland* (1936), a book still taken seriously. Muir said that 'the complete prohibition put upon drama by the Reformers just when it seemed on the point of developing' was''probably crucial for Scottish literature' and 'signalised the beginning of Scotland's decline as a civilised nation'. Poetic drama had a 'central and decisive' position in the development of English, French and German literature. Ergo, its absence, according to Muir, explained why Scottish literature was no damn good. Paradoxically Muir also upbraided his fellow-countrymen for not producing religious verse to match that of Donne, Herbert and so on: 'all that Scotland could show' in the age of the English Metaphysicals, 'was a metrical version of the Psalms, which is a curiosity'. This argumentation backs up Muir's notion that Scots were crippled by feeling in one language and thinking in another – his version of T.S. Eliot's theory about 'dissociation of sensibility' in English literature.

To start with that last point – I detect not the least sign of psychological crippledom in John Knox's own use of a Scottish English which is muscular, well-pointed, and actually well in front of most prose usage south of the border at that time. He anticipates the wonderful prose of the Authorised Version which is fundamental to English, as to Scots, literature. Writing and feeling are never the same thing for anyone, anywhere. A lot of Scots came to interiorise the language of the Authorised Version so that it seemed to represent their deepest feelings. English was not standardised as a language until the late seventeenth century. Up to then, good, pithy writing in Scottish English had as much authority as any other. An advantage of standardisation, which according to Eliot produced that deplorable 'dissociation' between feeling and utterance, was that English could replace Latin as the medium of scientific discourse. This remains an advantage, in so far as non-Lothian speakers might have trouble reading a paper in nuclear physics written in the idiom of Robert Garioch.

Now for Muir's point about poetic drama. Like Millar's equally idiotic view, this is based on simultaneous boast and cringe. Granted that Scotland is as big and important a country as England, it is amazing / disgusting / despair-inducing that it does not have a body of literature like that of England, conforming to the same supposed pan-European pattern of development. (Incidentally, why did Muir leave out Spain? Not read Lope, eh?) The fact that German poetic drama such as Muir approved of developed two centuries after the Elizabethans, in the era of Ossian, is, for Muir, neither here nor there. Nor is the fact that the ballad and song-making tradition of Scotland, the country's special glory, developed and proceeded apace through the seventeenth and eighteenth centuries, culminating in Robert Burns, a writer such as France, England, etc, have never had. According to Muir, the terrible fact that Scotland had no Webster (say), let alone Shakespeare, is the reason why our literature is stunted by comparison with England's. Cringe, cringe before the exemplary Southern neighbour...

But Scotland was in fact not a large nation hamstrung, but a nimble wee country with no more than one-fifth of England's population. A comparison with Scandinavian lands of comparable population is by no means to Scotland's disadvantage.

Facts about drama... In medieval Scotland, as elsewhere in Europe, there was 'folk drama' in the forms of plough plays and May games led by Robin, or Robert, Hood. There were Mystery Plays performed by craftsmen in towns, cycles representing Biblical events. And there were court entertainments – tournaments, dances, masques – with a dramatic character. One of Lyndsay's functions at the court of James v was to organise such things.

It can be said without the slightest reservation that the first impact of 'Reformation' on Scotland *encouraged* drama of a more intellectual and provocative nature. Knox approved of Friar Kyllow who presented a reforming Passion Play at Stirling in 1535 and got himself burnt as a martyr for his troubles. In Dundee in the 1540s, James Wedderburn unleashed reforming plays, now lost, well abreast of comparable developments in England. 'Reformation is a natural topic for the dynamic mode of drama', as Sarah Carpenter puts it in her authoritative survey of 'Early Scottish

Drama, (*The History of Scottish Literature*, 1988). Lyndsay's great
Satyre of the Thrie Estaitis may have begun life in partial draft at
Linlithgow Palace in 1540 as a play used by James v to warn his
Bishops to stay in order. But by the time the magnificent version
which survives was produced in the open air in Cupar, Fife in 1552,
it had become a huge piece of community theatre, incorporating
elements doubtless derived from rural and urban folk practices
with ideas about drama which Lyndsay had picked up in France,
and arguing exhaustively the case for reform of the church – as
must have done the presumably different version acted before the
Regent Mary of Guise in Edinburgh in 1554, for which we have
evidence of participation by craftsmens's guilds, as in Mystery Plays.

Lyndsay was not a proclaimed Protestant. Amongst goods he
left when he died was a rosary. His play perfectly represents an
exciting period in which serious Catholics were as fully convinced
as followers of Luther and Calvin that the Church needed
'reformacioun'. And around the very moment of Lyndsay's death,
in 1555, it was a Parliament under a Catholic Regent which banned
folk drama involving 'Robert Hude', 'Lytill John', 'Abbot of
Unresson', 'Quenis of May'. This didn't represent some specially
Scottish hatred of pleasure. It was part of the process which would
generate similar edicts all over Europe, Catholic as well as Protestant – the prime concern was with law and order.

Enter Knox. He approved of Lyndsay, as an ally in the days of
Beaton's murder, and his approval may have contributed to
Lyndsay's phenomenal popularity in post-Reformation Scotland.
Copies of his much-reprinted works were found in many country
cottages. People memorised great chunks of Lyndsay. In the eighteenth century, a writer noted that Lyndsay was 'little less necessary in every family than the Bible'. It is not surprising, though,
that Lyndsay's great play was never again performed after 1554.
Not only had it ceased to be topical, the resources of time and
effort required to stage it would always be in short supply, as indeed they are to this day. Knox disapproved of the masking that
went on in Mary's court, though he thought dancing, by an other-

wise sound, Protestant queen would be allowable. As for plays, near the end of his life, when civil war had prompted him to exile himself from Edinburgh, where his erstwhile ally, the turncoat Kirkcaldy of Grange, held the castle for MQS, Knox attended the wedding of one Colville, minister of East Kilbride. The celebrations included a play about the hoped-for storming and capture of Edinburgh Castle by the King's Party. The action culminated in a scene where Kirkcaldy of Grange and two others were hanged in effigy. Knox presumably watched with approval, for he had long been predicting that Kirkcaldy would be hanged 'in the face of the sun'. It seems quite baseless to suggest that Knox was opposed to drama as such.

As the King grew up, his court became a centre of dancing and entertainments. His consort Anne of Denmark, furthermore, was fond of such things. Scotland, to emphasise the obvious, did not have a huge capital city capable of supporting several public theatres as London did. Edinburgh was no mass market. The Court was the only arena in which drama comparable to Shakespeare's and Jonson's could have developed. The person who killed Scottish drama was not Knox, but James VI, when he removed himself to London to become James I.

It is undeniable that the temper of Presbyterianism in Scotland, as it shook down between 1603 and the Covenant of 1637, was antipathetical to drama and all carnal arts. But, to repeat crucial points – not only were the poems of Lyndsay, Dunbar, Henryson and James VI's Papist court poet Montgomerie – known and cherished by very ordinary people, but the wonderful language of the Authorised Version swept all before it, while the song tradition continued to flourish, and at the friendly frontier between folk and genteel culture Sir Robert Sempill of Beltrees wrote the poem in memory of his piper, Habbie Simpson, which gave Fergusson and Burns their 'Standard Habbie' metre. It is cringe that denies the song tradition its rightful pride of place in Scottish cultural history (the English see folksongs as simple stuff – they must be correct to think that odes are better). What further creates the impression that the period in Scotland between 1603 and 1707 was one of near-total cultural drouth is the venial but unfortunate conviction amongst generations, now, of literary intelligentsia, that Calvinism Was A Bad Thing. This means that interesting and powerful writings of the Covenanting period of religious dissension (1637–89) are routinely and completely ignored. They illuminate the soil from which later Enlightenment sprang, or, to vary the metaphor, display the midden from which it was fertilised.

Let us grant that Calvinism Is A Bad Thing, why did so many Scots (along with numerous English people, be it remembered, including the founders of Massachusetts) succumb to this Bad Thing? Firstly, it is intellectually the most coherent of theologies. If God exists, it is hard to deny that he must be as Calvin describes him. Secondly, because of this, it is better adapted than other theologies to rational procedures in business and science. Great success in these fields was barely open to Scots, at home, during the seventeenth century. But it could be said that a disposition to rationality, along with the commitment to education which Knox shared with fellow-Reformers and which was pursued by his successors, stood Scots in extremely good stead as their prospects improved in the eighteenth century.

But, thirdly, there must be some other reason, or set of reasons, why many Scots felt at home in this austere creed. It is arguable, 'counterfactually', that if Knox hadn't fallen under Calvin's spell in Geneva in the 1550s, Scotland's Reformation might have proceeded on Lutheran lines. But in terms of what is objected to nowadays – the evolution of a puritanical way of life – could the results have been any different? Lutherans also can be Puritans. Knox was nothing like Hitler in temperament, did not have at his disposal the modern mass media which reinforced Nazism, and could not conceivably, single-handed, or even with thousands of ministers exactly so-minded, have brainwashed the consciousness of Lowland Scots. Scots must have been tending anyway towards a social order in which literacy and thrift were prized. Along with these values went a spirit combining a strong sense of responsibility for others with a dogged commitment to personal dignity corresponding to that voiced by Knox in the interview when he made his Queen cry. His transatlantic biographer W. Stanford Reid is not exaggerating when he suggests in his *Trumpeter of God* that 'Knox brought into focus the Scottish concept of the right of the people to resist the Government'.

Descendants of the Lowland Scots for whom Knox was self-evidently a hero now share territory with the descendants of Irish Catholics entering *en masse* since the mid-nineteenth century, Catholic and Jewish immigrants from other parts of Europe, and people from the Indian sub-continent with altogether non-Christian traditions. One reason why revulsion against Knox and the Covenanting tradition is venial is that emphasis on them might seem to shut doors upon fellow-countrymen of non-Protestant background. But the history of Scottish culture simply cannot be understood if Reforming traditions are ignored or casually denounced.

To end on a purely personal note. When I was thirteen my parents took me to Geneva, where my father had work to do for the United Nations. We stayed a month. Geneva is not rich in spectacular artefacts. The one which would stick in my mind was the Monument to the Reformation. Large statues of Calvin and other Reformers are arrayed along a wall. One is of Knox. When I saw this first, I felt intense pride. Here, in this foreign city, stood a Scot, awesome.

2001

Describing Scottish Culture

IN THE SUMMER OF 1792, the Edinburgh lawyer, George Thomson, a clerk in the Board of Trustees for the Encouragement of Art and Manufacture in Scotland but also a keen amateur musician, wrote to Robert Burns, the famous ploughman poet, now an exciseman in south-west Scotland. His project was to produce a *Select Collection of Scottish Airs* and have them set by leading continental composers. Beside Haydn's star pupil Pleyel, he eventually enlisted Haydn himself and Beethoven.

Burns was already working as virtual editor of James Johnson's *Scots Musical Museum*, another multi-volume project, but he couldn't resist Thomson's appeal. Thomson offered 'any reasonable price' if Burns would write songs to go with melodies which he would send him, either amending old words or writing new ones. Burns was full of zest. He sternly insisted that he wouldn't provide *English Verses*. 'As to remuneration,' he went on, 'you may think my songs either *above* or *below* price; for they shall absolutely be one or the other. In the honest enthusiasm with which I embark on your undertaking, to talk of money, wages, fee, hire, etc. would be downright sodomy of soul!'

At this very time, the young Edinburgh lawyer, Walter Scott, admitted to the bar in July, was beginning his 'raids' into the Border country in search of old ballads, preserved in manuscript or heard from the lips of farmers, dominies, old beldames, bonnet lairds and labourers. Collecting oral tradition was for Scott also at this time a matter of pure enthusiasm. He had no notion that the *Minstrelsy of the Scottish Border* would make him famous. His literary energies over the next few years were concentrated on translations from the German of Schiller, Burger and Goethe, catching up with the *sturm und drang* proto-Romanticism of central Europe.

Not quite unknown to each other personally – Burns had met the boy Scott briefly – the two men were working independently and with almost equal disinterestedness on a project such as would fire many others in many countries: the retrieval and consolidation of national oral tradition.

In other countries, such work flowed over a political agenda: the assertion of national pride, as in the Russia of Pushkin and Gogol, or the aim of national independence, as in the smaller European countries freed by the Versailles settlement of 1919. In Scotland it seems on the face of it to have produced no more than the sentimental right-wing sub-nationalism of the middle and late nineteenth century, which generated monuments to Wallace and melodramatic history paintings and which was very, very belatedly followed by the establishment of a School of Scottish Studies at Edinburgh University after the Second World War. If Scotland in the 1790s could be seen as leading Europe in the recovery of national culture, it was not till the 1960s that something like a serious movement for political independence was in being. This has caused great retrospective anguish to Tom Nairn and other contemporary cultural nationalists. My purpose here is to provide a description of Scottish culture, historical and actual, which we might live with comfortably. Margaret Bennett, of the School of Scottish Studies, remarked in my presence recently that the Folk Song Revival of the 1950s seems to be the basis of our contemporary national consciousness and of what seems like a cultural renaissance. I think there are good reasons why this may be true.

I apply the term 'culture' in its broadest definition, to refer to all the customs, practices, activities and products in a given society which go beyond the barest requirements of survival and reproduction. Even the way in which a starving man catches and eats a fish will be culturally determined. Culture is a superstructure upon geography rather than on an economic base. In Marxist terms, it involves a form of false consciousness, when users of a certain language, living in a certain area, see themselves as joined in a commonalty irrespective of their diverse relations to the means of

production, distribution and exchange. It is so profoundly implicated in geography that the culture of settler or immigrant groups
– for instance, Scots in Canada – however much it preserves and
emphasises links with its culture of origin, rapidly becomes distinctive. Conversely, indigenous commonalties resisting accultura-
tion modify the cultures of dominant invaders. Sometimes incomers
may applaud and exaggerate this outcome, as when white New
Zealand rugby players rally in a Maori Haka, or English residents
in our Highlands become fanatical about the Gaelic language. Do
we now live in a postmodernist global village in which the current
phase of triumphant imperialism, associated with satellite TV and
with English as a *lingua franca*, will shortly obliterate all features
of local cultures which it cannot market as lifestyle or package as
'heritage'? I don't think so. China is the most populous country on
earth. Chinese culture is so ancient, so distinctive and so deeply
imbued with chauvinism, that the economic rise of China should
in itself guarantee the persistence of cultural plurality. Nevertheless, international imperialist culture has to provide the first of my
models.

The McDonald's hamburger epitomises this culture. In any city
anywhere one looks for a familiar logo and finds, reliably, the same
reliable products. (The french fries are so good, by the way, because they are cooked in the dripping from the beef.) Despite its
name, the chain has not the slightest Scottish association. Side dishes
and decor vary marginally to suit presumed local taste, but if much
were different one's small child, a demanding customer, would not
accept the place as a real McDonald's. I will not belabour the point
that Hilton Hotels and their competitors aspire to, and generally
achieve, similar universal blandness and comfort. The businessman and, perversely, the tourist expect and receive standard amenities. One of them is fluency in the English language on the part of
those in charge. This is the next stop after the airport, with its
stalls of world best sellers in English and its duty-free shop purvey-
ing some permutation or other of the brands of liquor, owned by
vast conglomerates, which, effectively detached from their origins,

signify varieties of good taste. Brands alter significance as marketing strategies dictate. It is a little known fact that Marlboro ciga-
rettes, possession of which is now a world-wide symbol that a
young chancer has made it, were advertised by Philip Morris in
1927 as a luxury brand aimed at women who were laggard as
consumers of the weed. 'Women, when they smoke at all, quickly
develop discriminating taste.' But in the 1950s it was snatched
away from women, given a filter but also its famous masculine
cowboy image, packaged in a flip-top, crush-proof box with distinctive red and white colours, and launched on its way to becoming the most popular cigarette, first in the USA (by 1976), then
internationally. Let us not deceive ourselves that the presence of
Glenmorangie whisky or Scottish smoked salmon in the airport
shops, means that an element of our own culture has international
valency. On the contrary, something we value for our own reasons
has been carried away from us to occupy such and such a vacant
or contested niche in the international market which trades in terms
of its own shifting system of differences.

We easily ignore how all pervasive, and yet how recent, this
international culture is. A hundred years ago there were very few
motor cars, radio and film did not exist and when white settlers
were establishing Kenya Colony, they traded in an oriental bazaar
set up by the Indians who came with them. All boats to China
were, by our standards, very slow. The Burns Supper in Sydney,
San Francisco, Buenos Aires, Calcutta and elsewhere was a strenu-
ous attempt to assert a universally-standard Scottishness in a variety of more or less alien environments. Now it is hard to distinguish
from other lifestyle choices, like the German food promotion in
the local bar or the film season put on by the Institut Français.
And it is not just airports and hotels which are internationally
standardised. 'There is no fixed time for breast feeding', as the
Ugandan poet Okot p'Bitek pointed out in the Sixties, subverting
with simple truth the impatient imperialist schedule. 'African time',
like 'Hebridean time', will insist that lateness for appointments is
normal and doesn't really matter. But both do so in the face of a

situation where restaurants, whatever cuisine they proffer, are expected to be open at midday and over a certain period in the evening. The customers expect to sit in chairs, items originally specific to Western and Chinese culture only, to use cutlery and to be offered three or four courses, followed by coffee. A restricted range of styles of dress is permissible. The usual credit cards are accepted everywhere. While native Malawians, for instance, relish a wide variety of grubs – I have a cookbook from that country which tells you how to prepare bee larvae, grasshoppers, termites, caterpillars and so on – you do not find these items on hotel menus in Malawi or in the small local supermarkets. They will arrive in Safeways, perhaps, one day, tinned like New Zealand oysters or French snails, or bagged like pork crackling, designated as exotic snacks or starters and so assimilated with international culinary norms. At the other extreme from Safeways, we have the primary culture of the Inuit of the North Shore of Alaska, as interpreted for us by Tom Lowenstein in his beautiful and remarkable book – *Ancient Land, Sacred Whale*. The people of Tikigaq lived on a peninsula which had once been a whale-like creature, slain by a shamanic harpooner. The bodies of whales hunted and eaten rejoined the mythic whale's body. Specific ways of killing, storing and eating animal food formed part of an ideological system which was articulated like a poem. Baked beans, which the Inuit eat these days, weren't, in terms of that system, real food at all.

Between the primary, elemental cultures of groups of hunter gatherers inseparable from the climate, terrain, fauna and flora of the commonalty's habitat, and the system of free floating signs in contemporary imperialist culture, there is a range of other models which have relevance for us. The settled agricultural civilisations of the ancient world – we could take ancient Egypt as an example – created cultures which involved articulations of difference affecting gender, occupation and status in systems that were tightly knit but not impervious to change over time. The culture of the ancient Greeks, peripheral to several such empires, borrowed hugely from Egypt, but also from the mobile Phoenicians (West Semites) who gave those who wrote down Homer their alphabet. Syncretic, adaptable, expansive, the culture of Periclean Athens, a small city by our standards, prefigured the patterns not only of later nation-state cultures, but of national-imperial ones. Famously, drama festivals, sporting events and political assemblies were institutions involving all citizens.

Rome developed the imperial aspects of the Greek model hugely. Here the distinction between 'high' and 'popular' culture which now confuses discussion, clearly emerges in the cynical wisdom so much admired by Edward Gibbon, with which Roman rulers, themselves free-thinking, encouraged the religious superstitions and calendar customs, however irrational they might hold them to be, which served to keep the populace subservient.

I will not dawdle through the Middle Ages. As we hop to the brink of the modern era, the Athenian republican model has been momentously developed in the city states of Florence and Venice, the Roman imperial model, in its own way, by the papacy, and the nation states of Western Europe are in formation. At this time – by the 1470s – the territory claimed by the Kings of Scots lies exactly within the borders of present day Scotland. The inhabitants speak a variety of languages and dialects, and their sense of common difference from the English is not fully developed. Gaelic speakers remain almost undistinguishably linked with their Irish cousins. Borderers, Scots and English, form part of a cattle culture involving endemic feuding but mutually resistant to the demands of Scottish and English Crowns for order and peace. Even the Scottish court is not very often in Edinburgh. In some respects, Scotland is less 'developed' than the polities centring on the cities of London, Paris, Moscow and even Stockholm. But it is geographically both extensive and compact, a different kind of arena from most of Europe which is patchworked with local authorities, cities, bishoprics, dukedoms, and so on, owing general allegiance, soon to be widely contested, to the universal Catholic church. At this point, I want to contrast the Scotland of James III, IV and V with two other models which emerged fully, elsewhere, rather later – the

Muscovite, Russian model, and the Bourbon French model. Russian speakers spread over a vast plain subject to raids from non-Christian Tartars and incursions by Catholics – Germans, Poles and Lithuanians – and by Swedes who were ultimately Protestant. Their capital, Moscow, was distant from all seas. Their culture, subject to oriental influence was nevertheless doggedly Christian, and in that respect 'European'. Their language spread with remarkably little differentiation of dialect wherever the tsars were able to establish a system which was squarely based on serfdom, a practice that inhibited the tendency of labourers to run away into the Cossack borderlands or push into scantily-peopled Siberia. The history of this highly distinctive culture is marked by famous turning points – Peter the Great's opening to the West and establishment of St Petersburg as a capital and port, Catherine's introduction of architectural and educational principles from the Western European Enlightenment and the rise, in the nineteenth century, of rich schools of literature, music and painting. We can attribute to the Russian sense of cultural commonalty both the extraordinarily broad humanity of Pushkin, Turgenev, Tolstoy and Chekhov, and the extreme chauvinism of Dostoevsky and Solzhenitsyn. It is now amply evident that Russian culture, Orthodoxy and all, survived the attempts of Stalin to replace it with secular and purportedly internationalist forms: indeed in 1941–45 Stalin himself, Georgian though he was, became perforce an extreme Russian nationalist.

It is obvious at once how this culture is different from our own. Scotland is slashed by the sea, has always given and taken influences across the waters and, by the seventeenth century, was dominated by a type of reformed Christianity which, whatever its totalising aspirations, proved particularly susceptible to transition to secular, capitalist values. Scottish culture is remarkably diverse within a relatively small area and any suggestion that it has ever been, or should be, 'racially' homogenous can only be dismissed with contempt. Like Russian culture, it is marked by a fierce sense of difference, but this is not difference from sharply distinct Tartars and Catholics but more elusive divergence from English people close in many ways, delimited by a border which has always been more like a revolving door than a portcullis.

The notion that Scots and French are somehow close may be true for many on a personal level. Culturally, it makes no sense: whereas our country has strong affinities with the Breton, Basque and Occitanian cultures included within France's longstanding borders. French culture, by the late seventeenth century, had been consciously fashioned as a model for Europe. Paris gave cultural laws. Versailles was the pluperfect monument to absolutist monarchy.

The French language was standardised and regulated for literary and intellectual purposes. Classicising rules were laid down for drama and poetry, and internalised even by the free-thinking Voltaire, who found Shakespeare wild and at times disgusting. The *Encyclopaedia* was a great project of the eighteenth-century intelligentsia to make all useful knowledge available in French, matched by Buffon's enormous, compendious Natural History. Love it or loathe it, this French metropolitan culture was immensely strong. The British Royal Academy imitated one of its centralising, regulating institutions, the *Encyclopaedia Brittanica*, founded in Edinburgh, emulated one of its major achievements. Enlightened people in clubs and masonic lodges all over the world knew the important French texts. Breaking from the dominant French model was important for intellectuals in Germany and Russia when they attempted to establish distinctive national cultures; but Goethe and Pushkin, as they strove to forge cultural independence, remained fluent in French and as readers of French texts. The use of French as the *lingua franca* of diplomacy is only now passing away. However, France, centralised though its rulers tried to make it, whether Bourbons, Napoleon or demagogic politicians, was, as an imperial state corrupted by elements which belong to a different model, that which Britain best exemplifies. Unlike many people in these parts, I admire English culture and even love it. I have to point out, though, that since the eighteenth century it has been only one element, and not always the dominant one, in British culture. The English confuse themselves – speaking of Britain as 'England' –

into imagining that the culture which has at its centre the music of a German, Handel, which was comprehensively influenced by the literary works of Burns, Scott and Carlyle, ideologically dominated in the mid-nineteenth century by concepts deriving from the Scottish Enlightenment, and shown its own face by a succession of great Irish playwrights – Farquhar, Goldsmith, Sheridan, Wilde and Shaw – can be accurately described as 'English'. It is British, and Linda Colley's splendid book, *Britons* (1992), demonstrates how a 'British' national identity was forged by ordinary people all over the larger island. She could have gone further to consider to what extent the Irish, or some of them, implicated themselves in this process, which created the metropolitan culture of the largest empire the world has ever seen. John Mackenzie, Professor of Imperial History at Lancaster University, has argued convincingly that patriotic Scots willingly submerged their national independence for the sake of the opportunities offered them by empire, yet remained a distinctive presence in that empire, bringing their own social ethos to play as administrators, finding their own special contribution to be expressed by the great and supposedly good explorer, Livingstone. It was possible as John Buchan demonstrated to be a thoroughgoing imperialist and a kind of Scottish Nationalist. Scotland could be viewed as a separate entity within the empire, like Canada and Australia, essentially equal to England, though less populous.

The absurd belief that Scots were brainy, the English merely instinctual and vigorous, accepted on both sides of the border, epitomised in Hardy's fable of *The Mayor of Casterbridge*, enabled Scots to think, not always without reason, that they were really in charge. Certainly, Scots had hands on many levers of propaganda, as newspaper editors, later in the BBC and in the film industry, as well as supplying leadership in political parties and trade unions, and in industrial board rooms. Colonial subjects we have never been.

Around 1900, then, Scottish culture looks like this both to Scots and outsiders – it is a component, at the very centre, of the British

Empire. Its heroes, Bruce and Wallace, are accepted as great men who struggled for liberty, which, embodied in the Mother of Parliaments, is, along with Christianity and juries, one of the good reasons why Britons deserve to rule the waves and much of the world's landmasses. Its national bard, Burns, and its national historian, Scott, are accorded reverence wherever English is spoken and taught, and a new hero, Stevenson, represents the romantic contribution of the Scot, both as a questing wanderer and supreme story-teller. Scottish country dancing will be taught to Africans by missionaries, black Africans and paler Chinese will learn to use the bagpipes in their military formations. Scots mountains are the playground of the empire's elect on holiday, Scotch whisky the man's drink in the clubs of the Raj. Scottish singers and comedians are popular throughout the English-speaking world. And beyond this, Scottish writers – not just Buchan, but Barrie and Kenneth Grahame – are performing the now traditional role, which goes back to Smollett, Boswell, Ivanhoe and Carlyle, of telling the English what they are like, just so's they know.

However, they aren't alone. The Pole Conrad, the Americans James and Eliot, and various Irishmen are also involved in defining English culture. It is characteristic of the 'imperial state' model that the peripheries invade the centre. (This happens in Paris, where the great Parisian school of painting is utterly cosmopolitan, where French composers play obsessively with Spanish themes and respond avidly to jazz, where Milhaud, adventuring musically into exotic places, also asserts his own Occitanian identity, and the black products of French colonial education which was designed to assimilate them completely – Cesaire and Senghor – are, before the Second World War, beginning to establish an 'African' presence in modern literature.) Towards the end of this century blacks and Asians from the former empire – Chaudhury and Naipaul, Walcott and Dabydeen – have joined in the game of explaining to the English who they are.

A typical Englishman, we might say, now eats curry and Chinese food frequently, supports a football team with a Scottish manager and an Irish, Welsh or French striker, with perhaps a Dutch or Zimbabwean goalie thrown in, and a cricket team largely made up of Southern African whites and people of recent Caribbean origin, and he watches with fascinated semi-comprehension Scottish actors in Taggart and the John Byrne series.

If he has literary tastes, he may well believe that the Irishman Yeats, the American Eliot and perhaps the Welshman Thomas are the major 'English' poets of the twentieth century. He may or may not realise that Anglo-Scottish origins probably helped to give Evelyn Waugh the angles on Englishness which make him so wickedly readable. Every so often, intellectuals of left or right rise up in exasperation to reassert truly English tradition – George Orwell, E.P. Thompson, Enoch Powell. But the task of separating that from the imperial culture has hardly been begun. Europeanisation and Americanisation complicate it excruciatingly. We Scots are much better off. We do not usually think so, perhaps because many of us measure our own culture against another model and find it wanting. This model is provided by the development, from the Napoleonic period onwards, of new nationalisms in Europe. Typically, these rally round a language spoken in part of an imperial state – Catalan in Spain, Finnish in the Russian Empire, Norwegian in the Danish polity, Hungarian, Czech and so on in the Austro-Hungarian Empire. Commonalties of language users inspired by Burns, Scott – and in most cases also by 'Ossian' Macpherson – reconstruct ancient epics, such as the Finnish Kalevala, collect folksongs, like Bartok and Kodaly, write historical novels and national anthems, and advocate national cuisines and styles of dress. Though intellectuals started the process, the results are not shallow. The Lithuanian song festivals, and their counterparts in other Baltic states, maintained national identity under the Russian occupation resumed by Stalin. The Welsh language has made very significant political gains though only a minority of Welsh people can use it. So have the Basques and the Catalans. Some people from these foreign commonalties find it impossible to understand why Scottish Nationalists and home rulers don't demand national status for Gaelic. Few are attuned to the ironies involved in the actual use, in the streets and in English literature, of Scots.

Set against this small-nation nationalist model, Scottish culture looks confused and incomplete. Apart from our self-expression in three or more languages (it's worth remembering, though, that some Finns write in Swedish and the Czech Republic's greatest dead writer used German), we have no vital nationalist school of music – people like McCunn and Mackenzie, early in the twentieth century, functioned as imperial composers, parts of the Scottish component of empire – we spurn or laugh at what is taken to be our national costume, except as regalia at weddings and at football matches, and we have never managed to acquire the habit of throwing bombs at the English or burning down the homes of English incomers. Our sounder intellectuals deny that there is a Scottish tradition of painting, separable from international influences, in the face of English cultural bureaucrats who want to give us a National Gallery of Scottish Art.

The story of Scottish painting actually points to a more general characteristic of our culture. It hasn't, like Czech culture (as we might see that), flowed in its underground channel from the Hussites to Janacek and Martinu and Vaclav Havel beneath various alien political and economic impositions. It does not rather straightforwardly centre on such a medieval corpus as the Icelandic sagas or on a body of folklore and nationalist music such as Finland's. It is made up of bits and pieces, striking and distinct in their own ways, which seem almost antagonistic to each other.

The creation in the seventeenth century of our national Church involved the abandonment of the rich tradition of writing in Scots in favour of the prose of the English bible. The great men of our Enlightenment strove to write perfect English while Ramsay, Fergusson and Burns revived Scots. Our hugest literary figure, Scott, the inventor of our history, was, pace his present day namesake Paul, a committed Unionist who forsook the national church for the Episcopalian rituals of the genteel. Our largest Victorian figures – Carlyle, Livingstone, Stevenson – were determined emigrants. Our greatest twentieth-century writer, MacDiarmid, denounced Burns and Scott, and more subversively still, Scottish folksong. Which brings me, not before time, to a crucial component in the model of Scottish culture which I now wish to offer you. Let us accept that Scottish culture is richly syncretic. By the middle ages, Celtic, Scandinavian and Norman English influences had marked it. It has continued to borrow not only from English culture but from Europe, from Dutch architecture in the seventeenth century, French painting around the turn of our own. It has been candidly open to American forms such as jazz and Country and Western music, and has been much quicker than the English to accept the end of the British Empire, hard though this bore on many Scots families and on the traditional markets for Scottish manufactures. But it has its own music and, associated with this music, words in Scots, in Gaelic and in English, which serve as a core of unexpungeable distinctiveness and profoundly influence many aspects of our culture. Our appropriation of the great 'Border' ballads could be seen as a case of brazen, successful cheek. It has been achieved because the persistence here of wandering tinker life on the edge of the commercial economy which emerged in the nineteenth century, and the thrawnness of Doric culture in the North East, permitted unbroken transmission, whereas in England the flow was broken. The national status – I mean Scottish national status – of Burns has clearly helped. Burns's greatest achievement, I believe, was not his revival, following Ramsay and Fergusson, of individualistic new verse in Scots, but his work for Johnson and Thomson in the preservation and enrichment of our song heritage. A vivid sense of this heritage explains a special virtue shared, in their different ways, by our greatest writers: their closeness to the people, to the crack of the pubs and the rhymes of the playground. It gives our literature some affinity with much American literature – the writings of Twain and Whitman and Carlos Williams and Faulkner and Tennessee Williams – with much Canadian and Australian writing, and with the vivid 'new writing' of the English-

speaking Caribbean. It moves, as it were, naturally between literary, genteel and demotic speech – a trick which some of the English picked up from Scott who, to be fair, had Shakespeare, the
Restoration dramatists, Defoe and Fielding as important exem-
plars, as well as his fellow countryman Smollett.

The status of poets in Scotland was both elevated and lowered
by Burns. In this connection, I remember a conversation in a pub
in West Lothian not long after MacDiarmid's death. One of the
regulars was a man called Frank who was, more or less openly, a
villain. He worked in what was euphemistically called 'civil engineering', that is on road-building, I think in haulage. He moon-
lighted as a hit man. He kept trying to persuade me to ghost his
memoirs, believing that his account of army experiences which
took him into every brothel from Cairo to Rome would make us
both rich as a pornographic bestseller. I mentioned that I hoped to
give a paper on MacDiarmid at a conference abroad. Frank said:
'Oh yes, MacDiarmid. He was a great man.' I can explain this
reaction only be attributing to him instinctive logic: 'Burns was a
famous poet. He was a great man. I have heard of MacDiarmid.
He was a poet. Therefore, he was a great man too.' I don't believe
there are many countries where a man of Frank's type would have
reacted thus. Bengal maybe. Certainly not in England. Professing
to despise folksong, even MacDiarmid positioned himself in the
dialogue with the Scottish commonalty. His powerful successors,
MacCaig, Morgan, Maclean, diversely do so, as, in a younger generation, does Tom Leonard. I can only think offhand of one indisputably major Scottish writer of the twentieth century – Edwin
Muir – who diverges from this into internationalist-English
Parnassian discourse. Stevenson most certainly did not: Byron's
address to his readers is one of the most Scottish things about him:
if we go way back to Dunbar, Lyndsay and Montgomerie, it is
striking how, unlike Wyatt and Sidney and Spenser, but like the
great Jacobean and Restoration dramatists, they escape from the
purlieux of court culture unashamedly into the streets and
farmtouns. Aristocratic women, as well as lowlier ones, have helped

preserve and have added to the song tradition, so that Violet Jacob's lyrics, for instance, are still sung around Montrose. I will not attempt to conscript either James Thomson of *The Seasons* or his namesake of *Dreadful Night* into this tradition; but, of course, both of them were based in London. The influence of Scott and Carlyle on Dickens partly explains his glorious transgressiveness and uninhibited demotic address; the scope of other great English nineteenth-century novelists was defined for them by Scott. But English literary culture in the age of Matthew Arnold and George Eliot prised high discourse from low, serious literature, and Oxbridge-dominated 'culture' from 'mass' understanding. One reason why Scottish writers have slumped in the canon of 'English literature' since is that they are associated with forms – rustic satire and simple song in Burns's case, historical romance in Scott's, boys' fiction in Stevenson's and 'funny dialect' in MacDiarmid's – deemed to be limited, sloppy or undignified, whereas Wordsworth's Cumbrian vowels and Keats's cockney were thought to have been sufficiently sublimated. Byron, of course, wasn't deemed high enough either to be truly, really, great, and his vast popularity came to be held against him. Better to be an ineffectual angel like Shelley.

I think we should cherish and enjoy our mongrel culture and its character which is established, in the renaissance of this century, as centrifugal *vis-à-vis* London and centripetal *vis-à-vis* the schools where Scottish children are taught and the pubs and halls where we sing. John Byrne is able to be as experimental with TV as Denis Potter without looking like an indignant anti-the-rest intellectual. No one seems to find it very odd that one of our rock stars has been a very serious Rector of Edinburgh University and another writes about Post Modernist culture for *The Guardian*. When Wendy Cope and Fiona Pitt Kethley produce funny poems, they marginalise themselves compoundedly as not only women, but light verse practitioners. Liz Lochhead centres herself in our culture with her serious jokes. Our more prominent younger painters, addicted to figuration, have returned to the Scottish habit of storytelling as exemplified in Wilkie and Orchardson. Our very impressive younger 'new music' composers – such as Judith Weir, McGuire, Sweeney, Macmillan – don't raid our folk music tradition but rather live in it. One can't imagine Ben Britten playing in a folk band like Eddie McGuire, or Johnny Taverner singing on that band's albums as James Macmillan has done. Neither Scot has thus compromised his 'international' standing. Both know that you can't be international if there are no 'nations', one of MacDiarmid's most important points. It is important that we don't discuss Scottish culture, or judge it, in terms of inappropriate models, taken to be not descriptive, but mandatory. I think the most clearly comparable culture to our own is the Irish, which has an overlapping musical tradition, a partly similar relationship to English culture, and a character marked like ours by waves of seaborne influences, though by even heavier emigration.

Set beside Ireland's, our culture competes, but cannot claim precedence in literature, probably stands more strongly in painting, architecture and decorative arts, is perhaps weaker in concert music, but at least even-stevens in popular cultural forms. Comparison with Wales reveals profound differences.

We have never had, nor should we now wish to create, a self-sufficient national culture like the French culture of Louis Quatorze and after. We have been enthralled by, but can detach ourselves from, the imperial-state culture of the London metropolis in which Scottish culture was a major component. We are less entangled with that, I fancy, than Ukrainians have been with Muscovite culture. We cannot now achieve, nor should we try to achieve, a language-based national culture on the Czech or Finnish model. Looking further afield though, there are helpful points of comparison and contrast with such cultures as those of Bengal and Catalonia, language based but located for centuries within larger encompassing political entities.

I should end with a word about the USA and our relationship to international-imperialist culture. The USA came into existence as a multi-ethnic nation, with elements of its settler population from every part of the north-west European archipelago, aka

'the British Isles', as well as German, Dutch, Swedish, French, His-
panic groups already within its borders or soon to be encompassed
by westward and southern expansion, and of course myriads of
Africans. The dominant communities during and after the revolution were heavily English, from New England and Virginia. But
the so-called 'Scotch-Irish' – in effect, protestant Scots who had
emigrated to Ireland then set off on a further migration – introduced whisky and began the transition from Anglo-Scottish folk
music to Country and Western as they rampaged down the Appa-
lachians slaying native American 'Indians'. There were also potent
affinities between presbyterian Scotland and congregationalist New
England. We have, I think, a fair claim to a large stake in the origins of US culture. However, European, Jewish and even East Asian
influences, together with the resurgence of African-American culture, give contemporary US culture such a character that we can't
assimilate its influences without threat to our own distinctiveness.
I think, though, that the pluralism of American culture (utterly
different from the centralist French model) makes it another impe-
rialist-state culture against which Scotland can hold out as its own
place. We cannot claim that we really run America, as we used to
claim we controlled England, but we can keep a consistent sense
of distance from the American ideology – we can place ourselves
in relation to it, but apart. The English (look at Thatcher and her
free market nonsense) are much more likely to get confused into
swallowing American assertions and pretending that they're part
of English heritage. In fact, much recent political struggle here can
be seen as involving resistance to Westminster's attempts to
Americanise Britain away from the Welfare State. We have allies in
Europe, even the French.

I don't think we'll lose our capacity to be different. My own
preferred notion of difference entails adaptation of the republican
model of society which had emerged in Macchiavelli's Florence
and was later expounded by the Englishman Harrington, and the
Scot, Fletcher of Saltoun, as well as appealing to other people all
over Europe. It involved not democratic but aristocratic control

over a state with no royal figurehead, or a ceremonial one. Those who owned land should meet to run the country. But this conception, both unappealing and unworkable now, elided into the eighteenth-century notion of the Republic of Letters, which is what people like Hume and Jeffrey believed they inhabited, and this further slipped towards the Burnsian point that a man (we would say 'person') is a man (or person) for all that. A radical re-interpretation of citizenship in a Scotland with its own parliament could draw on and adapt the ideas and temper of Fletcher and Hume and Adam Smith without reviving Hume's Toryism or succumbing to any simplistic version of Smith's economics.

I like to imagine Scotland as a nation re-asserting republican virtue against the corruption of the republican ideal in the USA.

1995

Scotland Since 1707

WELL, WAS THE UNION OF Parliaments in 1707 really the 'end of an auld sang', as Lord Seafield famously said at the time? An equally famous bon mot of the same period was Andrew Fletcher of Saltoun's statement that if he could make the nation's ballads, he didn't care who made its laws. As a law-making body, the Scottish parliament had not done much to sing about, before its final sessions which were graced by storming speeches from Fletcher and others against the idea of Union with England. Like other such institutions in Europe, the Scottish Parliament had represented propertied élites, not the people at large.

Scotland kept its ballads in spades. The century after Union saw marvellous efforts by Ramsay, Burns, Scott and others to preserve and extend the nation's heritage of song. Lairds and titled ladies, who wrote excellent lyrics, sang along, as it were, with their tenants and servants. By Treaty, Scotland preserved its own Established Church, governed since 1689 on Presbyterian lines which sharply differentiated it from England's, as did the character of its four old universities, open to all comers and ready to teach modern, practical subjects. Crucially, Scots Law remained separate. While Scots rose to the highest positions in the English legal system, no Englishman practiced in Scottish courts. Scots found parliamentary seats in England – there was no traffic the other way.

Our sense of history has been muddled by the picturesque Jacobite rebellions of 1715 and 1745. Bonnie Prince Charlie, who aimed to make his father King of England, was opposed by most Highland, as well as Lowland, Scots. His defeat came to symbolise the collapse of the old Gaelic order, but this was well under way before he arrived. Culloden was a victory for Presbyterian, Whiggish Scotland, which was still in practical terms its own nation after 1707, dominated by great landowners of old family and by clever lawyers of landowning stock. Politically, it was 'managed' for London governments by Scots who controlled the flow of crown patronage, in return for delivering the votes of Scottish MPs in support of English Prime Ministers. From the mid-1720s, John Campbell, Duke of Argyll, and his brother Archibald who succeeded him but is always referred to by his former title, 'Islay', presided for decades over an 'Argathelian' system which now seems monstrously corrupt, but which suited many Scots very well, in particular those who profited from a disproportionate siphoning of opportunities in the East India Company to avid aspirants north of the Tweed. There were plenty of Scots on hand to join in Clive's zestful Rape of Bengal after his victory at Plassey in 1757, and to do very well from the extension thereafter of British rule through India. From the 1770s, Scottish patronage was ordered by a lairdly lawyer, Henry Dundas, 'King Harry the Ninth', who became the most powerful man in British politics – not excluding his *protégé*, prime minister Pitt – through his near-absolute control over Scotland's few thousand parliamentary voters.

Dundas, who never set foot outside Britain, did everything he could to repair and extend Britain's intercontinental trade and imperial power after the loss of the Thirteen Colonies. No Scot had the least quarrel with such a project. Since the Union Scots had thriven mightily within the British, formerly English, Empire. Glasgow had won virtual monopoly over the rich trade in Virginia tobacco, which set it on its way to becoming a great city. It was said that a third of the planters on Jamaica, the wealthiest sugar-producing island in the British West Indies, were Scots. After Canada fell to Britain in 1759, Highland Scots came to dominate the North American fur trade. Fortunes earned, or pillaged, overseas were brought back to Scotland and applied to the startling 'improvement' of Scottish agriculture and the rapid rise of Scottish industry. Scots followed close on England's heels into the so-called 'commercial revolution' and if anything outstripped their Southern neighbours in the 'industrial revolution' which followed.

In Adam Smith, Scotland provided the prophet of a new world order, and the rapidly expanding middle class of his homeland throbbed with the pulse of prosperity. After Dundas's death, with final victory over Napoleon, Britain realised the old rogue's vision – a virtual monopoly of overseas colonies and advanced engineering technology, complete naval dominance in all oceans, and pole position in the new era of mass production in factories using steam power. It was extremely easy for Walter Scott to be both a devout Scottish patriot and a convinced believer in the Union with England, from which such benefits seemed to have flowed, along with a gratifying share in military and naval glory.

But Scott was at odds with the Whigs grouped around the *Edinburgh Review* who took the dismal science of Political Economy to the point where historic differences between Scotland and England seemed irrelevant in the new era of Free Trade and Utilitarian social policies. It was after such men had triumphed with Parliamentary Reform in 1832 and the *ancien régime* of Dundas, which his son had maintained, was finally scuppered, that Scottish self-command was jeopardised. The Disruption in the Kirk which produced the breakaway Free Church in 1843, represented and created unease, at a time when heavy Catholic immigration from Ireland was changing the character of Scotland's population. The new railways cut travel time to Southern England so sharply that Queen Victoria could make Balmoral her second home, and Englishmen could comfortably sit as MPs in Scottish constituencies for the Liberal Party which Scottish burghs now overwhelmingly favoured. Rich Scots sent their sons to English boarding schools, and the sporting estates of the Highlands became a favourite playground of their friends in the imperial ruling class and their foreign cronies. Edinburgh lost its position as a great independent capital of Enlightened thought, and its university gravitated towards English norms. Many of the best Scottish talents – Carlyle, Stevenson, Buchan, Barrie, the painter Orchardson, the composers Mackenzie, Wallace, McCunn and McEwan – would seek and find fame south of the Border.

Yet paradoxically the disproportionate Scottish stake in the overseas empire helped to maintain a strong sense of national distinctiveness. The local politicians who brought off the Canadian federation in 1867 were Scottish almost to a man. If Moffat, Philip and Livingstone worked in Southern Africa under the aegis of the London Missionary Society, Scottish missions and schools in India, Kenya, Malawi and elsewhere had sharp and peculiar impact. Scottish merchants flourished mightily in trade with the East, where Dundee, through jute, was in virtual symbiosis with Bengal, and the importation of tea became almost as fully a Scottish preserve as that of tobacco had once been. Above all, Glasgow, by 1900, revelled boastfully in its status as 'Second City' of the empire. Its shipyards sinewed the empire's commerce and navy. With its unique array of free and cheap municipal services, its wonderful art collections and its remarkable architecture, there was plenty to help its people transcend appalling standards of housing, far behind those of England.

In 1914, Scots were by and large complacent about their status in the world. Since Gladstone had put Home Rule on the agenda in the 1880s, on the grounds that if Ireland got it, Scotland should, there had been pressure, mostly from Liberals, towards it. But within the mighty British empire Scots believed, not without reason, that they provided the most enterprising businessmen, the most visionary industrialists, the most dynamic missionaries, the most skilful administrators, the most devoted and trustworthy professional men, and the best farmers. They had the most fish and superabundance of coal. They had developed the great tradition of working class self-help which informed the highly successful Co-operative Wholesale Societies, and which had inspired the creation of a Labour Party in Scotland ahead of England. Scotland had huge social problems, but Scots believed that Scots could tackle them. Onwards, as Ramsay Macdonald would put it, and upwards...

But by the time the confusedly idealistic MacDonald became Britain's first Labour Prime Minister, Scotland had been traumatised. It was not so much that the country had paid the price for disproportionate volunteering zeal with disproportionate casualties in the Great War. Scottish population actually rose between 1911 and 1921. Very suddenly, empire ceased to be a good deal. Scotland had depended on heavy industries and overseas markets. Post war slump hit these especially hard, along with coalmining, and the country was not well placed to acquire and build up the new light engineering, automobile and aircraft industries, which brought prosperity to large parts of England. As unemployment soared – to two-thirds at one point in Greenock – people drained away. Skilled and enterprising emigrants left despair behind them. Scots now had a grudge against history. This, not 1707, was the decisive watershed in Scottish attitudes. Boast gave way to whinge.

Though spite against Catholic immigrants persisted, and sectarian Protestant Parties briefly did very well in local elections in Glasgow and Edinburgh in the 1930s, the old religious spirit which had animated Scots and kept some of them sober was in decline. For many, Socialism became a substitute. The legend of the Red Clyde linked several discrete phenomena – the successful 1915 Rent Strike led by women which forced the Government to legislate against grasping landlords, the impalpable effects of John MacLean's adult education courses in Marxist economics, and the more tangible public response to his martyred imprisonment for his anti-war views, the agitation of shop stewards against deskilling of jobs in engineering under war conditions, and the sudden rise of Labour to dominance in the representation of the West of Scotland some time after the war, which reflected John Wheatley's success in switching the Catholic vote leftwards. 'Red Clyde' MPs thereafter formed a truculent element at Westminster, and more than incidentally tried to push through bills for Scottish Home Rule within the Empire. The rupture of the Independent Labour Party from the Labour Party in 1932, after Ramsay Macdonald had 'betrayed' the movement at the moment when Britain's economy felt the impact of the Great Depression, left Glasgow for a couple of decades with the only ILP representatives at Westminster, but otherwise under the control of Labour 'machine' politics, not very Red, but electorally dominant, from Paddy Dollan to Pat Lally, for the rest of the twentieth century. The tradition of self-help was travestied by a new politics of patronage, which eventually replaced bad old housing with disastrous new housing, and provided Labour with a stream of machine-made nonenties safely elected to seats at Westminster.

The Thirties, Forties and Fifties saw the climax of the Union with England. The administration of Scotland was devolved to Edinburgh's rather spectacular new Scottish Office, where Walter Eliott, wettest of Tories, made a start on the quangification of Scotland. Churchill selected Tom Johnston, erstwhile Red Clydesider, as Secretary of State in his Coalition Government. Partly by invoking the bogey of Nationalism, lurking ready to undermine the Imperial War Effort, Johnston was able to set up more quangoes. These did useful work, and reinforced the Welfare State which Labour brought in to popular acclaim after the war – in which Scots had fought and suffered alongside the English to win total victory over Nazism. Heavy industry had revived, and the country stood poised to accept gratefully Labour and Tory support for regional economies in the new era of full employment. In the 1950s, the great tradition of Scottish Liberalism finally collapsed, Conservatives won over half the vote in a general election, Labour abandoned its 70-year old commitment to Home Rule, and English TV magnetised every Scottish home. In short, Scottish political culture had plunged weightlessly into a Unionist vacuum...

So why do we have a new Parliament this week, elected on novel principles of proportional representation, certain to contain many representatives of the Scottish National Party and likely to have four women for every ten members? There are three possible reasons. One is the revival of Scottish culture from the 1950s, spearheaded by the folksong movement led by Hamish Henderson and Norman Buchan and vitalising the so-called 'Scottish Renaissance' in the arts proclaimed by Hugh MacDiarmid three decades before, but hitherto chiefly represented by his own lone efforts. Before long Scotland proved to have half a dozen or more major poets, brilliant painters revived the great Scottish figurative tradition and that Snark, the Great Glasgow Novel, was captured at last and proved not to be a Boojum. Secondly, the final breakdown of the British empire in the 1960s coincided with the achievement of independence by many poor countries, some less populous than Scotland, with the marching politics of CND, Black Power self-assertion in the USA and minority nationalist movements in several parts of Europe. Bright young men who might previously have looked to safe and lucrative employ in colonial administration, banking or commerce now perforce sought to realise ambitions at home. The Labour machine had no grip on urbanites decanted into New Towns. The Scottish National Party found a motley constituency, and its sudden rush of electoral success pushed Labour into schemes for devolution. But granted a century-long history of failure by caucusses and Conventions working to achieve Home Rule, after the debacle of the 1979 Referendum the issue might just have gone away. What made a new Parliament certain in the end was the way Thatcher rubbed our faces in the Democratic Deficit, and rallied up to three quarters of Scots behind the idea of Home Rule sufficient to prevent any future Government from thus imposing abhorrent policies by overruling the people's wishes. Edward I's arrogance forced Scotland into precocious nationalism, now Mrs Thatcher has ensured that we vote in the first ever democratic election for a Scottish Parliament.

1999

Livingstone, Self-Help and Scotland

IN 1859 LIVINGSTONE WAS making his way to Lake Shirwa in what is now Malawi. His companion was Dr John Kirk, and the two men got on well despite Kirk's reservations about Livingstone's leadership of the ill-fated Zambezi expedition. Kirk was less sympathetic than Livingstone towards Africans, whom he called 'niggers', and even allowing for the fact that those they met in a nearby village were middlemen in the slave trade he accosted them rudely. The language Kirk used in his diary ('blackguard', 'beast') can only be described as racist:

> We were rather wild at our reception by such a set of low rascals and they soon saw that we were rather up for fun and shooting or not shooting them was altogether indifferent to us and that if we had a good chance we would not lose it. Little did they know that it was our respectability in England and our wish to pass without getting a bad name that kept us back.

Kirk was from Forfarshire, like Livingstone a Scot, but his reference to 'England' as if it were their homeland is typical of Scots during this period. Livingstone himself would commonly conflate Scotland with an overall political entity called 'England' rather than 'Britain' and wrote from Quelimane to Edmund Gabriel in Luanda in 1856 about the Royal Navy's operations against slavers:

> If our cruisers have done nothing else, they have conferred a good name on the English... They [the natives] say, 'These English love the black people much.' This is so far in our favour in endeavouring to propagate our blessed Christianity.

The word 'our' seems to refer to 'the English', and he writes elsewhere of 'we English'. Livingstone continues:

> I feel convinced that God has gracious designs towards the Africans. They are an imperishable race... Then as our Burns has it: 'Then let us pray that come it may/For come it will for a' that/ When man and man the world o'er/ Shall brothers be for a' that.'

In 1859 Livingstone would write in his journal, 'There is room to spare for English emigrants to settle and work the virgin soil of the still untilled land of Ham.' But sharing his thoughts not long before with a fellow Scot, Sir Roderick Murchison (the distinguished geologist who presided over the Royal Geographical Society), he had been thinking of 'Scotch' settlers. 'The interior of this country ought to be colonised by our own countrymen... I think twenty or thirty good Christian Scotch families with their ministers and elders would produce an impression in ten years that would rejoice the hearts of all lovers of our race.' And asking Sir Roderick to find a job for Kirk after the Zambezi expedition foundered in 1864, he wrote: 'Being a Scotchman and really a very able and amiable fellow... I am quite sure he would be a credit to any appointment either at home or abroad.'

After failure in the 1690s to establish a colony in Central America, the Scottish political and commercial classes accepted Union with England in 1707, partly as an *entrée* to empire, for by that date the English had already begun to carve out a vast overseas empire. 'Clannishness' was not confined to Highlanders, and partiality for fellow Scots (which would later bind Livingstone, Kirk and Murchison) ensured that Scots became dominant in some parts of the empire, in others, merely influential. Within a few years of the Union, Scots were rampant on rich Caribbean sugar islands. Within 50 they owned about a quarter of all taxable land on the largest and richest of them all, Jamaica. After Wolfe's capture of Quebec, Scots moved in to dominate the Canadian fur trade, and by Livingstone's day a Highland Scot, Sir George Simpson (head of the Hudson's Bay Company), ruled an area comparable to the domain of the Russian Tsar while a black Scot, Sir James Douglas (son of a Scottish planter by a Creole Guyanese woman) was the first Governor of British Columbia. Dunedin, so named after Edinburgh, marks the Scottish impact on New Zealand. Scots were big in Australian wool and in the lucrative tea and opium trades with China.

From the Union onwards, Scots sucked in a disproportionate share of the rich patronage flowing from the East India Company. In the developing Indian Raj they came to form the 'core of the civil service'. Others grew rich as soldiers and traders. Even when Company rule was abolished after the Indian Mutiny of 1857 Scottish influence on the sub-continent did not abate. In 1865 Livingstone wrote drily to Kirk from Bombay that James Augustus Grant, another famous traveller in Africa, had been 'toasted in Calcutta' at a St Andrew's Day dinner. 'Scotchmen predominate there as well as here and all are pretty clannish.' Livingstone himself might be seen as yet another clannish 'Scotchman on the make', using England's power as a battering ram to smash open doors to opportunity. But in fact few career or commercial opportunities existed in Africa. Scots had to discover new opportunities for themselves, and Livingstone did not hope for a fortune and an estate back home in Scotland. He wanted to be God's instrument in saving the continent. It seems apt that four Scots – Livingstone, his brother Charles, John Kirk and George Rae – were the first white men known to have seen the glories of Lake Malawi, for Scots had played a disproportionate role in the opening up of Africa to European understanding. James Bruce (1730–94) was famous for his travels in Ethiopia, Mungo Park (1771–1806) for locating the River Niger; while Hugh Clapperton (1788–1827) and W.B. Baikie (1825–65) increased knowledge of West Africa. In the missionary field, where Scots were extremely prominent, even Robert Moffat, Livingstone's remarkable father-in-law, was dwarfed by the mighty John Philip, a byword for malice among Afrikaaners until the fall of apartheid and perhaps beyond because of his championship of native Africans.

Philip is an excellent example of 'self-help', a doctrine that was very important in nineteenth-century Britain but is easily misunderstood today. At a time when working men contended against the novel and often horrific conditions of life established by the new industrialism and the effects of great slumps in trade, self-help emphasised the virtues of hard work, thrift and sobriety as safeguards against destitution and as the means of rising to respectability and retaining it. But according to Samuel Smiles (1812–1901), the Scot who became the most famous exponent of the creed, the objective was not *nouveau riche* wealth. It was 'independence': the capacity to function freely and with dignity, without need to defer to aristocrats or unfair employers. Smiles, a doctor from the small Lothian town of Haddington, encountered self-help first, not as ideal but as reality, during the era of Chartism in Leeds, where he observed the passion for 'self-improvement' among working men who were defying conditions far worse than those which Livingstone endured as a child in Blantyre. Self-improvement entailed self-education. And the purpose of that education was not merely to improve marketable skills but also to permit appreciation of the arts (the poetry of Robert Burns was much loved in the north of England) and, above all, understanding of God's universe through science. Smiles's book *Self-Help*, published in 1859, drew all these elements together and gave them literary shape, using examples from the lives, factual or mythologised, of many well-known men and some quite obscure ones.

Though self-help had been a spontaneous response (throughout Britain) to industrialism, it was particularly congenial to the Lowland Scottish temperament. Philip was an early and awesome example. Born in Fife in 1775, the son of a handloom weaver with a serious library, Philip left school at eleven to work as a weaver himself but rose through self-education to become a mill manager. He resigned in disgust at his employer's attitude to child and female labour and trained for the ministry. Like Livingstone he was a Congregationalist, and like Livingstone, he was drawn to the London Missionary Society (LMS), whose projects he zealously extolled in his Aberdeen church. His captivated congregation were, however, incensed when the LMS asked him to go to South Africa to reform their missions, at that time racked by scandal. He arrived at the Cape in 1818 and at once entered political and social controversy which surrounded him for the next quarter century as he crusaded on behalf of the Khoikhoi ('Hottentots') whom the Boers had enslaved.

Livingstone should be seen primarily as momentously a self-improving Lowland Scot. It was commonplace at the time to compare the militant Xhosa of the Eastern Cape with Scottish Highlanders before Culloden – clans of cattle keepers who stole cattle but had martial virtues – and it is conventional now to attribute Livingstone's respect and affinity for African chiefs and native healers ('witch doctors') to his grandfather's birth on the Gaelic-speaking isle of Ulva. Livingstone boasted of his family's Highland origins and was delighted that he was cheered 'as a man and a brother' when he visited the Duke of Argyll in 1864. But he had been equally pleased six years earlier by acclaim from Lowland cotton workers. His reply to their address reveals the kind of Scot he was – self-improving, puritanical and dogged, with no yen to swagger about in a plaid or kilt:

> In Africa I have had hard work. I don't know that anyone in Africa despises a man who works hard. Eminent geologists, mineralogists, men of science in every department, if they attain eminence, work hard and that both early and late. That is just what we did...

Burns's phrase 'the man of independent mind' which Livingstone remembered at Quelimane, defines a major part of the self-help ethos. Smiles, indeed, quoted Burns approvingly in his book, at the head of a chapter on 'Money – Its Uses and Abuses':

> Not for to hide it in a hedge

Nor for a train attendant,
But for the glorious privilege
Of being independent.

However, Smiles felt constrained to add that 'unhappily' Burns's 'strain of song was higher than his practice: his ideal better than his habit'. This was grossly unfair, since Burns had worked very hard, farming, reading and writing, endeavouring to provide for his bairns. But he had celebrated the joys of tavern life and had been an open womaniser. Such 'habits' did not conform to the ethos. Livingstone, by contrast, seemed a perfect model of Smilesian self-help. To understand why, it is worth considering Smiles himself and some of his Scottish heroes.

According to a standard misreading Smiles was a zesty, blatant exponent of the idea that one should work hard, rise in life and make money. This falsification of his views, still prevalent today, was a source of some disappointment to the author. As a writer his speciality was biography, and he believed that the lives of worthy men would show others the true path, which was certainly not that of Mammon. In the 1870s he published three biographies. One, which he agreed to write only under pressure and with great reluctance, was of George Moore, a very successful warehouseman. In his autobiography Smiles mused:

With this exception, I have always selected my own subjects. It has been said that I wrote the lives only of successful men. This is, of course, a mistake. Robert Dick was not a successful man, for he died not worth a farthing. Thomas Edward was not a successful man, for he rarely made ten shillings a week by his cobbling.

Dick (1811–66), a Thurso baker, was fascinated by local fossils and became an indefatigable and quite significant geologist. He attracted the approving attention of the great Murchison himself but failed in his trade. As Smiles put it:

He was content to be poor, so long as he was independent, and free to indulge his profound yearnings after more knowledge. Though he attended carefully to his business... he was ruined by competition.

Smiles's lives of Moore and Dick appeared almost simultaneously in 1878. As Smiles ruefully noted in his autobiography, that of Moore went through many editions but the one edition of Dick's did not even sell out.

The Life of a Scottish Naturalist: Thomas Edward (1876) had fared better – a second edition was called for. Edward, from Banff, born in 1814, was a cobbler who studied 'beasties', as he called them, 'simply that I might learn all I could concerning the beautiful and wonderful works of God'. He was honoured in the naming of two tiny marine creatures, which he had found in the Moray Firth: *Conchia Edwardii* and *Anceus Edwardii*. Despite his low income he brought up eleven children 'respectably and virtuously'. He was highly regarded by Charles Darwin, who backed his successful claim to a Civil List pension, and he was elected to several learned societies. The story is inspiring even now.

The great Hugh Miller was a model for such men and personally encouraged Dick. The son of a Cromarty seaman, Miller (1802–56) developed a passion for geology while exploring his local beaches and rocks, and worked as a stonemason after he left school. He began to publish bad verse but good prose, and his fiery pen was put to use when controversy erupted in the 1830s over patronage in the Church of Scotland. A law passed at Westminster in 1712 permitted landlords to appoint ministers disliked by their parishioners. Leaders of opposition to such unPresbyterian goings on summoned Miller to Edinburgh, and he was put to work editing *The Witness*. A successful twice-weekly newspaper, it was a powerful influence contributing to the Disruption of 1843 when Thomas Chalmers led several hundred ministers and elders out of the annual General Assembly of the Established Church to set up a new Free Church. Afterwards, with spreading fame as a geologist,

Miller became Edinburgh's leading literary and scientific light. Smiles acknowledged his achievement in *Self-Help*: formed by his labours as a stonemason, Miller 'simply kept his eyes and his mind open; was sober, diligent and persevering; and this was the secret of his intellectual growth'. Unfortunately this great exemplar of self-help had blown his brains out on Christmas Eve not long before Smiles's tract was published...

Granted that Miller wasn't ideal, how would Thomas Carlyle, son of a stonemason, serve as an example in Smiles's catalogue? Smiles praised him in *Self-Help* for reconstructing the manuscript of his history of the French Revolution after his maid had used it to light the fire – 'an instance of determination of purpose which has seldom been surpassed'. But Carlyle, brilliant, sneering, hectoring (and virulently racist), was a controversial polemicist, about whom industrious folk might have doubts.

Livingstone, however, was to prove a completely edifying hero, not least because he persevered after the failure of his great Zambezi expedition and ended his days without European companions, chasing a geographical chimera through foul country and dangerous beasts despite his piles and fevers. He was Will personified.

When Thomas Edward addressed the boys of a school near Liverpool (in about 1880) he exemplified and extolled a virtue central to self-help: 'the will, the will to do and to win... Whenever I wished to do anything, I did it... The day never dawned, nor the night lowered, however stormy that kept me back.' One wonders if his admirer Smiles had ghosted the script for this man who spoke in the 'broadest of Aberdeen Scotch'.

Though Livingstone's tongue was also thick – 'it seemed almost foreign', one English friend wrote – no one would have been allowed to ghost for him. Men who worked, or tried to work, with him criticised Livingstone for many things, but never for lack of will. How could they, when he drove a small ship over 2,500 miles of ocean, from Africa to Bombay in 45 days, with no engineer, a crew of only twelve – of whom 9 were Africans, even more inexperienced than he was – and only fourteen tons of coal for when the wind failed? Even when Kirk was bitter about Livingstone's apparent lack of 'kindly feelings', he wrote privately that he still respected the man's 'energy and force of mind'.

Livingstone's love of 'independence' was extreme. Unlike Philip's, it led him away from confrontation with 'bad' men of his own colour towards a lonely martyr-like end. He raged, privately with extraordinary arrogance, against his colleagues on the Zambezi expedition, writing of himself in the third person:

> The whole of the exploration would have been more easily accomplished by the commander alone than when burdened by the baggage of his European underlings, and the unflinching energy with which he surmounted every obstacle and rendered the expedition so far successful would have received the approbation of his countrymen had he been alone.

A colleague at Kuruman, the Reverend Walter Inglis, while noting Livingstone's 'dry Scotch humour', remembered that his face 'wore at all times the strongly marked lines of potent will.' A religious journalist who saw him address a public meeting said that this face was 'typically that of a countryman from the North', meaning Scotland. And indeed, in Lowland Scotland there were ingrained traditions of dour stubbornness and wilful self-sacrifice. Livingstone by his own account resisted his father's efforts to make him read about the grim and gentry-hating lives of the seventeenth-century Covenanters who had resisted unto death by martyrdom the attempts of Charles II and James VII to destroy their Presbyterian faith. But in habits, if not in theology, Livingstone represented the Covenanting tradition.

Livingstone was brought up in the tradition of 'Independent' Puritanism. The 'Old Scots Independents', members of a little sect founded in 1768, were the originators of the Scottish Congregationalist tradition that Livingstone's father joined when he broke from the Established Kirk to attend a chapel in Hamilton. David

Dale, the philanthropic Congregationalist who opened the New Lanark mills (made so famous by his son-in-law Robert Owen) was a prominent neighbour, just a few miles away, of the Blantyre Livingstones, and George Shepperson is surely right to argue that this may have been 'more than a coincidence' in the formation of Livingstone's social conscience.

But the sect was galvanised and made prominent by the revivalism of Robert and James Haldane, of a prominent Perthshire lairdly family. While the Haldanes were moved by the French Revolution to reassert the democratic principles of Independency, once the creed of Cromwell's troopers, they coupled this with the evangelical and missionary spirit of the potent new anti-slavery movement, led by William Wilberforce. Though laymen, their preaching during a tour of the north of Scotland inspired a Society for Propagating the Gospel at Home, founded in 1797. Robert sold his estate to fund the Society and within a year this had germinated a Congregationalist body, with James as its pastor, and a Tabernacle in Leith Walk, Edinburgh.

The basic Congregational principle was defined as complete self-government by church members. By 1807 there were 85 more churches practising it. But the principle guaranteed splits, and when the Haldanes adopted Baptist views there was a rupture that left the 55 churches that had formed the Congregational Union in 1812 'independent' of the brothers, but stripped of funds. The Union persevered and grew.

This was the contumacious but relatively liberal minded and ecumenically inclined body to which Livingstone's father, Neil Livingstone, turned. Its strong connections with the LMS made it natural for David to seek employment from that Society. The Hamilton Congregational Church, which Livingstone attended, had been founded by James Haldane in 1807. Its meeting house was known locally as the 'Wee Kirk', being very small. However, its members apparently gave more than much larger congregations to collections for LMS missions abroad.

The Independent tradition was such that Livingstone cannot be described as heretical, though he eventually became so thoroughly ecumenical and so little concerned with formal group worship that he might be said to have moved away even from Protestantism itself. (Privately he suspected that his notion that the monastery of medieval Catholicism, in its original purity, was superior to the LMS mission would appal his 'stiff' Hamilton brethren.) On his return to Scotland as hero, in 1858, he stood before the members of the Hamilton Congregational Chapel – now a much larger building, erected in 1841 – and called for the 'sinking of sectarian differences in the proclamation of the same gospel which all the churches share'. Referring to the 1843 Disruption he said,

> I believe that every Scotch Christian abroad rejoiced in his heart when he saw the Free Church come out boldly on principle... I am sure that I look on all the different denominations in Hamilton and in Britain with feelings of affection. I cannot say which I love most. I am quite certain I ought not to dislike any of them.

In one of his last letters, written in 1872, Livingstone wrote:

> The religion of Christ is unquestionably the best for man. I refer to it not as the Protestant, the Catholic, the Greek or any other but to the comprehensive faith which has spread more widely over the world than most people imagine, and whose votaries of whatever name are better than any outside the pale.

He was not ready to slip into the liberal twentieth-century habit of seeing equal good in all faiths. Though he noted in 1863 that in Africa 'belief in one Supreme Being who made and upholds all things is universal', he was not reverting to eighteenth-century Deism either. He added that what Africans lacked was a 'correct notion of the controul [sic] he exercises over the affairs of the world' He retained a strong sense of God's Providence, though he was not inclined to use the term. God intervened in the world, and he could personally act for God. He was driven like a Puritan, but a non-Calvinist 'independent' one.

We must not fall into the error of seeing Livingstone as really, or merely, an imperialist seeking economic opportunity under the hypocritical mask of missionary evangelism. Gary Clendennen pertinently notes that 'One can easily detect the "hidden hand" of Adam Smith and the Scottish Enlightenment in... Livingstone's economic philosophy'. The political economist Smith, author of *The Wealth of Nations* (1776), had objected to slavery, as not only inhumane but also economically, as we would say today, counter-productive. Smith's vision, however, was coolly secular. His 'hidden hand' was at most the non-interventionist God of the Deists, the Divine Watchmaker who had made and wound up the world and would now let it run its own way which was the way of economic self-interest. Legitimate 'free' trade, Smithites argued, would quickly drive out the slave trade. And Livingstone did argue this. But he attached to this idea the notion of godly communities of missionaries and settlers led to Africa by him. God desired such colonies in order that people freed from dependence on Portuguese or Arab slave traders could be connected, as producers, with the world market.

Livingstone's obsessive quest for cotton, or at least the potential for cotton production, in the highlands of Central Africa, should not be seen as crudely 'imperialist'. Free trade did not imply unfair dominance, but the opposite. The cotton manufacturers of Lancashire to whose interests he appealed had been led politically by 'free traders' – Richard Cobden and John Bright – who were vehement opponents of empire. After the Indian Mutiny Cobden expressed to Bright his horror at the supposed atrocities of the sepoys but blamed them on the absurdity of British rule in India– 'based upon the assumption that the natives will be the willing instruments of their own humiliation' and deplored the unjustified contempt of 'niggers' shown by servants of the Raj. Even though these men lost to Palmerstonian Whiggery in the General Election of 1857, there was still no appetite for empire in the British parliament. Garrisons overseas were seen as a waste of money. The heyday of territorial imperialism had not dawned at the time of Livingstone's death in 1873 and the 'Scramble for Africa' had not yet begun. Livingstone's own logic was simply that cotton was the great commodity of world trade – comparable to oil today – and that demand for it would assist the great cause he shared with the Haldane brothers, with Philip, and with the Congregationalists of Hamilton: the ending of slavery.

In the first edition of *Self-Help* Smiles merely praised Livingstone briefly among other low-born missionaries. In later editions he gave him pages. Beside the hard work in Blantyre, the devoted reading and botanising, the manual work at the mission stations, Smiles extolled Livingstone's attitude to money. He needed a new steamship for African work at a cost of £2,000. 'This sum,' Smiles noted, 'he proposed to defray out of the means which he had set aside for his children arising from the profits of his books of travels. "The children must make it up themselves", was in effect his expression...' Livingstone was happy that his old friend James 'Paraffin' Young, who was the first oil mogul (through his exploitation of the West Lothian shale seams), should profit from his own observation of the potential of the coalfields of the Zambezi region in the dawning era of steam navigation. But, to quote Clendennen again:

> ... [his] analysis of Africa's economic potential contained precious few provisions for his own personal gain... As far as he was concerned, the economic development of Africa should benefit all Africans... as well as whomever among the Scottish poor migrated thither to work for the common cause.

God had made him His instrument. If his book *Missionary Travels* attracted attention to the author, it also drew interest towards Africa, and Livingstone could use his reputation as 'explorer' and scientist (he was appointed Fellow of the Royal Society in 1857) to further humanitarian aims far more extensive than David Dale's.

Though passionate interest in science was far from being a Scottish monopoly, the Scottish universities had put Scotland in the forefront of scientific enquiry and it excited interest at most levels of society. Another misconception about Livingstone, which must be dispelled, is that he had to struggle to reconcile science with belief in God. On the contrary: in his day to study the natural world was to affirm and consolidate faith in Him. Livingstone was a Christian. He was also a genuine scientist, as his day understood the term. There was no contradiction.

It is true that Livingstone's insatiable observations of geology, fauna and flora were sometimes vitiated by his obsession with his programme for helping God to save Africa. He was particularly interested in the tsetse fly and the way it barred the use of animals it attacked in certain parts of Africa, but he completely failed – refused – to grasp the similar role of mosquitoes bearing the malaria that could decimate the missionaries and settlers he wished to bring. This does not make him any less of a scientist than do errors deriving from prejudice in the work of such men as Murchison. (Indeed, in our own day political programmes and ethical considerations manifestly affect the work even of the most brilliant scientists.) When Murchison praised Livingstone above all for the 'astronomical observation' by which he had 'determined the longitude as well as the latitude of so many sites' he was not, as some have supposed, condescending to him as mere surveyor. He was associating him with Newton's astronomy and with the most prestigious and godly of sciences: physics.

Before Livingstone's death, Darwin's *Origin of Species* (1859), together with the professionalisation of science and its withdrawal into laboratories, was beginning to rupture the perfect union established between religion and the observation of nature. But Tennyson, who in famous passages of *In Memoriam* (1850) foreboded a rupture between science and faith was, like most very good poets, ahead of his time. And poets a generation earlier had not foreseen the divorce between science and poetry itself,

considered axiomatic after Darwin. When Livingstone was grow-
ing up, scientific knowledge, religious truth and poetic appreciation of nature marched together.

Reading his accounts of what he saw in Africa in his *Missionary Travels*, one is constantly struck by Livingstone's alternation,
from paragraph to paragraph, of precise observation with aesthetic
rapture. His memories of his early life explain this if we reread
them with the understanding that science, religion and poetry were
not then at odds. Thus he praises his father for providing at home
'a continuously consistent pious example such as that the ideal of
which is so beautifully and truthfully portrayed in Burns's *Cottar's
Saturday Night*'. Although his father wanted him to read stiff religious works, Livingstone preferred books about science and travel.
While the Congregationalist church deacon did beat his son for
this preference, there is no reason to believe that he opposed David's
discovery through 'the works of Dr Thomas Dick, *The Philosophy
of Religion* and *The Philosophy of the Future State* that my own
ideas that science and religion are not hostile but friendly to each
other [were] fully proved and enforced'.

A present-day Dundonian poet, W.N. Herbert, has fun at the
expense of a fellow townsman in his verse sequence 'The Testament of the Reverend Thomas Dick':

No irony could touch the telescopic length
of your desire to explicate space.
You sent theoretic steam engines to the stars
at twenty miles per hour, taking nearly
four thousand years to make your point and reach
Uranus. You were our McGonagall of science,
who inspired David Livingstone to
plunge through Africa's dark galaxy
spreading news of your Future State:
a Heaven of astronomers...

Herbert grasps at, yet misses the point. Yes, astronomy was the heavenly science. But for post-Newtonian, pre-Darwinian thinkers, the observations of physicists did actually display God.

Livingstone wrote about the 'intense love of nature' awakened and gratified in his youth by scouring the countryside for 'herbal simples'. He became a scientist with two aims. As a doctor he would try to cure those diseases that God had his own reasons for inflicting. He would never see any contradiction between tsetse fly and leprosy on the one hand and the idea of a Benevolent Creator on the other. 'Herbal simples', also sent by God, could cure diseases – the 'wise women' who practised in the Scottish countryside (like 'witch doctors' in Africa) could have assured Livingstone of this. Secondly, by observing the natural world he would obtain better understanding and love of his Creator, and bring these, through publication, to other people.

In his youth he came upon a limestone quarry where, like Hugh Miller, he was rapt. 'It is impossible to describe the delight and wonder with which I began to collect the shells of the carboniferous limestone which crops out in High Blantyre and Cambuslang.' Geology could be seen as the Scottish science *par excellence*. Though the claim that James Hutton of Edinburgh (1726–97) was the founder of modern geological science is inflated, it is true that his *Theory of the Earth* (1795) was immensely influential. This Newtonian 'paean to the beneficent intentions of the Creator', as it has been described, 'elevated geology among believers, to a prestige second only to that of physics.' Just as Newton had shown that the mathematical integrity of the solar system and stars proved the existence of a powerful creating mind, so Hutton presented geological phenomena as evidence that such a balanced and purposeful earth must be the result of intelligent design.

The notion of Livingstone as mere traveller upon the face of God's earth – not a real scientist, only a 'field worker' – is diametrically opposite to the thinking of the early and middle nineteenth century. He was, if you like, Thomas Edward in motion. Susan Faye Cannon argues that the great model for advanced scientists was Alexander Humboldt (1769–1859), the German traveller who went about with a large collection of scientific instruments attempting to cope with 'everything from the revolutions of the satellites of Jupiter to the carelessness of clumsy donkeys'. Such a scientist would discover endless miracles of perfect natural adaptation. Only a very intelligent, and essentially kind, Creator could be the 'great organiser' of such an amazing system of interrelations. The effect of Darwin's book and its reception was to destroy such confidence, since it seemed to show that natural selection was neither intelligent nor good. Livingstone's passion for detail in nature was such that he could write off the cuff to a correspondent who unexpectedly wanted his help in collecting examples of parasites:

> I never observed any parasitical insects on the elephant or rhinoceros, except a kind of worm between the eyeball and lid in the latter. I have observed the different kinds of intestinal worms in the bowels of the rhinoceros and zebra... On the wild pig a small kind of flea abounds.

He took a friendly interest in Darwin. But the man who had first described the Victoria Falls had been formed in an epoch when there seemed to be no conflict between aesthetic delight, religious awe and scientific discovery. In his account of his approach to the Falls he is in raptures over the beauty of the Zambezi:

> The whole scene was extremely beautiful; the banks and islands dotted over the river are adorned with sylvan vegetation of great variety of colour and form. At the period of our visit, several trees were spangled over with blossoms... The silvery mohonono, which in the tropics is in form like the cedar of Lebanon, stands in pleasing contrast with the dark colour of the motsouri... Some trees resemble the great spreading oak, others assume the character of our own elms and chestnuts; but no one can imagine the beauty of the view from anything witnessed in England... scenes so lovely

must have been gazed upon by angels in their flight.

But when he reaches the Falls themselves his description becomes as matter-of-fact as possible:

As [the mass of water] broke into (if I may use the term) pieces of water all rushing on in the same direction, each gave off several rays of foam, exactly as bits of steel, when burnt in oxygen gas, give off rays of sparks... Of the five columns, two on the right and one on the left of the island were the largest, and the streams which formed them seemed each to exceed in size the falls of the Clyde at Stonebyres, when that river is in flood.

'England' is positioned in relation to the Falls aesthetically: Scotland is the homeland where Livingstone learnt to think in terms of mensuration, 'scientifically'. But he is also the countryman of Walter Scott, whose techniques of description he imitates (they derive from conventions of the 'picturesque' in landscape gardening and landscape painting). And one is reminded also of Scott's twentieth-century successor as the dominant figure in Scottish arts and letters, C.M. Grieve (Hugh MacDiarmid), a Marxist and materialist who attempted in his later verse to put poetry and science together again after their rupture in the late nineteenth century.

In his combination of inspiration and matter-of-factness Livingstone prefigures characteristics of twentieth-century Scottish intellectual life. This is not surprising, for he was formed in, and extended, Scottish intellectual and social traditions. The image of steel burning in oxygen would have appealed to MacDiarmid.

1996

The Disruption in Fiction

A HUNDRED YEARS AGO, few educated Scots would have doubted that the Disruption of the Church of Scotland in 1843 had been a major event in Scottish history – even in world history – as important as Bannockburn and Culloden.

The purity of Presbyterianism, as established in Scotland, had been sullied, as many Kirk members saw it, by the right legally accorded to landowners, by 'patronage' to impose their own preferred preachers on congregations rather than allowing members free choice. The issue boiled over around the time when the emergent British bourgeoisie, in a rapidly industrialising nation, contested the entrenched power of the landed aristocracy and secured the Reform of Parliament in 1832 and the abolition of the protectionist Corn Laws in 1846. A fervent Evangelical wing of the Kirk, led by the saintly divine Thomas Chalmers, energised by the writings of Hugh Miller, having failed to get support for their case against 'intrusion' from the Westminster authorities, took extreme action: 470 ministers, over a third of the total, seceded from the Kirk, hundreds of them marching out of the General Assembly in the Church of St Andrew and St George in Edinburgh's New Town to a hall downhill where they founded a Free Church. The members of the new church were rich enough to replace buildings and livings thus forfeited, and to compete in the mission field with the Established Church. Free Churchmen in general were not extreme puritans like the small rump of 'Wee Frees' which dominated the north-west Highlands and Islands in the twentieth century, remaining thrawnly distinct after the Free Church had first amalgamated with the United Presbyterian Church, another large dissenting body, in 1900, then reunited with the Established Church of Scotland in 1929. Men central to Scottish life had been Free Church members, proud of the men of 1843 who had stood out for principle.

So why does the general or common reader in Scotland now possess no myth, however remote from documented fact, of the great Disruption? Why has an event which engaged the minds and passions of men regarded as great in their generation have almost no resonance for our contemporaries, even in Edinburgh – which saw the climactic drama – a city not backward in emphasising historic traditions, nor, of course, in selling them to tourists?

Michael Fry argues in *Patronage and Principle* that the Disruption was one of those episodes of a 'Scottish Revolution' in the 1830s and 1840s 'qualified by the destruction they wrought in an ancient polity to stand with almost any other of the national revolutions in Europe during the previous fifty years'. This is not an exaggeration. Many historians now see this as the period in which Scottish independence was at last, and decisively, lost. Yet our children don't know who Miller was, let alone Chalmers.

Several causes can be suggested for this national amnesia. The most obvious is the rapid secularisation of the Scottish intelligentsia after the First World War. Traditions of religious revolt, which had obsessed even the aesthete Stevenson, became increasingly unmentionable. By the last quarter of the twentieth century, a notion that ministers, of every denomination, were and always had been, enemies of radical thought and rebellious behaviour was taken for granted. Knox could not be ignored and was ritually lampooned (as in *Mary Queen of Scots Got Her Head Chopped Off*, that popular play from the 1980s by Liz Lochhead), even by those who had no sympathy at all for Tory, Catholic or Episcopalian counter-traditions. But the Covenanting rebels of the seventeenth century were deprecated when not wholly occluded: the spate of publication and republication of works about and from their crises dried up in the 1930s. By the 1980s, memoirs of once famous missionaries turned up for a few pence in jumble sales. The otherwise admirable movement to create a secular, pluralist, independent nation shuddered away from the Presbyterian themes of the past as if all Calvinists had been Orangemen, all elders Holy Willies.

The churches themselves, for the most part, now doctrinally evasive and resolutely ecumenical, had no interest in countering such absurdities. Your best chance of getting a sight of relevant books was in a Free Presbyterian shop in Stornoway. So a second cause of amnesia was the reticence of those who knew most. Even the amazing Hugh Miller, whose works of autobiography and natural history had retained for decades 'classic' status, had eventually to be rescued from the waters of Lethe by a journalist, George Rosie, who prefaced his biography and anthology of 1981, *Hugh Miller: Outrage and Order*, with the point that none of its subjects' books were now in print.

But these factors would have counted for much less had just one potent work of fiction fixed, mythologically, an image, however much at variance with documents, of the drama of 1843. Though Scott, from the 1930s on, fell steeply from fashion himself (a turgid Tory tartaniser, as the nationalistic radicals misconceived him), *Old Mortality* continued to present a projection of the Covenanters, and those who now perversely chose to elevate Hogg and even Galt critically above the Wizard of the North, rediscovered notable counter-fictions by these men (*The Brownie of Bodsbeck, Ringan Gilhaize*), dealing with the same matter. So, playing off all three, Harry Tait, produced a memorable rewriting of myth in his *Ballad of Sawney Bain* (1990). The Covenanters retain mythic presence; the clerics and laity of the Disruption have lost it.

Fictions about the latter's doings have been few. It would be facile to suggest that this is because those most inward with Disruption values had wholesale contempt for literary and other arts, or that the most talented writers of the Free Church heyday were completely alienated from it. Margaret Oliphant, one of the most accomplished and prolific Victorian novelists, came from a Free Church family. Stevenson, self-exiled from puritan Scotland, was nevertheless touched by tales of the Covenanters. The problem is not that the men of the Disruption and their heirs were unbendingly puritanical in their rejection of fiction, it is, rather, that they proved to be too reasonable, too worldly, even too Laodicean, to be ranged with Bruce's soldiery, diehard Cameronians and doomed Jacobites in the 'pageant' of Scottish history. They contended in debate, they chose 'sacrifice': but they landed comfortably poised on their feet. They challenged the premises of the British state, up to a point, but they did not shake the class structure emerging with industrialisation. None of their missions had the glamour attached to the wanderings of that independent Scottish Protestant, Livingstone. Their intellectual, architectural and social achievements merged into the mass of Scottish 'Victorianisms'; their diverse polemical positions into the complexities of sectarian and political debate. Their nemesis was that the fundamentalist hardliners of 1900 eventually came to replace them in the Scottish mind – men who, however rebarbative, clearly stood for something distinctive.

Three notable novels present the events of 1843. Lydia Miller's *Passages in the Life of an English Heiress, or, Recollections of the Disruption Time in Scotland* was published in 1847, just after the death of the great Chalmers, who features not unvividly in its strange pages. Lydia Miller was Hugh's wife, and her book illuminates positions which he did not disavow, even if he did not fully share them. Since it vanished without trace after one edition (the one copy in the National Library of Scotland [NLS] is falling apart), it cannot be seen as an ideological agent of any importance. Its interest, on the contrary, lies in its air of having been ideologically acted upon: it reveals cultural cross-currents moving hither and thither the thinking of bourgeois Free Churchers in Miller's Edinburgh.

William Alexander's *Johnny Gibb of Gushetneuk* (1869–70) was, in contrast, highly successful, in newspaper serial form and in popular and deluxe bound editions. In the introduction to its seventeenth edition (Edinburgh, 1912), Alexander Mackie hailed it as a 'local classic... a work of undoubted genius'. He foresaw, however, that its rich use of Aberdeenshire Doric would present a problem for new readers: 'The dialect will not die yet awhile, but there is little doubt that under a compulsory English education its purity and breadth of vocabulary are already on the wane.' Unsurprisingly, this very factor has educed lavish praise from nationalistic critics in the last couple of decades, and the work is now re-established as a 'Victorian classic' (albeit, out of print). Alexander was a left-liberal journalist, editor of the *Aberdeen Free Press*, and his view of the Disruption as it affected the rural parish of his own youth was undoubtedly influential. It provides us, *inter alia*, with an opportunity to assess Hume Brown's judgement in his still more influential *History of Scotland* that the Evangelicals of the 1830s and 1840s characteristically asserted 'the rights of the people in opposition to the privileged classes'. If we accept Alexander's fiction as documentary (and it was certainly intended to be so), the verdict will be yes, up to a point. Alexander, in fact, makes the Disruption seem incidental in changing relationships in the countryside involving the Anglicisation of lords, the growth under them of big farmers and the invasion of commerce.

Alexander begins the 26th of his 49 chapters (each originally seen as a self-contained episode in the bi-weekly *Free Press*): 'In the parish of Pyketillim the great event of the Disruption was not seen in any of its grand or striking features.' Quite so. One of the book's many merits is that it conveys how the Disruption, occurring along existing fault-lines in class-divided Scottish society, nevertheless did not 'disrupt' communities traumatically. Wholly sympathetic to the Free Church as Alexander was, he was far too shrewd and humane to idealise its beginnings as millennial, or even, at grass roots, wildly exciting. His plotting involves quiet use of an Anglicised pro-Establishment laird as deus ex machina distributing just deserts, so that the story's very shape resists the egalitarian animus of its eponymous, unheroic, hero.

The Disruption is the subject of Robin Jenkins's *The Awakening of George Darroch*. Soon after its appearance in 1985, the jury of a national literary prize, wishing to consider *Darroch*, found that its publisher had gone bust and all remaining copies were warehoused in south-west England. Luckily, a Penguin paperback was already on the way, but the book never made the splash which its vast merits deserved.

Jenkins is interested in what might be called the 'problem of Good' and the damage which seekers of extreme 'good' can do in a 'relative and conditional universe'. He presents the Disruption in a starkly dramatic way, at times in scenes recalling those of late-medieval morality plays, except that he deploys the psychological insights of a post-Freudian novelist. In 1982, before *Darroch's* publication, he went on record in 'Speaking as a Scot' about his view of its subject. Working on the Disruption, he 'very soon became aware that it had not really been a passionate spiritual crusade but merely a gentlemanly disagreement over theological matters'. Except in one respect, the Evangelicals:

> ... all wholeheartedly supported the Establishment, and when they spoke of their religious beliefs they did so in stilted, stereotyped, lifeless language... You may imagine I found this a drawback, for my hero was an Evangelical and to make him representative I had to have him too speaking in that dreary conventional way.

Hoping to find an epic crusade, Jenkins found only 'genteel' argument. If he had read Lydia Miller's novel, this would have confirmed him in his judgement that the Evangelicals were disastrously timid and respectable.

It is worth recalling the juncture in the history of prose fiction at which Lydia Miller's book appeared. As Ina Ferris has shown in her brilliant study, *The Achievement of Literary Authority* (1991) – subtitled *Gender, History, and the Waverley Novels* – the vast critical success of Walter Scott had depended in part on the conviction that he had rescued the novel form from female practitioners who had confined it to the presentation of domesticised society under conventional restraints. According to the orthodoxies of critics, who were almost invariably male, female novelists were indecent when, like Lady Morgan, they ventured on to high historical ground and dealt with sexual passion; boring, if worthy, when, like Maria Edgeworth, they moralised didactically. Francis Jeffrey had damned Edgeworth with faint praise: 'she scarcely makes use of a single tint that is warmer than real life'. As Ferris puts it, 'the writerly fitness of women was perceived as a function of their enclosure'.

Lydia Miller was unfortunate in that she launched herself as a writer of fiction in 1847, the very year that saw the publication of *Jane Eyre* and *Wuthering Heights* by Charlotte and Emily Brontë, respectively, novels which showed how the discourses of Romanticism could be stirred-in with domestic matter to profoundly exciting effect, and a year before Mrs Gaskell's *Mary Barton*. Lydia Miller's available models were Scott and Galt for 'manners painting' of Scottish life, Austen and Ferrier for drawing-room scenes, and nobody of great merit for the serious treatment of church affairs in a contemporary context. Her *Passages* have the awkward character of a 'historical' fiction grafted together with a novel of contemporary domesticity and a 'novel of ideas' of the kind familiarised by the age of Enlightenment. Their 'historical' import is signalled by the full title: *Passages in the Life of an English Heiress, or, Recollections of Disruption Times in Scotland*. Only four years after the event, Miller is claiming to 'recollect' the Disruption as Scott and Galt had memorialised the transition to industrialism. She is laying claim to the high ground of 'history'. Occupying this, Scott had satisfied critics that the novel, associated with the typically male discourse of history, could provide more than mere amusement in an idle hour. Miller's need to maintain an elevated, quasi-male stance in judgement is one reason why her heroine, a fount of 'historical' judgement, cannot be allowed any girlish passion or domestic interests, despite her youth. Had Miller held back for a decade or two, the examples of the Brontës, digested, might have shown her how to use a first-person female narrator judgementally (*Jane Eyre*) or how to intercut points of view to achieve 'historical' depth (*Wuthering Heights*). She displays at various points in her novel qualities of a successful 'realist' writer of fiction: descriptive passages are conventional but sturdy, she has some ear for dialogue and she can present 'character' vividly. But it may be doubted whether she could ever have engaged without reservation in the dangerous trade of novel-writing. She, like her husband, might be called a 'liberal intellectual', at ease in 'polite society' with civilised adversaries. But as we shall see, *Passages* rises at one point to a frenzy of hysterical sectarianism, and its author must always have been aware of the deep prejudice against fiction which was instinctive in Evangelical circles. As William Donaldson puts it in his essay 'Popular Literature', (*The History of Scotish Literature*, 1988):

> To the extreme evangelical fiction was simply a lie and as such intrinsically immoral. Indeed, the form was regarded with varying degrees of distrust by religious activists of every kind. Fiction corrupted the reader. It inflamed the passions and made vice interesting.

The liberal wing of the movement, nevertheless, would move cautiously into the arena of didactic opportunity created by the newspaper press from the mid-1850s. A serialised novel could inculcate good evangelical principles. Donaldson, however, cites the instance of the greatly popular, now forgotten David Pae, author of some 50 full-length serial novels:

> Despite his sincere desire to make evil serve the ends of good Pae was caught in an insoluble dilemma: the more deeply he entered the imaginative domain the more important fictional elements became. In engaging with fiction at all he tacitly endorsed the very things he wished to destroy.

Lydia Miller was less daring than Pae. Her novel betrays overweening consciousness on her part of what she should NOT do, with moral and political imperatives interfused. She should not risk titillating erotic passion. She should not, in the age of Chartism, abet stirrers of class discord. Over and beyond this, she should not, by offering any elaborate, suspenseful plot, draw readers too far into the shadow-world of novelistic fiction. She must provide the literary equivalent of the vegetarian haggis.

What we know about Lydia Miller herself indicates that she could draw on personal experience of the Highland rural society in which her novel opens, of the fashionable Edinburgh society to which it moves, and of the southern England in which it ends; but also, that she was not fully at home in any of these spheres.

Lydia Mackenzie Fraser was the daughter of an Inverness businessman who lost his fortune. While he was in trouble, she was brought up by relatives in Surrey. She also sojourned in Edinburgh, staying with Burns's publisher, George Thomson, and mingling with the second rank of literati – the Ballantynes, Mrs Grant of Laggan, Tennant who wrote 'Anster Fair' and the painter Thomson of Duddingston – if not with the aristocrats whom she presents in her novel. After her father's death, her mother, who had her own income, went to live in the bustling little town of Cromarty. Lydia was excited to learn that a stonemason of the town, one Hugh Miller, was publishing poetry. The Burns cult was well developed. She sought to attract Miller's attention, and he was soon smitten with her 'petite figure, waxen clearness of complexion, and childlike appearance'. Despite her mother's disapproval, romance blossomed. By Hugh Miller's own admission she 'taught him to understand the love poetry of Burns'.

Miller determined to marry her only when his station in life was more respectable. In late 1834, after three years of courtship, he was offered and accepted the post of accountant in a bank. They finally married in January 1837. Despite a hostile account of her 'evil' personality, left by Miller's nephew Hugh Williamson and discovered by George Rosie in the National Library of Scotland, they appear to have been a close and harmonious couple. In his cryptic and agonised suicide note of 1856, Miller addressed her as 'Dearest Lydia... My dear, dear wife...' She was at his side in Edinburgh when he edited the new Evangelical newspaper, *The Witness*, from January 1840 through the stirring events of 1843 and beyond, and she was accordingly close to the leaders of the new Free Church. She clearly held her own in a demanding arena of debate.

She prepared her novel, published anonymously, with the claim that if its pages had any value, it was 'as a faithful record of personal experience'. She modified this when she added that 'In the earlier chapters I have not introduced a character which I had not familiarly known, and scarce an incident which did not occur in real life.' The later chapters were admittedly fictional. So, manifestly, were the earlier, since Lydia Miller was not the descendant of a Norman Conqueror or the daughter of a wealthy English Whig landowner. Jane Hamilton Leigh inherits the property of her father, who had run his estate, Chester-Lee, and governed her education by strict principle:

> Strange as it was, he made the science of ethics the basis of all her acquirements – the centre from which all other knowledge radiated. Two questions he constantly kept in view as the grand problems of life,–'What is in itself good?' and 'What is the method of producing the greatest amount of practical good in any given circumstances?'

Bereaved of this admirable parent, she goes to stay with her mother's brother, a Ross-shire 'reue' (sic), Sir Duncan Ross. 'Every inch of wall' in his house, Rosemount, is covered with paintings. His taste in these is admitted to be fine, but he has been morally corrupted by dissipation in Paris and Rome. He is 'half a Catholic on the Continent, and nothing at home'. His lairdly neighbours are less exotically delinquent. Davidson of Kilblair, their leader in 'county matters', reviles the Evangelical party in the church. The Moderates, he avers, 'have something more of gentlemen about them'. Our grave heroine asks how they show this:

> 'Why', said Davidson,'they don't meddle with what does not concern them. They can sit quietly while their superiors stow

away a couple of bottles or so (though I hold that to be too much for them, as the times go at any rate); they can sing a good song, take a hand at Whist, and in short, be friendly and social in their way: and then, you know, it is natural that, after all that, they should tip the wink at certain gentlemanly follies.' He winked at Sir Duncan as he spoke. 'You have enlightened me on the subject of Moderation, and on that of patronage too', said Jane, her eye giving out an indignant flash, as it was wont when she detected anything radically false and hollow, but giving no other sign of emotion. 'But you will pardon me', continued she, 'if I think that those accomplishments you have mentioned are not the chief ends of a clergyman's life.'

Davidson, not wishing to alienate a wealthy heiress, backtracks at once. He suggests the clergy should be 'moral... in order to set a good example to the lower orders'. 'Ay, the rascal multitude', begins Sir Duncan. Jane interrupts: 'I have not been accustomed to speak of the rascal multitude' – but her uncle goes on to deplore that the rascal multitude has left Scotland almost without 'decent' churches since the Reformation. Jane argues that the people were right to attack popery, that the Reformers didn't instigate iconoclasm, and that it was a pity that the images went out with the popery.

Conversation flows on to the topic of patronage. Davidson flies into a rage on the subject of non-intrusion. 'The Church may go to the bottom, before I lose my patronages. Did I not pay £400 only two years ago for Cambusnethan and Kilrathy? It is downright swindling to speak of it.' When Jane argues back, he asserts that he and his kind are 'not so helpless' as she thinks. 'Excellent fellows' among the Moderates are working on their side. 'It were odd if they didn't, since we gave them their livings and have got those of their sons in our hands. What between our power and their art, we must gain over the young men by shoals.'

At the end of this unedifying evening, Jane returns to her room gloomily asking herself whether morality be really 'the chief end of existence'. She undergoes what might be described as a 'conversion experience'. She asks her 'little' Highland maid, May, 'What is the chief end of man's being?' May replies 'To glorify God, and to enjoy him forever.' Asking where May learnt that, Jane discovers it was in a 'worn and half dirty pamphlet', the Shorter Catechism:

> 'These are extraordinary views' said the young lady, as she finished reading the pamphlet for the third time, 'and an extraordinary peasantry they are who hold them. They do love good... It is with me writing on a slate, which may be effaced. It is engraven somehow on these people's hearts.'

Praying that night, she feels unprecedented awe.

The next chapter connects May to the Covenanting tradition. She is seen reading *The Cloud of Witnesses* to her dying grandfather John Morrison, who explains Erastianism to her and blesses the Lord that he has 'lived to see the day when the root of bitterness is about to be taken out of Zion when Erastian patronage shall be digged out and cast away'. He tells May how her own mother was killed as soldiers shot at the people resisting the intrusion of one Donaldson by a Catholic laird. Then he has a fatal stroke. Lydia Miller now introduces her own 'stroke'. She has promised in her preface:

> ... to introduce to the reader a class of humble individuals with whom he has probably heretofore had but little acquaintance. They are the relics of a primitive age extinct everywhere except in those parts where a different language has preserved the manners and customs of the olden time from the inroads of change. Marked by peculiarities, assuming in some districts, it has been said, a less agreeable aspect than in others, I am far from advocating their support when the necessities of the past have ceased to exist. Certain it is,

however, that they have lent most material aid in evangelising the Highlands of Scotland.

These 'humble individuals' are 'The Men'. Four of this 'class' gather round old John's deathbed in his crude cottage: a catechist, two crofters, a shopkeeper. They come from an unofficial order of Churchmen below ministers, elders, and deacons permitted, in Rossshire, to take a share the public exercises of the church and utter their thoughts on scriptural texts. (Lydia Miller reassures us that this 'prophesying' is allowed for in the *Book of Common Order* and the *First Book of Discipline*, though now confined to the north of Scotland.) Over their dying fellow the Men now pray, read the Bible and sing psalms. Next day, in Jane's presence, John dies pronouncing a kind of prophetic curse on Donaldson's son George, who has joined the villagers around him.

By far the most interesting pages of the novel explore Lydia's conception of The Men. Though she claims, as we have seen, that these passages are documentary, her discourse, deriving more from Scott than Galt, is ultimately Ossianic. She assimilates The Men with the Highland romance of the Ossianic noble savage.

It is worth mentioning here Peter Womack's *Improvement and Romance*, a searching analysis of the Highland romance as it developed after 1746 through Macpherson, Scott and lesser writers:

It is the ideological function of the romance that it removes the contradictory elements from the scope of material life altogether; that it marks out a kind of reservation in which the values which Improvement... suppresses can be *contained* – that is preserved, but also imprisoned... Officially, Romance and Improvement were opposites: native and imported, past and present, tradition and innovation. But in reality they were twins.

That is, the sentimentalisation of the Highlands supported, ideologically, the capitalism of the Lowlands. It is, in a way, to Lydia

Miller's credit that she is explicitly uneasy about this twinning. In so far as The Men are part of an 'ancient' order hostile to market forces, free trade and improvement, she is clear in her Preface that they must become extinct: 'I am far from advocating their support when the necessities of the past have ceased to exist.' Yet when she elaborates on the case of the pious shopkeeper Munro who attended Morrison's deathbed, her tone is quite different. He also owns a 'small but very excellent farm': 'He was thus a wealthy man in his way, and an excellent specimen of that worthy class which the remorseless spirit, misnamed improvement, has so nearly swept from the country.'

Though Lydia Miller wants to make them also the guardians of the Lowland Covenanting tradition, men of this 'class' are now usually Gaelic speakers. When they gather from as far as forty miles away in the shopkeeper's house, on the occasion of a half-yearly communion at Glenmore (the parish where Rosemount is situated, and where the minister Dr Blair is famous for piety), they speak English in deference to 'one or two of the company' not fluent in Gaelic. Miller's suggestion that the Lowland Covenanting tradition found a strong fortress at last in the Gaeltacht makes historical sense. She produces, however, an idealised image of The Men and their people as essentially 'primitive' (a word flavoured in this connection by its usage in 'Primitive Church'). When Jane passes at this time a gathering of 'thousands' singing psalms, in Gaelic, in the open air, the music is 'simple in its scale, like the melodies of all primitive people, but rapid and involved in its transitions'.

As the patronage issue impinges directly upon her, she recognises in this 'primitive' fervour something of far greater spiritual weight than the gentility of Moderates. Her 'madcap' young soldier cousin, Harry McLeod, divulges to her that Sir Duncan has sold the presentation of Glenmore to his father. Harry himself has made his father promise to give it to young Donaldson, a college friend, whose eye he put out with a fork in a romp. Jane is appalled – 'could she doubt that this George Donaldson was immeasurably inferior, both morally and intellectually, to many of her humble friends?' But old Dr Blair, knowing his death is near, has already pleaded with his congregation that there should 'no riot and confusion' when his successor is installed. We learn that when Mr McLean was intruded into the adjacent parish of Dalry, the people were so law-abiding that they tholed this: 'the church remained empty, that was all'. Lydia Miller's comment is:

> to submit to unrighteousness personally or locally, may be virtue; to submit to it nationally is either insensibility or cowardice... When the nation's cry against iniquity arises, the 'power that is' is the awakened strength and integrity of a great people, the enlightened, determined conscience of a nation – in which is the voice of God.

Leave it to Dr Chalmers and his colleagues.

The Revd Dr Blair himself is allowed to expound the reasons why popular choice should prevail in the appointment of ministers. Even presbyteries are likely to act at times from 'corrupt' motives: members 'might accommodate one another'. However, the power of the church to license ministers ensures that the people can only choose from among candidates of sound doctrine.

We are now over a quarter of the way through a novel of 429 pages. So far we have been given 'scenes', not story. These scenes set up starkly the contrast between utterly admirable Gaelic Christians and generally corrupt Anglicised gentry, and we have learnt that the former represent the true Scottish nation. The beautiful Jane has acquired correct Non-Intrusionist opinions. Now, for better or worse, Lydia Miller has to cope with the promise implied when she gave her heiress youth and beauty: a novelistic development must be essayed.

At once she demonstrates that she could cope, but won't. A young English lieutenant, a comrade of Harry's, falls wordlessly in love with Jane. They go with Sir Duncan and a party of young officers to visit the Intruder, Old Donaldson. The trip takes them into fine Highland scenery, ambitiously described. Old Donaldson is a grotesque, in whose potential Walter Scott would have revelled. He dresses like a 'gardener', speaks in broad Scots, convincingly rendered, and has married his serving lass as his third wife. He is by far the most vivid – and hence, for novel-readers, the most appealing – character so far presented. But we only get one taste of him, and no more is heard of Jane's military admirer. Further frustration occurs when Jane, sallying forth to read Mrs Hemans, her favourite poet, at a favourite scenic spot, rashly loses herself in the mist after ascending a mountain for the view. She is rescued by Evan Munro, son of one of The Men, who is destined for the ministry. Surely romance must blossom? Not likely. Jane goes off to stay in Ainslie Place, Edinburgh, with Lord and Lady Lentraethen, for whom 'good' is little more than taste. Lydia Miller's mode switches from scene-painting in a Romantic environment to the territory of 'comedy of manners'.

She shows evidence that she might have succeeded in the medium of Austen and Ferrier. We get a vivacious account of a discussion at a society dinner where Jane makes play with the fact that Jeffrey and Cockburn side with Chalmers over patronage. However, her happy fate is to be taken in hand by Lord Lentraethen's pious brother, General Maitland, who lectures her at length on church affairs. Greatly daring, Lydia Miller gives him a past – he married at nineteen, in India, an extravagant 'baby-wife' now long dead. What attracts Jane to this austere character (whose physical characteristics, save his 'penetrating gaze', are not described) is, primarily, his relationship with his daughter by this marriage. A psychologist might be interested as to why Lydia Miller, herself the offspring of a failed man, should attach such extraordinary importance to the father–daughter relationship. After meeting Maitland's daughter and taking to her, Jane weeps 'bitter, orphan tears' on her pillow and 'images of General Maitland and his child' mingle 'strangely and uneasily in her dreams' with those of her own beloved father.

Meanwhile, young George Donaldson has been 'intruded' by

Davidson at Glenmore, following Dr Blair's demise. In an other-wise passive demonstration, a snowball knocks off Davidson's hat. This leads to a stand-off with young Kenneth Ore, previously iden-tified as swain of Jane's servant May, when Davidson orders him to pick it up:

> Kenneth folded his arms and stood erect. 'Pick it up for your-self, Mr Davidson', he replied quietly but haughtily, 'or or-der your footman to do it. I am no man's footman'. Davidson stepped up to him, almost beside himself. 'If I had my pis-tols here', he vociferated, 'by —, I would send a bullet through you.' The low and somewhat mean figure of Davidson, and his face purple as it was with rage, presented rather a curi-ous contrast to the manly form, the handsome features, and contemptuous lip of the young Highlander. The latter cer-tainly looked for that moment the aristocrat.

At the moment when George Donaldson is to be ordained, the congregation stages a mass walk-out, but those who remain in the gallery howl out their feelings. Hence Kenneth Ore and old Samuel, one of The Men, are sent for trial in Edinburgh as representatives of the rioters. Maitland brings Samuel into the Lentraethen draw-ing room after their acquittal, and Jane, conversing with him, is 'struck with that sense of the grave sublime, which an adequate faith in omnipotence never fails to inspire; and which she knew deeply pervaded the minds of the Christian mountaineers'.

But such virtuous folk now feel impelled to emigrate. Lydia Miller had some understanding of the processes involved in the Clearances. Samuel told Jane, back in the Highlands, that 'distress and poverty are making many of us look to a foreign land', and Kenneth has spoken more forcibly about landlords who use their people 'worse than brutes'. But Miller suggests, through Samuel, that people would not bring themselves to leave the place of their fathers 'so long as the preaching of the gospel' continued there, making young Donaldson's intrusion spur these men overseas.

Miller implies that the Clearances involve choice by the emigrants, and that the victory of true religion would keep them in Scotland.

This is in line with the views of Thomas Chalmers on poverty, which Maitland expounds to Jane. He believes that 'spiritual philanthropy' rather than cash is the answer. Once the poor are converted, 'self-help' will raise them from pauperism. His millennial aim goes beyond Chalmers' godly Commonwealth towards the vision of a fully Christianised world: 'Why confine our wishes to Scotland?'

Jane is now closely involved in Church of Scotland matters. She meets the great Chalmers himself, whose simplicity of dress betokens 'a toilet devoid of concentration'; but 'with him the sense of duty itself was absorbed in the higher principle of *love*'. She hears deliberations on the issue of patronage at the 1841 General Assembly, and sits till the conclusion of debate at 3.00 AM. Then, very abruptly, she and her General are married, and she returns with him to her English estate.

This proves to comprise a never-never portion of England, sagely governed by her late father. The land is rich. Life is idyllic. Paternalistic local manufacturers now provide employment for the surplus rural population, Jane's father having talked them into responsible behaviour. The interests of landlord and tenant here are identical. Jane, whose mansion has a gallery of ancestral portraits of 'noble knights and ladies' suddenly becomes Countess of Lentraethen on the demise of Maitland's brother. But she grows discontented with the 'rich Epicureanism of England', as compared with the 'hut on the Highland mountain' where old John Morrison had lived and died. Furthermore, her land steward has carelessly sold the living of the parish church to the highest bidder and he – horror! – is a High Churchman. 'Figments of popery... the grossness of Romanism' can be seen in the church and after attending one service there Jane and her husband decide that if the 'plague spot of Popery' spreads throughout the Church of England, they will lend aid to forming a purer 'Free Church of England', 'unfettered by State support', a 'purified' Church which might 'one day be adopted by a regenerated State as her true help-mate'.

Here Miller entertains the remarkable idea that there is actually a 'Popish Plot' involving not only the High Church faction in England but also the Moderates in the Kirk. The Romish vicar of Jane's parish, Edward Clayton, is unmasked to her readers as a Jesuit – a tortured soul, an ex-criminal who flew to Rome for mercy. We are treated to an exchange of letters between him and the Scottish Moderate leader 'Bremner' who likewise has 'a secret in Rome's keeping', and is presumably acting under threat of blackmail. Alas, Miller does not develop this remarkable fantasy.

The tell-tale correspondence (unknown, of course, to the novel's other characters) immediately precedes a routine, hagiographical, distant description of the scenes of Disruption in Edinburgh. Now God's providence ties up the novel's loose ends. Sir Duncan Ross is 'assassinated in the streets of Rome, at midnight, by a disappointed rival'. Jane, who has bought out poor Clayton and settled a good Evangelical person on her English estate, inherits Rosemount and returns there to the plaudits of 'a picturesque population full of motion and enthusiasm'. Alas, Clearance has wreaked its havoc. The pious Mrs Munro, wife of the shopkeeper (whose son Evan is dying, partly from studying too hard, partly, it is suggested, for hopeless love of Jane) tells the Countess how lordly persecution drove the Ores, Samuel and others to emigration – 'They'll turn the land into the land of the stranger and the sheep'. But under the friendly rule of the new owners, Rosemount now prospers, with 'smiling cottages... ease and plenty'. Only the manse, occupied by the unregenerate George Donaldson, remains un-improved, its lawn 'rank with unsightly weeds'. Naturally, the emigrants, funded by Jane, will return to join in open-air Free Church worship under Charles Blair, son of the good old minister.

Why, we must wonder, does Lydia Miller not end her heiress's story here? It is because her novel is directed as an appeal and an inspiration towards the English reading public. It was published in London. Its last fictional chapter is set in Jane's English estate at Chester-Lee, where her tenants celebrate the first public appearance of their Countess's son and heir 'Lord Arthur'. A bizarre conjuncture of discourses closes the book. While on 'far Highland Mountains' Kenneth Ore and others light bonfires to hail the birth of the young master, that fortunate babe lies in the ancestral drawing room in a 'sculpted cradle of mother of pearl', surrounded by lamps 'fed with perfumed oil' and by 'gems of art... costly luxuries from the courts of foreign princes', while his parents earnestly discuss the laws of property. Miller's final chapter resumes her own position. She tells her English readers: 'The progress of Popery on the one side of the kingdom – the creation and vital energy of the Free Church on the other, are the grand antagonistic movements of the powers of good and evil in our day.' The planting of ministers among the indigent and outcast will save a 'social fabric tottering at its base' by mediating between rich and poor. Meanwhile, members of the Free Church, no doubt as attentive as the Lentraethens to the laws of property, have already poured £1.5 million into its coffers.

Miller, it emerges, has conscripted the noble savages and natural aristocrats of Ross-shire to serve the ends of bourgeois evangelisation – and has not quailed from enlisting in the same cause a dream of 'Merry England' governed by wise landlords of ancient chivalric lineage. This enterprise was never likely to succeed novelistically. The great English public would prefer the more erotic imaginings of the Brontës and the better-submerged earnestness of George Eliot. And it has to be added that Miller's device of a 'Popish Plot' was many years past its sell-by date: Chalmers had spoken in favour of Catholic emancipation, Hugh Miller had favoured it, and Lydia Miller's introduction of this motif paradoxically reinforces something on which her text strives to be silent, but (with its ultimate 'mother of pearl' and 'gems of art') cannot avoid blurting out – the devilish attractiveness of Rome, its rituals, and the rich artistic production associated with them. If only, she clearly wishes, one could have the images without the popery. But meanwhile, her own fiction's lumpy eschewal of erotic plotting in favour of dry argumentation, suggests that for Free

Churches that happy day is far ahead. To write a fully novelistic novel would betray the cause. This fiction is designed, it seems, to reassure English persons that the Free Church is a true friend of social stability.

It has been necessary to quote and summarise Lydia Miller's novel at length because it is now almost unavailable. Alexander's *Johnny Gibb of Gushetneuk* is far easier to find. This is paradoxical, since it was addressed not even to the whole Scottish reading public, but only to those who perused the *Aberdeen Free Press* and would understand the dialect spoken by most of its characters. Alexander, when he wrote it, was recalling his own early years in the parish of Garioch. He was relaxed and experienced within the conventions of producing fiction for newspaper serialisation and can be called a master of his own peculiar variant of the novel-form. Furthermore, he wrote a quarter of a century after the great Disruption crisis, and already felt no need to pillory Moderates, let alone taint them with Romish associations. Unlike Lydia Miller, he does not go in for lengthy Evangelical effusions, and he certainly does not idealise the adherents of the new Free Church in the parish of Pyketillim.

Dr Donaldson, author of a pioneering account of Alexander's career, sees him as a 'realist' working within the same literary movement as Tolstoy and Zola, but especially concerned with documentary veracity (so far as Victorian prudery allowed) in the presentation of language in all its spoken registers. *Johnny Gibb*, in Donaldson's account, emerges not as the one-off novel of a distinguished journalist – it was the only fiction by him of such length which Alexander allowed to appear in book form – but as merely a small part of a fiction-writing career which extended over several decades, from the mid-1850s. In particular, Donaldson places *Johnny Gibb* as the central section of an epic sequence nearly a quarter of a million words long, encompassing almost a century of change and development in the rural north-east; beginning with the novel *Ravenshowe* (*Free Press* 1867–68) and completed with the last of the short stories collected as *Life Among My Ain Folk*

(1875). This sequence deals with the agricultural revolution in Aberdeenshire, in which initially, small tenant farmers like the author's own parents reclaimed 'acre by acre' featureless expanses of moss and moor, only to be ousted by 'muckle farmers' arising under the big landowners, and engulfed in the railway – which speeded a new world of commerce and industry. Alexander, as Donaldson shows, was deeply critical of capitalist values and emphatically on the side of the class of small tenant farmer represented by Johnny Gibb – 'the last defence of traditional decencies and a human scale of values in the rural economy'.

The novel deals mostly with the estate of Sir Simon Frissal of Glensnicker and two of his tenant farmers, Johnny Gibb and his neighbour Peter Birse, the farmer of Clinkstyle. Birse, a weak man, and his feckless elder son are driven by his wife to aspire to the status of muckle farmers, and she plots to absorb Gibb's farm when his lease expires. Gibb seems to play into her hands, openly voting against the laird's candidate in elections, building a voluntary 'venture school' in opposition to the Moderate parish schoolmaster, and steering Non-Intrusionist parishioners through the Disruption into their own Free Kirk. He is, furthermore, elderly and childless. But he has lent money to the laird – not yet repaid – and the Birses are discomfited when Sir Simon not only gives the lease of Gushetneuk to Johnny's nominee – the husband of his own 'adopted' niece – but consigns a tongue of Birse's land to Gushetneuk by way of rationalisation.

Douglas Gifford has seen Johnny Gibb as typical of the 'mythic' figures in nineteenth-century Scottish fiction who 'in being themselves' are also 'being Scotland' – sound men in a sick society – and has proclaimed the novel to be a 'mythic masterpiece'. This could create a false impression: Alexander is doggedly matter of fact, leaving it to his readers to find 'symbolic' value, if any, in such details as the absurd second-hand coach which the memorably grasping and snobbish Mrs Birse makes her husband buy in anticipation of a rise in status. This is a dry book about dry people, and Johnny Gibb himself is presented foursquare, 'a

short, thick-set man', within obvious limitations: he is literate but
reads little; devout but uninterested in proselytising for his opinions; content to do what he can in his own small parish.

Nor is the Disruption 'mythologised' in any usual sense of that
word. Johnny's contempt for lairds precedes the Intrusion controversy and exists irrespective of their religious opinions:

> The tac half o' oor lairds is owre the lugs in a bag o' debt. I
> wud hae them roupit oot at the door and set to some eesfu
> trade... Stechin' up a kwintra side wi them, wi' their peer
> stinkin' pride... an' them nedder able to manage their awcres
> themsel's, nor can get ither fowke that can dee't for them.

Though he has a 'very good balance' at his banker's, Johnny
continues to live simply and at kirk or market 'will accost any
dyker or ditcher in the parish on terms of perfect equality'. His
politics are 'advanced Liberal', though the term is not used in the
late 1830s when we first meet him. His honest tongue ensures that
the Revd Gregory Sleekaboot refuses him an eldership. So he is
predisposed to interest when he hears – on his annual excursion to
Macduff, where his wife takes the waters for her health – at first
hand about the Marnoch Intrusion case from Maister Saun'ers of
that parish, who inveighs against 'A man wi' nae gifts fittin' im for
the work forc't upon an unwillin' people, i' the vera teeth o' the
Veto Act... after the noble struggles and sufferin's o' our
convenantin' forbears to maintain spiritooal independence.' They
discuss the idea of abandoning the defiled Kirk and worshipping
on the hillsides in seventeenth-century fashion.

This meeting stirs Johnny's 'zeal in the Non-Intrusion cause'
far beyond his 'previous state of hazy, half-informed rebellion
against Moderate domination'. He is further 'politicised' by following the progress of the Marnoch case, and by 1842 he has 'learnt
clearly to distinguish between 'Moderates' and 'Evangelicals', and
those words [are] frequently on his lips'. He feels he must stand up
against Sleekaboot 'for the good cause' and with his ally Roderick

M'Aul, souter in the hamlet of Smiddyward, invites an unattached Evangelical minister visiting the area to preach in the independent 'venture' school.

The brief description of this important occasion exemplifies Alexander's humorous detachment. Sleekaboot reads every week, from a 'well thumbed ms', a sermon regularly repeated:

> But the Rev. Alister Macrory, albeit a little uncouth and violent in his manner, and given to shaking his fist and staring directly forward at a particular point in his audience, as if he wanted to single you out individually to be preached at, was, to all appearance, a man really in earnest...

Alexander is certainly not the man to separate Evangelical sheep from Moderate goats in any crude way. His picture of the convivial, tolerant Moderate schoolmaster, the Revd Tawse, is very sympathetic. The appalling Mrs Birse has fallen out with Tawse on account of his failure to drum education into the head of her stupid younger son Benjie, whom she wants to make a lawyer. Sending Benjie to the venture school as an alternative, she associates her family with the Evangelical side and, as an opponent of an individual Moderate, decides to go to its second unofficial prayer meeting.

In the controversy which inevitably follows these meetings, the laird's 'ground-officer' (sub-factor), David Hadden, moves to prevent an Evangelical pow-wow at the Smiddyware School, and it is transferred to Johnny's barn, where locals sign a paper adhering to Non-Intrusion principles, which seems to Johnny himself 'a process very nigh akin to signing the solemn League and Covenant'. But this point is offered with gentle irony. The next chapter emphasises that the Disruption was not so very disruptive in Pyketillim. A parishioner witnesses and reports an intrusion at nearby Culsalmon which provokes a riot. Hearing of a later intrusion into a Strathbogie parish where the Moderates called in soldiers though there was no riot, Johnny Gibb begins to talk in millenarian terms, declaring that 'things could not stop short of a rebellion which would put that of the '45 in the shade'. But after events in Edinburgh take their course, all that happens is that the new Free Church of Pyketillim begins to meet in his barn, pending erection of a kirk, while he, a 'Disruption leader' *de facto* rather than by 'intention', negotiates for a supply of preachers. Sandy Peterkin, the 'free' master, is expelled from his venture school but finds employment in the shop. And the laird, shrewdly proposing and disposing, frustrates the ambitions of Mrs Birse. Sleekaboot stays in his own kirk, keeps his manse; the representative of peasant independence, Johnny, stands at peaceful truce with his landlord, while the new Church which he more than anyone has promoted co-exists alongside the old. As Donaldson points out, Johnny's childlessness may be felt as symbolic: he represents a dying class. But we leave him in prosperous retirement on the land which he has personally improved, an elder of the Church which seems to him to represent his own democratic ethos.

In its own mode, *Johnny Gibb* is a virtually flawless work of fiction. Extracting the 'Disruption' episodes from it misrepresents a book in which earnest religious controversy emerges from a vividly 'heard' flux of local gossip, talk of farming practicalities, alcoholic convivialities and exuberant wedding customs. Set beside Grassic Gibbon's Sunset Song which deals with similar countryside, attitudes and people decades later, *Johnny Gibb*'s radical thrust seems restrained and its social criticism gentle. Mid-Victorian 'equipoise' seems to condition its virtual truce with time and change. Its slow, though not laboured, English narrative voice strongly affirms the best values of Doric-speakers who are heard in their own voice, and in its genial complicity, implies confidence that these values and that language can survive – in or out of the Free Kirk which gives them place.

Robin Jenkins, in contrast, wrote *The Awakening of George Darroch* with an agonised sense that true 'Scotland' had slipped away. Reading it after *Johnny Gibb*, one might well marvel at the swift suppleness of narrative available to twentieth-century writers.

Jenkins is able to present, in far fewer pages than Miller or Alexander, a great range of characters, milieux, arguments and striking events. Though he knows that he has to introduce the subject of the Disruption itself to readers who mostly know nothing about it, he is able to move with apparent ease from efficient exposition to critical analysis.

George Darroch is the minister of a mediocre parish in industrial Lanarkshire. He has a large family – his wife is pregnant for the fifteenth time. Seven children survive, including mentally-retarded Sarah who will need attention all her life. His sons are contemptuous of the agonised conscience which has led him to subscribe to the Evangelical manifesto and contemplate leaving his manse. His brother-in-law, Robert Drummond, is the urbane Moderate minister of a wealthy Edinburgh parish and is able to dangle before him the promise of a rich living offered by a patron in rural Lothian. Furthermore, George is racked by private self-contradiction. In his early forties, he is highly attractive to women. His wife has always refused to take pleasure in the sexual act; so has Drummond's, who has given him only one child. But whereas Robert relieves himself with strong drink, George fantasises about Eleanor Jarvie, the wife of a neighbouring minister, of immigrant Italian family. She is built, in his eyes, like the voluptuous goddess seen painted on a ceiling at the laird's house, 'lying on a bank of flowers and being nuzzled by fawns no more naked than she' – Eleanor, 'grave, slow-moving, brown-eyed, dark skinned and spicy breathed…, whose beauty was exotic and mysterious, redolent of frankincense, pomegranates, and the cedars of Lebanon'.

Jenkins has shrewdly noted the tension in Evangelicalism which we have seen emerging in Lydia Miller's final endorsement of beautiful luxury. Much of the imagery of the Bible itself attaches spiritual significance to sensually potent things and people. While George feels impelled to dedicate himself to the poor and outcast, he is also hauled by his libido towards notions of running away to Italy with Eleanor. But when Jenkins, outside the pages of his novel, referred to George as 'a rather peculiar type of hypocrite', he was probably not thinking of these furtive sexual drives, nor of the blindness which makes him impervious to the fact that his wife is dying through the effects of yet another unwanted pregnancy. What seems to fascinate Jenkins is the spiritual arrogation of this mild, friendly, sincere man. Can his earnest desire to serve Christ and the poor be separated from a craving for distinction? His schoolboy son, James (an endearingly complex character, destined for the ministry, yet a devotee of Hume's, a Moderate in his views, yet stubbornly honest), is 'white with despair' when he sees his father walk out of St Andrew's church on 18 May 1843, the first of the 'unknowns' to follow the famous leaders...' Given the best opportunity of his life to show off, his father had not been able to resist it. For the sake of a minute's vanity he had sentenced his family to years of hardship.' But matters are more complex than James realises. The charming neighbour, Mrs Wedderburn, who has recently married his cheerful sailor uncle, reassures him that his father will inherit Mr Jarvie's Church, larger and more convenient than his present one in Craignethan. 'Unfortunately it would allow his father to devote more time, devotion, and money, to his Pauper's mission, and to have himself appointed chaplain to the prison, where he would carry out his duties with absurd seriousness. He would become busy, ambitious and false...'

Jenkins's title must refer to the point in his novel where George, we must understand, undergoes change at the basis of his character. This is the crisis where Jenkins's method most strongly echoes late medieval Morality. Eleanor Jarvie, though vivid enough, is hardly 'plausible' in routine novelistic terms. It is not explained why this strong-charactered, voluptuous woman consented to marry the unseductive and latterly fat and impotent Revd Jarvie and live in a small provincial town. However, as clearly as Sensuality in Lyndsay's great *Thrie Estaites*, she represents Temptation. After his colleague's death, George goes to Jarvie's manse with the notion of enjoying the widow's body very much in mind, though he has been legitimately invited to make a selection from Jarvie's books. Eleanor is drunk but has no trouble putting him in his place.

His own wife has died: he should marry his plain but sensible house-keeper. As for herself, she is off to Italy. In Jarvie's library, George reaches a 'turning point in his life'. He recognises that he had in-tended to have 'carnal relations' with Eleanor. 'Only the lack of a bed or couch had prevented him from making the abominable at-tempt.' But Christ is merciful, and now in his pain and confusion he hears 'the voice of God, with a message'. It tells him that he has been 'picked to turn the Kirk of Scotland away from arid theol-ogy' towards 'compassionate and responsible involvement' with the outcast poor. Since he has this divine mission, it would be bad if his lust towards Eleanor was revealed. For that reason the Lord has 'put it in her head to go to far-off Italy'. When Eleanor rejoins him she notices his changed state and is puzzled. 'Others were go-ing to be similarly perplexed.' Now, confident of his mission, he will set out cunningly to beat 'the hypocritical world at its own game'. When Eleanor, not without affection, calls him a 'crafty little rogue', he does not feel discomfited. 'He would never be dis-comfited again.'

Jenkins is setting up George, in fact, as an unusually subtle ver-sion of the 'justified sinner', a type prominent in Scottish writing from Burns's Holy Willie to Spark's Jean Brodie. What he takes to be the voice of God spurs him to calculated, antinomian, devious-ness. Jenkins's reader is likely to sympathise with George's ardent commitment to the poor, which draws him into earnest prayer in the Cadzow jail with a woman who has murdered her prosti-tute daughter and survived after cutting her own throat, and which has earned him the approval of the democratic agitator, Taylor, whom he permitted to take sanctuary in his kirk. His mis-sion, unlike Chalmers', is not constrained by theology. But Jenkins knows, and reminds us, that just as Chalmers' vision of godly Commonwealth was unrealisable by the Free Church which he founded – not least because the Disruption itself deprived Pres-byterians of unchallenged leadership in Scottish affairs – so George's really anticipates the work of Socialism, and the prophet of Socialism is the unbelieving Taylor. George's kindness may touch the poor, but his God will not prevail through him.

On first reading of the novel, it seems to be very much on George's side against his brother-in-law. Yet rereading establishes that Robert Drummond, a kind man with artistic tastes, is, beneath the gaze of eternity, no more contemptible than Darroch. They have in common the burden of wives schooled to reject pleasure in sex – and at least Drummond cares deeply for his sister, whose life is blighted and at last terminated early by Darroch's imperious physical attentions. Drummond doesn't really like George but, as a Tory in the Dundas tradition, is prepared to put himself out to help his relative towards wealth and ease. Jenkins's presentation of the Disruption is finely poised between recognition that real agony, real sacrifice, real nobility were involved on the Evangelical side and judgement that its values were fatally narrow and imperfect. George himself recognises this – yet, 'ambitiously', chooses to scheme within the new Free Church. Amongst all these creatures of a bygone era, Jenkins may seem to invite us to confer fuller approval on Mrs Wedderburn, who frankly likes sex, and George's seaman brother, Henry, who is happy to go along with her: yet his trade involves him in Far Eastern transactions in the period of the Opium Wars, and the secular hedonism of this couple, tested by Jenkins in that context, would surely prove equally unacceptable as a basis for morality. However, Jenkins has revived the drama of the Disruption with an imagination well informed by reading in social history and with a serious interest in the ideas and dilemmas of Presbyterians in that period.

1993

When was Scotland?

OVER THE LAST THREE DECADES, many Socialists in Scotland have committed themselves wholeheartedly to 'Home Rule' (a traditional Labour Party objective, of course, though abandoned in the late Fifties) and some have gone further, to call for 'independence'. Tommy Sheridan's Scottish Socialist Party might or might not be called 'Nationalist', depending on how that term is defined, but a 'myth of origin' for its stance can be found in John MacLean's call for a Scottish Workers Republic in the 1920s. Journalists have chattered freely about a 'nationalist wing' of the Labour party and with more justification about Socialists in the SNP.

There are strategic and even tactical reasons why Socialists should have worked to help create the new Edinburgh Parliament, and why independence for Scotland might further Socialist practices. I will come back to these later. Meanwhile, all talk about Scottish 'nationality' – such is the nature of ideology, such are its inevitable overhang and undertow – plays off and is played with by powerful myths. Tartan, which was hardly innocuous when it was the garb of the most ruthless troops at the disposal of the British empire, may now seem to be no more than a harmless 'lifestyle choice.' But the idea that Scotland is an ancient nation 'colonised' by England, that the English tried to deprive us of 'our language' (Scots, or Gaelic), to brainwash us as they are held to have done to Kikuyu and Luo, that we therefore have a natural affinity with the oppressed and wretched of the earth, our fellow victims – this sturdy phantom has potentially very dangerous implications, the chief of which is anti-English racism.

People other than Socialists are heard to utter such nonsense. The notion that Hanoverian operations in the *Gaeltacht* were equivalent to Hitler's Final Solution has recently been aired repeatedly in the normally sane letters-columns of the *Herald*. The problem with such talk – and this is an insight I owe to a brilliant young black man brought up in Scotland – is that sooner or later it implies that the true bedrock of Scottish 'nationality' is a language which very few of us can speak and which is self-evidently not native to people born here with dusky skins. Likewise, the Scots Language purists who accuse Anglicised Quislings, since 1603, of suppressing the true leid of the Scottish People, are pushing an essentialist line which can topple into racism.

There were racist implications in John MacLean's belief in an aboriginal Celtic Communism. Left wing conceptions of Scottish identity may be seen as related to that, though their expression is not racist. Whereas Bruce is held in some suspicion, as an Anglo-Norman aristocrat, Wallace is thought to have mobilised the common folk in a precocious 'nationalist' movement. It is widely – even generally – believed that clansmen before the '45 were living 'as families', quasi-socialistically, until Cumberland's troops moved in, after which their chiefs, corrupted by capitalism, set about re-placing them with sheep. More immediately, it has been thought that Scottish reaction against the policies of Thatcher and Major – which must certainly be seen as the proximate cause of Home Rule as we now have it, since it led to the electoral destruction of the Conservative and Unionist Party – was fuelled by an especially Scottish 'civic' consensus which favoured public ownership of essential utilities and amenities, higher spending on health and education, and a more generous attitude towards the wider world.

Meanwhile, our purportedly generous, enlightened, left of centre populace permits to continue the obscene deformation of life in Castlemilk, Easterhouse, Muirhouse and other unspeakable schemes. It gets agitated over the high proportion of students from England in certain Scottish universities, not about the inevitable decline in standards resulting from too few academics enduring bigger and bigger workloads. It agonised over the loss of Ravenscraig steel and is now mortified by the threat to what remains of the 'historic' Clydeside shipbuilding industry while ignoring the decimation of the textile industry on which Border towns have depended. At least, these are the attitudes which one deduces from the news media. The shibboleths of 'nationhood' ensure that more attention is paid just now to a crisis in 'tourism' than to the ongoing scandal of homelessness. 'Nationhood,' to adapt Johnson, is the last refuge of the clueless chancer.

So Neil Davidson's book on *The Origins of Scottish Nationhood*, published recently by Pluto, is extremely timely. The gist of his thesis may seem to some over-technical. He argues on classic Marxist lines (with a bit of help at one point from Trotsky) that 'nationalism' is a product of capitalism and a developed bourgeoisie, that it can be said to have existed in England by 1688 and emerged in France a century later. The term could not be associated with the opposition in the Scottish Parliament to amalgamation with Westminster in 1707. Scotland down to then had not experienced even a successful absolutist kingship, centralising power, and overriding contumacious regional overlords. It remained a collection of still-feudal territories where magnates made their own law. Lowlanders left Highlanders out of their vision of 'their' country and vice versa. Yet by 1820, when Davidson's study terminates, there was undoubtedly a sense of Scottish 'nationhood' shareable within the whole area denominated 'Scotland.' The Tartan kilt, proscribed after Culloden, had become the garb of regiments victorious in the the Napoleonic Wars, and a proud symbol of Scottishness. Lowland and Highland, Campbell and MacDonald, even Catholic, Episcopalian and Evangelical Protestant, were integrated in a conception of Scotland which, while it was crystallised in the all-conquering novels of Walter Scott, could not have been so had there not been solid preconditions for its acceptance, fully met.

Davidson's argument is that Scottish nationhood was not something denied by the Union of 1707 – it arose out of it. While he is sharply critical of Linda Colley's justly influential book *Britons* (1992), he utilises very well her main argument that the later part of the eighteenth century saw the emergence of a common 'British' identity. England led the world, with its constitutional limitation of monarchical powers generating 'Liberty', its commercial prowess and its advanced agriculture. Scottish landowners, merchants, industrialists and intellectuals were avid to catch up. They craved 'assimilation'. The English did not bully Scots into changing the ways they spoke and wrote. Scots took elocution lessons of their own accord and strove to purge their prose of 'Scotticisms'. It was no accident that a Scot, James Thomson, wrote the words of 'Rule Britannia' (1740). The national effort to catch up with England succeeded. Fusion occurred not just at the levels where aristocrats from Scotland and England intermarried, where traders from both countries cooperated in the East India Company and the rape of India, and where the London Missionary Society facilitated the work of Scottish missionaries. The radical working class movements in the two countries interchanged rhetoric and symbolism. Burns in his poem *The Dumfries Volunteers* called for the defence of 'British ground' against the 'foreign foe'. After the Napoleonic Wars were over, radicals, and later Chartists, in Yorkshire and Lancashire played and sang 'Scots Wha Hae' with gusto at their rallies.

'It is not simply,' Davidson writes, 'that Scottishness is part of Britishness – a point most people would concede – it is also that Britishness is part of Scottishness and the latter would not exist, at least in the same form, without the former.' Shock, horror! (Or Jings! Crivvens!) This man says we owe our 'nationhood' to our fusion in one state with the Auld Enemy!!! Yet, once one has dispensed with the ludicrous notion that Scotland was 'colonised' by England – the brief spell of Cromwellian conquest in the 1650s did not entail *colonisation,* and anyone who still thinks that 'the English' beat 'the Scots' at Culloden is an irredeemable numpty – Davidson's case seems unassailably strong. One could argue that in Bruce's day a high proportion of the Scottish nobility showed a strong 'national' disposition to stand together against the English king. One could discuss at some length the sense of a 'national' calling by the Lord God embodied in the rhetoric of dedicated

Covenanters, and one could investigate, as David Allan has done, the fascination of Scottish intellectuals, from the sixteenth through to the eighteenth century, with their country's history. But an ample 'Scottishness' uniting Lowlands and Highland was impossible until the latter had been, first, subdued, then, through Macpherson's *Ossian*, turned into poetry which haunted contemporaries, including Burns, then Scott, who incorporated it into their own potent visions of Scotland. Both writers were determined to preserve the Scottish heritage of poetry and song, and to immortalise Scottish heroism. Both accepted that Scotland was changing fast and endorsed change. Burns wanted his country, still controlled politically by a tiny oligarchy of voters (the entire Scottish county franchise in 1790 was 2,655, slightly smaller than that of the town of Preston in England, and only 33 people had the vote in Edinburgh) to move towards democracy. Scott had no stomach for that, but with pangs and reservations endorsed the industrial revolution. Near the end of his epoch-making *Waverley* (1814), his narrator observes that since 1746 and the crushing of the Jacobites, 'The gradual influx of wealth, and extension of commerce, have since united to render the present people of Scotland a class of human beings as different from their grandfathers, as the existing English are from those of Queen Elizabeth's time.'

Notice that Scott knows that the English have changed, too. And of course since 1814 both Scotland and England have undergone further enormous transformations. Neil Davidson's account of the role of Scots in the conquest and exploitation of the British Empire, despite a few blemishes attributable, I fear, to weak editorial work by Pluto, is as good a summary as I've seen of the suture which fixed Scottish 'nationhood' proudly together with 'Britishness'. To suggest, as so many have done, that Scots were tools of the English in their expansion is ridiculous. To call them 'junior partners' is more plausible, until one notices that in certain areas (American tobacco, Canadian furs and politics, African exploration, Bengal jute, and so on) Scots indisputably ruled the roost. What has happened since the dismantling of empire, effectually completed in the 1960s, is that more and more Scots have detached their 'Scottishness' from their 'Britishness'. However confused common notions about 'Scottish identity' may be, we tend more and more to 'know' that we are different and to take some pride in that. What Davidson does not discuss is where this leaves the English.

'English' culture has been saturated in Scottish influences. (Burns on Wordsworth, Scott on the Brontës, Carlyle on Dickens – such a list could go on and on.) The current travails of English intellectuals, left and right, as they clutch for what is specifically 'English' to match the 'Scottishness' embodied now in in the Edinburgh Parliament, will be eased if they accept that English 'nationhood' also has, since the 1780s at any rate, been modified and transformed by 'Britishness.'

But why should Socialists bother with all this ideological blether? Class interests unite Scottish capitalists with English, and Scottish employees should cooperate with counterparts south of the Border. In so far as the Edinburgh Parliament is a product of a sense of 'nationhood', I suggest that Socialists can make use of nationhood. Strategically, a country of five milllion people with traditions, however sentimentalised, of fellow feeling across classes is more likely to foster social experiments involving Green policies, cooperation, public ownership and generosity towards poorer nations, than that much more complex UKanian entity, with ten or eleven times the population, which is bottom heavy with south-eastern suburbia. And experiments successful in Scotland may be imitable in England. Tactically, Socialists can seek to use the Edinburgh Parliament to expose, by defiance and contrariness, the inanities of Neo-Blairism and whatever comes next. But those who might idly suppose that Scottish 'nationhood' is static, unchanging, a 'given' entity to slot some day 'independently' into Europe are romantics ignorant of the history which Neil Davidson has so acutely sorted out for us.

2000

Imperialism and Scottish Culture

THERE ARE THREE EMINENTLY contentious terms in my title. Definitions of 'imperialism' abound. 'Culture' can be applied narrowly to the folk arts and/or 'high arts' of a particular aggregation of people, or exhaustively to all their lived practices. And the delimitation of 'Scottish'-ness is not easy. I hope that what I say later may helpfully ease us through these problems of definition, but I am going to begin exactly where you might expect me to start – with popular fiction by one of Scotland's best-known and best-loved authors, who was happy to call himself an 'imperialist' and lived and wrote in the heyday of 'imperialism', whether this is defined as the dominant ideology of the British state, as a phase in Western capitalism, or merely as a phenomeon in popular culture.

John Buchan began to publish thrillers featuring Richard Hannay – later, General Sir Richard Hannay – during the First World War. *The Thirty-Nine Steps* came out in 1915, *Greenmantle* in 1916 and *Mr Standfast* in 1919. All three feature conspiracies by diabolically clever master-spies against British power. Their plots depend on amazing coincidences and involve nightmarish sequences in which Hannay is pursued over awkward terrains by fiendish adversaries, changing clothes and accents repeatedly to disguise his identity. In his dedication of *The Thirty-Nine Steps* to Thomas Arthur Nelson, in whose publishing business Buchan had been a partner, he confesses to his affection for the works of light fiction known as 'dime novels' in the USA and 'shockers' in Britain – 'where the incidents defy the probabilities and march just inside the borders of the possible.' His short novel derived from a serious bout of illness in which he felt 'driven' to write a 'shocker' for himself. But now, with the Great War raging, 'the wildest fictions are so much less improbable than the facts'. So he has it both ways. He admits that his fiction is not serious in its intention, yet insinuates that it somehow corresponds, albeit inadequately, to contemporary reality... Buchan, overage for service, and initially unfit, did not enjoy the Great War at all when he finally found his way to France as an Intelligence Corps Officer. Numerous dear friends, including Nelson, were killed. But Buchan's faith in the British Empire, its peoples and its beneficent destiny, enabled him to present the war, in his 'shockers', as a contest between victorious Good and thwarted Evil.

Having it both, or all, ways turns out to be typical of Buchan's discourse, matching salient features of his biography. Born in Perth, a son of the Manse, in 1875, and schooled in Glasgow, he nevertheless identified most strongly with the landscape and traditions of the Borders where he spent boyhood summers. From Glasgow University, he proceeded to Brasenose College, where he shone academically and socially and acquired an abiding devotion to the landscapes of Oxfordshire. He diverted from his chosen career at the London Bar to serve Lord Milner, the statesman sent out to reconstruct South Africa after the Boer War. He was not the first or the last Scot to fall in love with Africa, where, employed on various administrative tasks over a couple of years, he roamed vast unspoilt tracts of 'Nature'. His first famous novel, *Prester John*, had an African basis. His Hannay is an idealised self-projection. Hannay is not a deep intellectual, like Buchan. His posture as a self-proclaimed bear (as it were) of very little brain at times recalls his exact fictional coeval, P.G. Wodehouse's Bertie Wooster (like Hannay created with the American market very much in mind – a Brit for Yank consumption). Hannay shares Buchan's own devotion to field sports. Unlike Buchan, though, he is a serious fighting army officer. He has been formed by years roaming the Southern African veld, and has spent relatively little time in the Scotland of his forebears. But he is as much at home as his creator in rugged Scottish landscapes and with Scottish people of all classes.

Indeed, the notion of 'Scottishness' which Buchan's shockers communicate virtually assimilates it with the famed capacities of the chameleon. Hannay's friend, Sandy Arbuthnot, another Anglo-Scot with whom he teams up in *Greenmantle*, is an astonishing linguist and master of disguise who is able to lead a cult of Middle-Eastern devotees and pass himself off as a Mohammedan Messiah. In Turkey, Hannay refers to 'straths' and 'glens' as features of the local landscape, but everywhere he is haunted by memories of the South African karoo, revived for him by his close comradeship in thwarting Kaiser Wilhelm with an ageing Boer big-game tracker, Pieter Pienaar. Scotland might be said to represent Ancestry and Danger, South Africa Beauty and Freedom. But Hannay, in *Mr Standfast*, falls for a perfect English Rose, identified in his imagination with the spot in the Cotswolds where he first meets her, and where they settle when married.

Just before he is introduced to Mary Lamington, to whom Buchan rather impishly gives the name of a Scottish Border village, Hannay has:

> ... a kind of revelation. I had a vision of what I had been fighting for, what we were all fighting for. It was peace, deep and holy and ancient, peace deeper than the oldest wars, peace which would endure when all our swords were hammered into ploughshares. It was more; for in that hour England first took hold of me. Before, my country had been South Africa, and when I thought of home it had been the wide sun-steeped spaces of the veld or some scented glen of the Berg. But now I realized that I had a new home. I understood what a precious thing this little England was, how old and kindly and comforting, how wholly worth striving for. The freedom of an acre of her soil was cheaply bought by the blood of the best of us.

Yet when Hannay later, in a tight corner, is restored by the thought of Mary 'looking again beyond the war, to that peace which she and I would one day inherit... a vision of a green English landscape', there comes to his mind 'a line of an old song, which had

been a favourite of my father's: There's an eye that ever weeps and
a fair face will be fain/ When I ride through Annan Water wi' my
bonny bands again!'

Buchan called his engaging autobiography *Memory Hold the
Door*. But his own identity seems to go round and round in a revolving door. Oxford, he claims:

> ... enabled me to discover Scotland. Before I came [n.b. not
> 'went'] up I had explored a great part of the Lowlands with
> the prosaic purpose of catching trout; but apart from my
> own Borders, the land, though I was steeped in its history,
> made no special appeal. Scottish literature, except the bal-
> lads and Sir Walter Scott, was scarcely known to me, and I
> had read very little of Robert Burns. But now as a tempo-
> rary exile I adopted all the characteristics of a Scot abroad.
> I became a fervent admirer of Burns and a lover of Dunbar
> and the other poets of the Golden Age. I cultivated a senti-
> ment for all things Scottish and brought the Highlands and
> isles into the orbit of my interest.

The physical self-transformations of Hannay – rarely seen in
the same clothes for more than a few pages at a time – match the
psychological prestidigitation of his creator. 'Empire' gave Buchan
an umbrella of identity under which he could identify passionately
with South Africa and, later, with Canada, of which he was appointed Viceroy, while promoting the publication of new verse in
the old Scots tongue (some of which he wrote himself) and professing a Scottish patriotism which verged on outright nationalist
sentiment – all the time responding wholeheartedly to that vision
of Deep England which inspired the English Nationalist school of
composers – Elgar, Vaughan Williams, Butterworth, Moeran, and
others. Buchan can only be called a 'racist' in so far as he traffics
freely in the racist stereotypes of his day – the brutal, methodical
German, the foppish but vicious Turk, the honest Boer in tune
with the natural world, and so on. He is avid to find good in all

'races' – Hannay admires the spirit of a 'Portuguese Jew' who conflates in one person two often despised racial types.

Buchan's idealisation of England, as transmitted through Hannay, suggested that it represented past peace, enduring peace, and the future peace of a world civilised by the British Empire. Reminiscing in 1940, he wrote of his South African days when:

> a vision of what the Empire might be dawned upon certain minds with almost the force of revelation... I dreamed of a world-wide brotherhood with the background of a common race and creed, consecrated in the service of peace; Britain enriching the rest out of her culture and traditions, and the spirit of the Dominions like a strong wind freshening the stuffiness of the old lands. I saw in the Empire a means of giving the congested masses at home open country instead of a blind alley... Our creed was not based on antagonism to any other people. It was humanitarian and international; we believed that we were laying the basis of a federation of the world.

While the idealism of Milner's 'Round Table' group of imperialists, so named after the journal which it published, belonged very specifically to a particular historical conjuncture, marked by the achievement of Dominion status by Australia, New Zealand and South Africa, following Canada, and early steps towards Indian home rule, the terms on which Buchan embraced England and Englishness had been long prefigured in the writings of fellow Scots and admitted by sometimes-envious Englishmen. In the novels of Buchan's boyhood and lifetime hero, Walter Scott, the peace and prosperity which had followed the suppression of the last Jacobite Rebellion represented a necessary accommodation of Scottish violence, clannishness and fanaticism with English stability and commercial prowess. Thomas Carlyle had extolled the dumb strength of John Bull, great doer, not great thinker, with the implication that he needed Scots to intellectualise for him. David Livingstone, passionately Scottish in spiritual and intellectual formation, was usually happy to be regarded as an Englishman. In Thomas Hardy's great fable, *The Mayor of Casterbridge*, a charming Scottish wanderer named Farfrae literally takes over a Wessex, West Saxon, Deep English town, representing the success of many 'Scots on the make' in English, Welsh and Irish trade and industry, in the City of London, and perhaps above all in the Colonies. Buchan flourished and wrote at a moment when the English public boarding schools exercised cultural and political hegemony, when wealthy Scots sents their sons to them, then on to Oxford and Cambridge Universities, and when a composite British ruling class moved freely between clubs in London and sporting estates in the Scottish Highlands, both shared and shared alike between Anglo-Scots and their wealthy English friends. English toffs had learned to play golf; Scots played cricket. But the chameleon Scot might be seen as acting a part which the Englishman performed naturally. He could equally well identify with South Sea Islanders, like R.L. Stevenson, with the wilds of North America, like John Muir, or with the Workers of the World like R.B. Cunninghame Graham, 'Don Roberto' to admiring Argentinians who named a city after him.

So far what I have said might seem likely to produce an argument as follows: in the heyday of the British empire some Scots attached to the British ruling class and its strategies, represented – with charm and idealism – by Buchan, who was both politician and bestselling writer, infected Scottish culture with imperialist ideas. Along with Buchan one might range the distinguished Scottish composers Alexander Mackenzie and Hamish McCunn who contributed, with Edward Elgar, compositions performed in the Empire Pageant at the 1924 British Empire Exhibition at Wembley – Mackenzie was represented by his *Britannia Overture* and McCunn by *Livingstone Episode* and *Camp and Kaffir Melodies*. One might mention Harry Lauder, the former coal-miner, knighted in 1919, who sang Scottish songs all over the Empire to thronged halls and was delighted in Rangoon to meet Mr Lim, 'known all over India as the Sugar King' and 'reputed to be one of the richest Chinamen in the world', who greeted him in his opulent mansion, 'Man, Harry, it's a braw, bricht moonlicht nicht the nicht, is it no? Hooch aye,' and proceeded, 'Say, Harry, ma cock, hoo wad ye like me to gie ye a blaw on the pipes?' – upon which he performed in fine style, confiding later that he had been Pipe Major in the Dollar Academy pipe band. One might further allude to the high-minded John Reith directing that great institution the BBC as it linked the Empire through the airwaves and promoted a homogenised Standard Received Pronunciation, and the equally stern John Grierson, pioneering British documentary cinema at the Empire Marketing Board, and moving on via the GPO Film Unit, to develop documentary cinema in Canada.

But the idea that Scotland's destiny lay within the English-speaking 'Commonwealth of Nations' – the very term had been coined by a Scottish politician, Lord Rosebery, in the 1880s – was not confined to people obviously hitched to the imperial Establishment. One might discount as Establishment axe-grinding a prominent feature of the Scottish National War Memorial unveiled in 1927 in Edinburgh Castle, where above the the door of the innermost Shrine the branches of the Tree of Empire supported the arms of Scotland along with those of the Dominions and India. However, the Memorial, under the overall charge of the architect Sir Robert Lorimer, and realised in detail by distinguished sculptors and craftsmen inspired by the Arts and Crafts movement, was far from being a crassly jingoistic project. In that decade when Presbyterian clerics inveighed darkly against Catholic immigration, it was not surprising that the arms of Eire, a Free State within the Commonwealth since 1923, were not represented. But that status achieved by southern Ireland seemed to some a precedent for a self-ruling Scotland. In 1928 the Reverend James Barr, an Independent Labour MP, supported by the so-called 'Red Clydesiders' (Maxton, Johnston, Kirkwood and all), put forward a bill in the Commons designed to give Scotland self-governing status within the empire, and this was hailed as a proposal 'within the true lines of Imperial development' by none other than C.M. Grieve, whose verse in Scots as 'Hugh MacDiarmid' Buchan had encouraged, and who shortly figured as one of the founders of the National Party of Scotland. For Grieve, Scotland was 'one of the great founder nations of the empire'. So one might say that the ideology of empire as a beneficent force permeated even oppositional elements in Scottish political and artistic culture. Pittendreigh Macgillvary (1856–1938), though nationalistic as artist and poet, had been honoured with the title King's Sculptor in Scotland in 1921. He was naturally asked to join the General Committee organising the British Empire Exhibition at Wembley. He resigned when his suggestion that Scottish sculptors should be exhibited separately from English colleagues was turned down. But it seems just as significant that he had agreed to join the committee in the first place.

It seems to me that all that I have so far suggested might seem embarrassingly self-evident. In a period when Glasgow was proud of being the Second City of the empire, and would host its own impressive Empire Exhibition as late as 1938, when Clyde-built ships were sinews of imperial commerce and the Royal Navy, when a century of large-scale emigration had linked Scottish families to far continents, when Scottish missions and the schools attached to them were profoundly influential in India and Africa, when Scots contributed a disproportionate number of regulars, volunteers and casualties to the British military effort on the Western Front of 1914–18 – Scottish culture at all levels was affected by imperial sentiment, and even the opposition to the war by John MacLean was garnished by the boast that Glasgow, so important in world trade and industry, could become a second, bigger and better Petrograd. Only retrospectively could ignorant people suggest that Scotland had been a colonised country, a victim of the English imperial drive in which, in fact, Scots had very willingly participated.

Analytically, Scotland's position in the empire had been utterly different from that of Ireland, a country colonised and subordinated by England from the sixteenth century, and indeed from that of Wales, a backward region where industrialisation from the eighteenth century had depended on English – and Scottish – capital.

During a period of resurgent nationalism in all three Celtic countries, Michael Hechter's *Internal Colonialism: The Celtic Fringe in British National Development* (1975) gained a certain amount of credence and fed into ideas suggested by Immanuel Wallerstein's theses about core and periphery in capitalist expansion. But the differing courses of politics in the three countries since then can only be explained by Scotland's lack of any overall history of colonial oppression and exploitation. While Ireland's heritage of violent resistance had a grisly sequel, and the language issue and English immigration had explosive, and divisive, power in Welsh political life, Scotland proceded decorously, without any serious violence, towards the recovery of its own parliament in 1999. As a nation, Scotland had never ceased to exist. Under the 1707 Treaty of Union it had retained its own established Church, its own system of education and crucial, its own law and legal system. MacDiarmid's claim that it had been 'one of the great founder nations of the empire' would not have seemed at all absurd to a Canadian, New Zealander or Malawian.

I will now retreat, as I promised, to the problem of definition. I will try to be summary without being clumsy but I hope you can forgive my simplifications.

Let us run with the broad definitions of terms. When we speak of a 'native American culture', we refer to all the lived practices of an aboriginal people. 'Scottish culture' would accordingly refer to everything we do in Scotland – how we drink, how we marry, how we sing. Attempts have been made to isolate 'imperialism' as a recurrent phenomenon in human societies which can be studied from ancient pre-capitalist examples as well as modern ones. But it seems wisest to apply the term to the processes which first created the development of modern capitalism in Europe, from the fifteenth century, then generated industrial revolution, which permitted European powers and the USA, in cooperation as well as rivalry, to dominate, in effect, every part of the world and opened up virtually all the earth's material resources, and most of its human populations, to profitable exploitation by metropolitan capital. 'Globalisation' such as we live with today is the latest phase of this process and I myself would readily describe it as intrinsically 'imperialistic'.

In this context, to differentiate between Scottish 'culture' and those of other industrialised Western cultures will be difficult. As both Marxist and 'social scientific' approaches to history and society have insisted, the situation of a factory worker or typist in Scotland is very similar to that of counterparts elsewhere. Differentials such as literacy rates and mortality statistics may suggest local peculiarities. (Russians clearly drink too much vodka.) Deep-fried Mars Bars and Haggis suppers are no doubt rare in Milan, but McDonald's hamburgers are now eaten in every modern city. For several centuries a Western lifestyle has been emerging which is now adopted in Eastern societies and by Southern elites and could be described as 'Americanised', with the qualification that the American lifestyle has incorporated or adapted features from many other cultures. Curries and paellas assort with pizzas and fried potatoes in our post-modernist world of instantaneous worldwide communication. Country and western music, perversely deplored by some in Scotland as an American intrusion, is in fact a development from Scottish, Irish – and English – musical styles. Harry Lauder's Mr Lim had as much right to his bagpipes as we have to Peking Duck.

But geographical and chronological factors have given Scotland a peculiar position in the history of imperialism-stroke-globalisation which makes it analytically possible to assign special characteristics to Scottish culture. They also serve to explain peculiarities in the work of great Scottish storytellers – Scott, Stevenson and Buchan.

Geographically, Scotland is a country slashed deeply by the sea with a relatively low ratio of fertile land. These factors have made emigration salient in history and culture. It is estimated that before 1641, 100,000 people emigrated to Ireland from Britain. Thirty thousand of these were Scots, and concentrated in Ulster, they had a disproportionate effect on Irish and then, by further emigration, on North American history. But in the first four decades of the seventeenth century, greater numbers of Scots – 40,000 – are said to have emigrated to Poland, and a further 30,000 to Scandinavia. Though the population of Scotland at this time was less than a million, this effusion was not of course comparable to the mass exodus from Ireland during and after the mid-nineteenth-century famine. But it did mean that the Wandering Scot – soldier, farmer, trader – was a well-established as prototype by the seventeenth century. Nationalists in Scotland have latterly said a lot about our– 'European' outlook as compared to the insular English. One might extrapolate backwards from, and forward to, the fictions of Smollett and Scott, Stevenson and Buchan and argue that Scots, often short of opportunity in their own land, have long been at-tuned to accomodating themselves to foreign tastes, prejudices and customs. An interesting example would be Episcopalian clergy-men, of a persuasion first unpopular, then, after the Glorious Revo-lution, outlawed, in Scotland itself. Such Scots could find employment abroad, as chaplains in the unsavoury forts of the Royal African Company, or emissaries in America of the Society for the Propagation of the Gospel. The first Episcopalian bishop of the infant USA was accordingly consecrated, after the American Revolution, in Aberdeen.

Another geographical factor was proximity to England. This had the effect in the fourteenth century of exciting Scots to a pre-cocious nationalism and moving them towards the potentially revo-lutionary doctrine that kings ultimately had authority only through the consent of the people. Emulation of a dangerous and richer southern neighbour helped to inspire notable Scottish achievements around 1500, when William Dunbar consciously developed from and vied with the great master Chaucer, when James IV's navy pre-ceded the Tudors' in solving the problem of how to mount a really heavy gun on a sailing ship, and Scottish seamen were developing a lead over English in the arts of deep sea navigation. While Tu-dors planted English colonies in Ireland, James VI came up with the notion of colonising the Scottish Gaeltacht. His exploitation, after the Union of the Crowns, of English conquest of Ireland gave scope for fellow Scots in colonisation, and some proceeded later in the seventeenth century to make East New Jersey a distinctively Scottish colony on the American seaboard. After such experience, the idea of creating a Scottish colony on the isthmus of Panama was not so daft as historians of the Darien Company of the 1690s have tended to assume. Its failure merely matched those of attempted settlements by English and other European peoples in various parts of the tropical world in the early phases of capitalist imperialism.

The English could not have stopped Scots penetrating their colonies in the seventeenth century even if they had seriously tried to do so. The exclusive, 'mercantilist' English Navigation Acts from 1651 onwards did not check the probes of Scots interlopers. From the Union of Parliaments in 1707, Scots were entirely within their rights to operate as equals in any British settlement. They developed overweening influence in some of the West Indian sugar colonies and, as every schoolboy should now know, Glasgow rose to opulence on the basis of a virtual monopoly position in the trade in Virginian tobacco. No Scottish port specialised in the slave trade, but through sugar and tobacco, African slavery was as important to Scotland's economic progress as to England's. Burns was drawn to the idea of mending his fortunes as an overseer in a West Indies sugar plantation and Scott was permanently mortified by the cowardice displayed by his brother when he confronted a slave rebellion in just such a position. As early as the 1720s Robert Walpole saw East India Company patronage as an aid to making the Scots amenable to Whig government and we can descry the first fabulous fortunes accruing to lucky Scots in the East. Overseas fortunes, brought home, energised improving agriculture and modern industry in Scotland.

By the nineteenth century, disproportionate Scottish influence in British trade, soldiering and politics in India were taken for granted, as was the dominant position of Scots in the fur trade of the vast region now included in Canada. Much has been made of the plight of Highland Gaels forced into emigration after Culloden and in the 'Clearances' of the nineteenth century, but it has to be said that they were normally likely to prosper more overseas not only than impoverished Irish Gaels, but than their compatriots at home. Scottish regiments and their wailing bagpipes developed fierce and proud traditions within the British Army. It has been customary for nationalistic historians to suggest that the Scots were recruited as mercenaries and, as it were, upper servants, of the English in the dirty work of Empire. This seems more plausible as a view of the Irish contribution to British expansion overseas. Ireland fed men disproportionately into the British Army, though it must be added that Ireland, too, supplied colonial governors, generals and entrepreneurs to the imperial project.

Scots, with traditions of a war of liberation against English rule, conscious of links with a doomed aboriginal Gaelic culture, and with chameleon-like propensities, were perhaps imaginatively predisposed to greater sympathy with native Americans and Maoris, Sikhs and Bantus than many English readily displayed. John Mackenzie has argued that Scots brought a distinctive vision of civic morality to the government of overseas empire which so many of them found themselves conducting. But only a gross aversion to blatant evidence could sustain either the notion that Scots were less zestful in empire than the English, or that their attitude to the English involved cultural cringe. Scotland's middle classes on balance did very well indeed out of empire and its labouring classes were largely sustained by industries exporting from the empire or importing from it.

If England seemed to a man like Buchan a centre of calm and a reservoir of spiritual values at the heart of empire, this must have been partly because the Scots were dashing about so conspicuously far and wide to energise it. Surely no English city, after Liverpool lost its slave trade, lived in symbiosis with tropical empire matching Dundee's with Bengal? In 1937, Evgenia Fraser, daughter of a Russian father and a mother from Broughty Ferry, reared in Scotland, arrived to join her husband Ronnie on the banks of the Hooghly. He was the kerani in charge of the office of a jute mill and all its clerical staff:

> The keranis of all the mills, up and down the river, were young men recruited from Dundee and its district. Most of them had a grammar school background and had served their apprenticeship in the offices of jute mills and brokers. They had also attended the Dundee technical college... Usually after a certain time working as keranis in the mill offices they were promoted as salesmen in the various head offices, situated mostly in that promised land of Clive Street, Calcutta. The other men, the overseers, in different departments of the mill had held similar positions in the mill in Angus and had also attended the technical college.

Beside geography, the other factors differentiating Scottish culture from English imperialism, and European imperialism in general, were asynchronicity and ideology, closely related to each other. Seventeenth-century Scotland had close links with the Netherlands, at that point leading Europe not only in intercontinental trade and colonisation, but also in advanced agricultural methods. The English, with their greater resources, were temporarily better placed to imitate, then surpass, the Dutch. But when agricultural improvement and overseas trade rather suddenly began to burgeon together in Scotland towards the middle of the eighteenth century, Scottish economic and social thinkers were well placed to discuss the resulting industrial revolution, its theoretical dimensions and its moral implications. The achievements of the Scottish Enlightenment resulted from this conjuncture. In the same country, Scottish thinkers saw co-existing the traditional economy of the *Gaeltacht* and the cutting-edge practices of trade in tobacco, the Carron ironworks, Lothian husbandry and new textile technology. Watt's steam engine and Adam Smith's political economy coincided with the world-wide impact of Macpherson's versions of Gaelic poetry and, not long after, the Scots verse of Robert Burns and his wonderful reworkings of traditional song. Scotland had the unique and unrepeatable distinction of pioneering simultaneously in the recovery of traditional cultures for modern man and the spelling out of the gospels of economic and technological progress. Walter Scott, bringing all these elements together in a genre of historical realism in fiction which he effectually invented, established parameters for Scottish identity within which his fellow-countrymen lived comfortably for a century.

The Scottish past was wondrously lively, an incomparable source of song and story, but self-interest dictated that Scots should abandon heroics and lost causes and accommodate themselves with commerce, industry and the British imperial project. Storytelling, which in Scott, was still at first geared to experience – he had spoken to old Jacobites and living devotees of the true Covenanted faith – led in less factually-rooted romances by him to variations on the theme of the Wandering Scot, transmuted in Stevenson and Buchan into a wholly freewheeling type of adventure narrative which might be seen as achieving its final sublimation in the ahistorical but in a sense historic creation by an Anglo-Scot, Ian Fleming, of James Bond 007, duly fixed in global culture by our incomparable Edinburgh milk-roundsman 'Big Tam'. And aptly so. Sean Connery, never able to escape his Lothian accent entirely, whatever nationality producers have cast him into, has been an ironic obverse of Hannay and Arbuthnot, masters of disguise: the Scot who cannot be other than he is and now indignantly demands the severance of his own country at last from England – but also the Scot who defined triumphant Englishness for moviegoers worldwide, tacitly usurping the imperial mastery of the Southron at the moment of its terminal decline after the Suez fiasco. This is perhaps a lesser feat than the usurpation of the English literary tradition and the English language itself by Yeats, Joyce and Heaney. But it is one of many examples of twentieth-century Scottish creativity which make it meaningful to discuss Scottish culture as a distinctive element within the post-modernist global pot-pourri.

1999

Poetry, Language and Empire

JOHN AUBREY RETOLD the old gossip that Sir Walter Ralegh once aborded one of Queen Elizabeth's maids of honour, got her against a tree and had his way with her. As her excitement mounted her cry of 'Sweet Sir Walter' became 'Sweesir, Swatter! ... Sweesir Swatter!'

> Speaking broad Devonshire,
> Ralegh has backed the maid to a tree
> As Ireland is backed to England
>
> And drives inland
> Till all her strands are breathless:
> 'Sweesir, Swatter! Sweesir, Swatter!'
>
> He is water, he is ocean, lifting
> Her farthingale like a scarf of weed lifting
> In the front of a wave.

Seamus Heaney's poem, 'Ocean's Love to Ireland', translates the real or apocryphal bodily act into a metaphor about language. Ralegh, the great poet, who wrote, flattering his Queen, 'The Ocean's Love to Cynthia', punned on his own name: he was 'water', he was 'ocean'. He was also a vigorous and ruthless coloniser, acquiring and exploiting a very large estate in land conquered from the Irish. He was, further, the Captain presiding over the massacre at Smerwick of a force sent by the King of Spain to aid the native Irish. Heaney puts these histories together:

> Yet his superb crest inclines to Cynthia

Even while it runs its bent
In the rivers of Lee and Blackwater.

Those are the plashy spots where he would lay
His cape before her. In London, his name
Will rise on water, and on these dark seepings:

Smerwick sowed with the mouthing corpses
Of six hundred papists, 'as gallant and good
Personages as ever were beheld.'

Ralegh's ravishment of the maid of honour is compared to
Ireland's rape by England. His work in Ireland, however, is service
to the Queen herself and to the Tudor State. Ireland is a 'ruined
maid'. (Those who know Hardy's poem of that name reflect here
that being 'ruined' is not always such a bad thing.) The English
iamb supplants the measures of Gaelic. Deprived of their role in a
social hierarchy which has been destroyed, Gaelic poets became,
as we say, 'wankers':

The ruined maid complains in Irish,
Ocean has scattered her dream of fleets,
The Spanish prince has spilled his gold

And failed her. Iambic drums
Of English beat the woods where her poets
Sink like Onan. Rush-light, mushroom-flesh,

She fades from their somnolent clasp
Into ringlet-breath and dew,
The ground possessed and repossessed.

Ralegh's penetration, unlike that of the prematurely ejaculat-
ing Spanish prince, has been complete. Yet – and the punchline
bears strongly on the argument of this essay – the ground thus

possessed by Ralegh is repossessed by the Irish. They recover it using the English language which Ralegh and his friend and fellow-colonist Spenser gave them. 'An image out of Spenser and the common tongue – Yeats's line almost casually assumes that the marginalised, increasingly de-Gaelicised, Irish population owned and developed the language of the Elizabethans.

Joyce inherits from Shakespeare more directly than Noel Coward (say) does. Quite clearly, Heaney himself, a Catholic from Northern Ireland 'possessed' of no Gaelic, asserts, by the very force of this poem and of the volume *North*, published in 1975, in which it appears, the right of his Irish people to their English language.

Twenty years ago I returned to Nairobi, where I had taught for three exciting years, as part of a British Council tour. Ngugi wa Thiong'o, a colleague with whom I'd previously been on warm terms, was head of the Literature Department at the university. He had led it in a particular Marxist direction. I was lecturing on the great twentieth-century Scottish novelist Lewis Grassic Gibbon, and I thought I had got this across to him. But misunderstanding persisted. The students who at first packed out a large lecture hall had been told I was going to talk about Conrad and Kipling as Imperialists. They began to walk out very soon after I launched into my lecture, and in the end there were few left. Ngugi, however, stayed and voiced his own objections in question time.

I had said things about the 'authenticity' of Gibbon's use of a narrative idiom based on north-eastern Scottish speech and queried whether African writers born into non-English speaking communities could achieve this. Ngugi at that time still agreed with Chinua Achebe's position that Africans had every right to use English: indeed, in Nigeria, it was necessary. Almost the first question I'd asked him when we'd first met seven years before was why he didn't write in Kikuyu. He had said that it was because English was the language in which he'd learnt to read and write fiction. I had come to think this illogical – that a Marxist nationalist should write in a language not read easily, if at all, by most of the ordinary people around him.

The sequel is well-known. Three years later Ngugi and a co-author staged a play, before a popular audience, in Kikuyu. For this he was thrown into jail for nearly a year. He emerged vowing to do no more creative writing in English. His debate with Achebe eventually became very fierce indeed.

I would no longer use the term 'authenticity' unless I were talking about the genuineness of, say, a rare stamp or a manuscript. But I still believe that writers should be in touch with the speech of the people they live among. Manifestly, a poem or a novel isn't remembered, or even much read in the first place, if it doesn't communicate with a public. Translation's a fine thing but it's not where a text starts, where its energy comes from.

In the British Isles, or the north-west European archipelago, as some of us have begun to say, literature – published writing – is produced in a number of languages. Three are very old – Welsh, Irish Gaelic (gay-lick) and Scottish Gaelic (gar-lick) – branching from the same trunk. Two are old but more recent – English and Scots – some are still young, like the Glaswegian of James Kelman and Tom Leonard and (new in Britain at any rate) the idioms of Caribbean British and Asian British poets and novelists. All these are clearly hybrid: thus the 'Shetlandic' used by some recent writers is a mongrel Scots/Norse idiom. Obviously, each of the tongues I've mentioned has a regional base. Equally clearly, they're not confined to use only in their regions of origin. Meg Bateman, who learnt Scottish Gaelic as a second language, writes strong poetry in it and has taught it to classes in Edinburgh, where the genteel speech of Anglicised Scots and of numerous English incomers rubs shoulders with that local demotic so ferociously displayed by Irvine Welsh.

There are dialects in England, too, of course. A dense Geordie speech from the north-east can be almost incomprehensible to outsiders from other parts of Britain, though Tommy Armstrong, the coalfield balladeer, penned brilliant song lyrics in it a century ago and singers from other parts have learnt to voice them. Television represents nightly the still-great diversity of English speech in accents, rhythm, lexicon.

A man from St Asaph's in north Wales whom I met recently described to me a language frontier I'd never heard of. He comes from the corridor north of the mountains which stretches from Welsh-speaking Anglesey and north-west Wales across to Liverpool, where so many Welsh people have settled, contributing to the wondrously vital tongue of that city. The frontier on this corridor is between 'Nylanders' and 'Mainlanders'. The Mainlanders are English-speaking Welsh people who know no Welsh language. The Nylanders are Welsh who speak Welsh, so called because they end every sentence with 'ny'.

In Ireland, beside the tradition of Gaelic poetry successfully revived in the last few decades – with women to the fore, though in older Irish communities the production of poetry by women was banned – successful work is extant in the Scotch-Irish dialect of the Protestant north. Two melting pots bubble on each side of the Irish Sea. Exchanges between them occur all the time. So many Irish people work in England. Liverpool, where Scots threading down the line of the M6 (the quickest route out of their country by road) have historically converged with Welsh up from the valleys and Irish from the ferries, with African seamen and now with Caribbean and Asian immigrants, could be described as the linguistic epicentre of the north-west European archipelago.

Of course, all the languages of the archipelago are in motion. The oldest of them have been in motion for a couple of millennia, English and Scots for hundreds of years. How does such motion occur? Much of it comes, of course, from literature itself. From taught Latin comes Johnson's Augustan prose, which leaves indelible traces even on Charlie Dickens. Locutions from Shakespeare. locutions from Burns, slowly or rapidly penetrate spoken language – there are 'images from Spenser and the common tongue'. But a still more important force is what happened in market places, in the middle ages and later. Another is what has happened in education. A third, in our own century, has been the impact of new media – film, radio, TV – facilitating what we call 'Americanisation'.

In market places people from different areas with different

tongues met physically. Necessarily, to do business, they had to find means of linguistic communication. The processes of pidginisation and creolisation occurred within the north-west European archipelago. Education, before those abominable acts of 1870 in England, 1871 in Scotland, made it universally compulsory, was a very complex story. There were more or less dignified grammar schools, high schools, and what in England are misleadingly called 'public' schools where you had to learn Latin. Rich parents employed private tutors. So did some poor ones, like Robert Burns's parents. There were 'enterprise schools' to which parents of middling and small means sent their sons to learn practical skills which would help them make their way in the world. But all education involved transactions with polished or at least with 'standard' English. You did not learn to spell in Ayrshire Scots or Yorkshire English.

The twentieth-century mass media have had contradictory results. Notoriously, Sir John Reith's BBC, from the 1920s through the 1930s, eschewed regional accents, let alone idioms: the former became fully acceptable on radio only during the 'People's War' of 1939–45. Yet meanwhile American movies were introducing all sorts of new idioms. Television, ultimately committed to narrative realism in soap opera and drama, has had to accommodate accents, and to some extent idioms, such as men and women do really use. A recent extreme instance has been the highly successful series *Taggart*, featuring a Glasgow cop and set in Glasgow, where Glaswegian voices, thick as fruit scones and fish suppers, baffle yet enthral auditors from other airts. So while the new media must, to a greater or lesser extent, generate standardisation, they also create or represent deviation.

The main point I am working for here is that the English which came at the empire, as Ralegh came at the maid, was not, and is not now, a monolithic 'standard' tongue. Ralegh, as Heaney emphasises, spoke 'broad Devonshire' though what he wrote contributed to a standardisation – *pro tem*, transitional – of English as a medium for poetry. And an Irish or Welsh planter in the West

Indies – let us be clear that such people existed well before the end of the seventeenth century – or a Scottish soldier of fortune in India later, did not voice, even if they could write, the current standardised English idiom. This had implications displayed in Cassidy and Le Page's great dictionary of Jamaican Creole.

In terms of consciousness where did such people stand? That Ireland was colonised admits of no doubt. Strongbow's Anglo-Norman invaders of the middle ages were absorbed, Gaelicised. De Burgos became Burkes. To a remarkable extent the English planters of the sixteenth century were absorbed, Catholicised. The focus of oppression in the eighteenth century was primarily religious: there was a Protestant ascendancy which included Irish landlords whose genealogy went back to the days of Brian Boru and the High Kings. Irish nationalism, as it developed from the 1790s onwards, was never a purely Catholic affair.

For that matter, after Catholic emancipation in 1829, Catholic as well as Protestant Irishmen became loyal servants and soldiers of empire. Either way, to speak of a 'colonial mentality' seems ridiculous. 'Provincial' might often be more to the point; so, sadly, must 'sectarian'.

The Welsh, after their medieval conquest by the English, were reconquered in a sense in the sixteenth century, when the Tudor State started trying to bring them to order, with a formal Act of Union in 1536. But note the irony: the Tudors were Welsh, and Welsh intellectuals exulted in that fact. They saw the Ancient Britons as having got their own back, and one of them, Dr Dee, Elizabeth's court magician, actually coined the term 'British empire'. Crunch point for Welsh consciousness came in the era of evangelical Christian revival and industrial revolution. While great Methodistical preachers gave the Welsh commonalty a new, non-Anglican, version of Christianity, capital from outside, largely Scottish, came in to transform quiet valleys into centres of coal production and iron making. The upshot was to generate a sense that the Welsh were all basically common, as it were working class, and those who weren't common were bloody English.

Lowland Scots were never in any sense colonised. They were avid colonisers. From the middle ages, when they overran the ancient Norse communities of the Northern Isles, to circa 1600 when James VI sent the Fife Adventurers off to colonise the Hebrides, through the plantation of Ulster, so largely by Scots, and then, after the Treaty of Union of 1707, the overweeningly disproportionate share of the spoils of empire taken by Scots in the West Indies, India, later Africa, lowland Scots were victimisers not, vis à vis the outside world, victims. (That working class Scots were victimised by their fellow countrymen is another matter.) The people who were colonized in Scotland were the Highland Gaels: sometimes shovelled off their land to make way for sheep and sporting estates, their language devalued and even, as education had its horrible way, forbidden. But who took over the North American fur trade from the French Canadians after General Wolfe's conquest? Highland Gaels. Who was the most influential of early governors of Australia? Lachlan Macquarie, a Highland Gael. Whose bagpipes, through their ferocious regiments, spread terror all over the world in the service of empire? Highland Gaels. For those who doubt that the Highland story is much more complex than the poignant oft-told tale of Clearances suggests, I recommend a fine article by Eric Richards, 'The Highland Passage to Colonial Australia' in the 1995 issue (volume 2, number 1) of an excellent journal, *Scotlands*, partly founded and subsidised from the University of Waikato, New Zealand. As Richards puts it:

> The out-reach of the Highlanders eastwards was part of the imperial agenda of the nineteenth century, driven by trade, conquest and the idea of a civilizing mission. In the previous century Highlanders in the American colonies seemed to be the 'shock troops' of empire, deep in the backwoods, doing the rough work of pioneering and confronting the indigeneous people. In Australia and New Zealand, in the Victorian age, Highlanders were again involved on the savage frontier of settlement, thrusting into aboriginal space

and taking appalling toll of human life. Highlanders on the Antipodean frontiers, as in the more formal battlefields of Empire, were undoubtedly red in tooth and claw.

A very great proportion of emigration from the Highlands was wholly voluntary, or even if impelled by poverty, opportunistic. The myth of the Clearances was largely created and sustained by the sentimentality of Lowland Scots on the one hand and the guilt of expatriate, colonising Highlanders who'd done well out of emigration.

Let's now consider a further force making for motion in language: borrowing. It is an insult to the vitality of colonised peoples to imagine that the impact of tongues from the north–western European archipelago on them was that of a steamroller, squashing them, and that linguistically they got none of their own back. Our Englishes now accommodate words like bungalow from India, safari from East Africa, barbecue from the Caribbean, as part of any standard which may be deemed to exist. All right: you might argue that these words were stolen, appropriated. But consider the word 'curry' and what it stands for. Curry is something which the British in India learnt to love eating. Now every town in Britain has Indian restaurants. The possessors were actually possessed.

One of my objections, the most severe one, to 'post-colonial literary theory' is the way it tends to privilege writing in English, or Englishes. Yet the exclusion of writings from former empires in many other languages is actually essential to its terminological coherence. It would be absurd to apply it to writings in Irish or Scottish Gaelic, twin languages far older than English, or in Bengali or in Swahili, which had literary life before imperialism. The very use of these languages expresses pre-coloniality. It seems to me that Ngugi's turn to Kikuyu – a language of possible popular resistance to neo-colonialism or, as I would prefer to say, resistance to the present day persistence of imperialism after 'decolonisation' – is an entirely logical one. But the positions adopted by Heaney, by Derek Walcott, by Achebe and by Soyinka, are not illogical either.

The English, or Englishes, which we use are not a simple instrument, or set of instruments, of oppression. We can distinguish the tongue, or tongues, involved in and now emerging from territorial imperialism from the brutalities of that process. I will list again those forces making for motion.

The Market Place. In the East in particular, imperialists and natives trading, traded language. Look at the rich idiom of Rudyard Kipling. Education. Always in the age of imperialism a vehicle of oppression, not least within the north–west European archipelago. But the oppressed often seize from it what they want, as Ngugi seized the novels of Joseph Conrad, a comprehensive influence on him at Makerere University.

Mass Media. Flux. Unpredictable permutations of influence, from America, from elsewhere. All languages, English, non-English, within the former empire now suffer these influences in parallel, simultaneously.

With these forces active at the same time within the north – west European archipelago, and the former empire which people from all those islands colonised, we are talking about a wonderfully complex and rich phenomenon, these many Englishes. The ground which was possessed may be repossessed in various ways. I'll begin to conclude by quoting an article by Alan Riach, 'Language Rules' (*Scotia Pacific* no. 2, 1995), and then one of my own, (*Chapman* 82, 1995). Riach writes:

> Scots are well known for bad language. Swearing is what a lot of our people do, but the Scots language itself is a kind of rebarbative diction, full of ochs and achs (also known as 'velar fricatives'). To speak the tongue you have to use your tongue and throat and saliva – your body goes to work. It's not the Latinate cerebral language of oh-so-precise 18th century gentility or the proper received pronunciation of the old BBC or the high nasal diction of condescending British politicians (of whatever party). Even without velar fricatives, the Scots tongue can sound harsh and combative, yet it is

also capable of subtlety... That's why there's no such thing as a 'pure' Scots language. There's too much energy in it.

In my own article, 'Scots Language in Transition', I consider the attempt, around the middle of the twentieth century, to standardise Scots literary expression in a synthetic medium, 'Lallans' – Lowland Scots. I express no regret that it broke down. On the contrary, my argument is that the Scottish Folk-song Revival, from the 1950s onwards, may, along with the use of Scots on TV, have helped writers see Scots speech, Scots tongue, as it has been, as it actually is, in all its varieties:

Take, for instance, Robert Alan Jamieson's debut volume, *Shoormal* (1986) containing poems in what we outsiders might call Shetlandic, but he calls Norrona/Scots. Jamieson remarks in his introduction that 'Whilst the poems in Norroena/Scots may be artificial, their language is still more natural to my tongue than that of those in English.' 'Song oda Post War Exiles' is perhaps the most accessible of these poems. A couple are leaving their small island for a 'cooncilhoose in Scallwa' (the relative metropolis, Scalloway!) The wife is eager to go, her man grieves:

Dat last faent glisk o wir croft de da shore,
Aa quhite-washed clean, brukk gien fae da door,
I'll never forgit it, I canna forgit it,
For days an nichts hit's wi me alaek
Dat last rummit stane I touched or wir daek,
Dat last faent glisk as I pulled on da oar,
Aa quhite-washed clean, brukk gien fae da door.
Hit med me greet t'see it.

Whatever (admitted) artificiality there may be in an idiom which Jamieson himself calls 'a synthetic Shetlandic using some Norn words and phrases bound together with Scots', it is emphatically not Alexandrian Lallans artificiality. The aim is not to represent a revived tradition but to give voice idiosyncratically to the experience of living in a particular place within Scotland's territory at a particular time.

Typically, current Scottish writers employ Scots as it suits them, when they need it. Even Tom Leonard is not a diehard user of the Glasgow phonetics which spring to mind when his name is mentioned. 'Much of his best verse is in standard English. But the effect of his Glaswegian utterance has been enormous... The impact in Scotland has been such as to liberate voices in Muirhouse as well as Castlemilk, east as well as west, free them to make literary use of the demotic of the schemes:

right inuff
ma language is disgraceful
ma maw tellt mi
ma teacher tellt mi
thi doactir tellt mi
thi priest tellt mi ...
sum we smout thit thoat ah hudny read chomsky tellt mi
a calvinistic communist thit thoat ah wuz revisionist tellt mi
po-faced literati grimly kerryin thi burden a thi past tellt mi
po-faced literati grimly kerryin thi burden a thi future tellt mi ...
even thi introduction tay thi Scottish National Dictionary tellt mi
Ach well
all livin language is sacred
fuck thi lohta thim

('The Ghostie Men')

Leonard jests in deadly earnest on the language issue. Like James Kelman, whose influence on prose has equalled Leonard's on younger poets, he would see formalised, institutionalised Lallans as just as oppressive as standard English. People have a right to their own speech, their own culture, which nationalist as well as internationalist grammarians, and their allies in education and the media, seek to deny them. The use by these writers of specifically Glaswegian demotic has been an example for Irvine Welsh and Duncan MacLean on the east coast – and could supply a model anywhere in the country where local speech differs markedly from standard English.

I have emphasised in this essay the local, the incidental, use of language, its multifariousness even within the long-settled and much-educated islands of the north–west European archipelago where those processes of imperialism began which have made English a 'world language'. It is a 'world language' because airlines and airports use it, hotels use it, rock songs use it. But it has not supplanted, and will not supplant Spanish, Portuguese, French, Russian, let alone Japanese and least of all Chinese. There will continue to be many languages, and several alternative 'world languages'.

And there is, I believe, one singular, true 'world language'. It is the language of poetry from which the languages of fiction and drama, of all literary expression, ultimately derive.

The Scottish poet Edwin Morgan helps me to explain what I mean. Fertile in the generation of languages – it was he who wrote 'The Loch Ness Monster's Song' – he provides in his poem 'The First Men on Mercury' a hilarious model of what happens on language frontiers, where intruder and native come together. The piece begins:

– We come in peace from the third planet.
Would you take us to your leader?
– Bawr stretter! Bawr. Bawr. Stretterhawl?
– This is a little plastic model
of the solar system, with working parts.
You are here and we are there and we
are now here with you, is this clear?
– Gawl horrop. Bawr. Abawrhannahanna!

Mutual pidginisation sets in fast. In the end the arrogant earthman is sent on his way by a Mercurian fluent in English:

– Banghapper now! Yes, third planet back.
Yuleeda will go back blue, white, brown
nowhanna! There is no more talk.
– Gawl han fasthapper?
– No. You must go back to your planet.
Go back in peace, take what you have gained
but quickly.
– Stretterworra gawl, gawl ...
– Of course, but nothing is ever the same,
now is it? You'll remember Mercury.

In an article on 'The Translation of Poetry' (1976: reprinted in *Nothing Not Giving Messages*, 1990) Morgan has written:

Without desiring to be mystical, I believe there does seem to be some sense (and it is a sense unlocked not even by the devoted critic – only by the translator, who is committed to an action in a way that the critic is not) in which the poem exists independently of the language of its composition... At times when states are anxious to express their national identity and to prove the virtues of their language, they have very often in history indulged in widespread translation from other cultures; yet in the process of doing this they subtly alter their own language, joining it in many unforeseen ways to a greater continent of almost undefined and non-specific human expression.

What Morgan says is true of the culture of Ralegh and Spenser in the great era of Elizabethan translation, and of Russian culture in the epoch of Pushkin. It can be stretched, without strain, then modified, to apply also to what are called 'new literatures in En-

POETRY, LANGUAGE AND EMPIRE

glish'. The idiom of Derek Walcott involves translation from French-based St Lucian *patwa* and Trinidadian creole, into which his English, one infers, is translated back again by silent Caribbean readers. This English, in any case, has been created by innumerable encounters of a kind of which Morgan's 'First Men on Mercury' provides a paradigm: between, for instance, Saxon and Celt, Anglo-Celt and Dane, Irish and English, English and Scots, and then between the bearers of rich mongrel'English' tongues and peoples in every continent, where the Portuguese, in particular, had often established the pidgin medium of European contact.

> I have Dutch, nigger, and English in me,
> and either I'm nobody, or I'm a nation ...

Walcott's Shabine says in 'The Schooner Flight'. In fact, in Caribbean and other post-colonial nations, the 'English' component is itself hybrid. Language is not a fatality, predestining. It is firm yet fluid, shaped, reshaped, reshaping. No chosen tongue is exclusively one thing, itself. If it communicates at all, it redeems Babel.

1996

Index

Some other books published by **LUATH** PRESS

The Souls of the Dead are Taking the Best Seats: 50 World Poets on War
Compiled by Angus Calder and Beth Junor
1 84282 032 X PB £7.99

From the clash of steel to the rumble of tanks, the sights and sounds of war have inspired poets of every nation since conflict was invented. In this timely new anthology, respected poet and historian Angus Calder and anti-war activist Beth Junor have drawn together a representation of war poetry from nations and cultures across the globe. Shared experience and powerful imagery combine to give this collection of poems an immediacy and poignancy that illustrate both the horror and the humanity that are distilled by the events that humankind calls war.

I highly recommend this collection of poems: they are as vivid as they are thought-provoking.
COLONEL CLIVE FAIRWEATHER, CBE, SCOTTISH APPEAL DIRECTOR, COMBATSTRESS

Sun Behind the Castle: Edinburgh Poems
Angus Calder
1 84282 078 8 PB £8.99

This is a lovely book. If only every city in this land had a poet like him, what a richer country it would seem.
ANDREW MARR

The Edinburgh of Angus Calder's poems is not the city of summer tourism and landmark buildings. It is the all-the-year-round arena of lingering mists or brilliant sunlight on grey stone, where seagulls and pigeons command the early-morning streets, curlers sweep their ice at Murrayfield and coarse sportsmen revel on the Meadows. World famous Sandy Bell's is not the only pub evoked, and Bread Street features more strongly than Princes Street. This is because the centre of Calder's Edinburgh is Tollcross, terrain of theatres and cheap shops, ethnic restaurants and lapdance bars, just south-west of respectability. The culminating sequence of *Sun Behind the Castle* transports to Tollcross the ancient Roman poet Horace, modernising completely more than a score of his famous *Odes*, with their gossip and lyricism, fatalism, political comment and hedonistic moralising.

Carpe diem. Enjoy this delicious biscuit.

old Scotland new Scotland
Jeff Fallow
0 946487 40 5 PB £6.99

old Scotland new Scotland is a powerful and provocative portrayal of Scotland's past and present in graphic form. This fast-track guide is the quick way to learn what your history teacher didn't tell you. Scottish politics have never been more exciting. Fallow's finger is on the pulse. He catches the mood of a nation on the move. old Scotland new Scotland is essential reading for all who seek an understanding of Scotland and its history. Jeff Fallow takes us on a graphic voyage through Scotland's turbulent history, from earliest times through to the present day and beyond, pushing cartoon into a new realm of radicalism. He captures the soul of a nation, political rebellion always close to its heart.

At times like this you suddenly realise how dangerous the neglect of Scottish history in our schools and universities may turn out to be. MICHAEL FRY, THE HERALD

...one of the things I hope will go is our chip on the shoulder about the English... The snp has a huge responsibility to articulate Scottish independence in a way that is pro-Scottish and not anti-English. ALEX SALMOND, THE SCOTSMAN

This book shines a new light on events in Scottish history of which generations of Scots have been largely unaware. Eschewing the romanticisation of his country's past, Fallow offers a new perspective on an old nation. Too many people associate Scottish history with tartan trivia or outworn romantic myth. This book aims to blast that stubborn idea. JEFF FALLOW

Reportage Scotland: History in the Making
Louise Yeoman
Foreword by Professor David Stevenson
0 946487 61 8 PB £9.99

Events – major and minor – as seen and recorded by Scots throughout history.

Which cardinal was salted and put in a barrel?
Which king was murdered in a sewer?
What was Dr Fian's love magic?
Who was the half-roasted abbot?
Why did Lord Kitchener's niece try to blow up Burns's cottage?

The answers can all be found in this eclectic mix covering nearly 2000 years of Scottish history. Historian Louise Yeoman's rummage through the manuscript, book and newspaper archives of the National Library of Scotland has yielded an astonishing range of material from a letter to the king of the Picts to Mary, Queen of Scots' own account of the murder of David Riccio; from the execution of William Wallace to accounts of anti-poll tax actions and the opening of the new Scottish Parliament. The book takes pieces from the original French, Latin, Gaelic and Scots and makes them accessible to the general reader, often for the first time. The result is compelling reading for anyone interested in the history that has made Scotland what it is today.

Marvellously illuminating and wonderfully readable ANGUS CALDER, SCOTLAND ON SUNDAY

A monumental achievement in drawing together such a rich historical harvest CHRIS HOLME, THE HERALD

Scotland, Land and People
An Inhabited Solitude
James McCarthy
0 946487 57 X PB £7.99

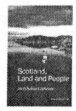

'Scotland is the country above all others that I have seen, in which a man of imagination may carve out his own pleasures; there are so many inhabited solitudes.'
DOROTHY WORDSWORTH, journal, August 1803.

In this informed and thought-provoking profile of Scotland's unique landscapes and the impact of humans on what we see now an and in the future, James McCarthy leads us through the many aspects of the land and the people who inhabit it: natural Scotland; the rocks beneath; land ownership; the use of resources; people and place; conserving Scotland's heritage and much more. Written in a highly readable style, this concise volume offers an understanding of the land as a whole. Emphasising the uniqueness of the Scottish environment, the author explores the links between this and other aspects of our culture as a key element in rediscovering a modern sense of the Scottish identity and perception of nationhood.

...an engaging introduction to the mysteries of Scotland's people and landscapes. Difficult concepts are described in simple terms, providing the interested Scot or tourist with an invaluable overview of the country. The interdependent links between land and people are convincingly pointed up. Scotland's diverse culture, wildlife and landscapes are properly celebrated throughout. This is a book which will appeal to a wide audience. It fills an important niche which, to my knowledge, is filled by no other publications.
BETSY KING, Chief Executive, Scottish Environmental Education Council.

But n Ben A-Go-Go
Matthew Fitt
1 84282 041 1PB £6.99

The year is 2090. Global flooding has left most of Scotland under water. The descendants of those who survived God's Flood live in a community of floating island parishes, known collectively as Port.

Port's citizens live in mortal fear of Senga, a supervirus whose victims are kept in a giant hospital warehouse in sealed capsules called Kists. Paolo Broon is a low-ranking cyberjanny. His life-partner, Nadia, lies forgotten and alone in Omega Kist 624 in the Rigo Imbeki Medical Center. When he receives an unexpected message from his radge criminal father to meet him at But n Ben A-Go-Go, Paolo's life is changed forever. Set in a distinctly unbonnie future-Scotland, the novel's dangerous atmosphere and psychologically-malkied characters weave a tale that both chills and intrigues. In *But n Ben A-Go-Go* Matthew Fitt takes the allegedly dead language of Scots and energises it with a narrative that crackles and fizzes with life.

I recommend an entertaining and ground-breaking book. EDWIN MORGAN

spellbinding... an assured novel of real inventiveness. Be prepared to boldly go ELLIE MCDONALD

Easier to read than Shakespeare, and twice the fun. DES DILLON

Bursting with sly humour, staggeringly imaginative, often poignant and at times exploding with Uzi-blazing action, this book is a cracker. GREGOR STEELE, TIMES EDUCATIONAL SUPPLEMENT

Luath Press Limited
committed to publishing well written books worth reading

LUATH PRESS takes its name from Robert Burns, whose little collie Luath (*Gael.*, swift or nimble) tripped up Jean Armour at a wedding and gave him the chance to speak to the woman who was to be his wife and the abiding love of his life. Burns called one of *The Twa Dogs* Luath after Cuchullin's hunting dog in *Ossian's Fingal*. Luath Press was established in 1981 in the heart of Burns country, and is now based a few steps up the road from Burns' first lodgings on Edinburgh's Royal Mile. Luath offers you distinctive writing with a hint of unexpected pleasures.

Most bookshops in the UK, the US, Canada, Australia, New Zealand and parts of Europe, either carry our books in stock or can order them for you. To order direct from us, please send a £sterling cheque, postal order, international money order or your credit card details (number, address of cardholder and expiry date) to us at the address below. Please add post and packing as follows: UK – £1.00 per delivery address; overseas surface mail – £2.50 per delivery address; overseas airmail – £3.50 for the first book to each delivery address, plus £1.00 for each additional book by airmail to the same address. If your order is a gift, we will happily enclose your card or message at no extra charge.

Luath Press Limited
543/2 Castlehill
The Royal Mile
Edinburgh EH1 2ND
Scotland
Telephone: 0131 225 4326 (24 hours)
Fax: 0131 225 4324
email: gavin.macdougall@luath. co.uk
Website: www. luath.co.uk